T0355465

How We Read Now

*Strategic Choices for
Print, Screen, and Audio*

Naomi S. Baron

OXFORD
UNIVERSITY PRESS

OXFORD
UNIVERSITY PRESS

Oxford University Press is a department of the University of Oxford. It furthers
the University's objective of excellence in research, scholarship, and education
by publishing worldwide. Oxford is a registered trade mark of Oxford University
Press in the UK and certain other countries.

Published in the United States of America by Oxford University Press
198 Madison Avenue, New York, NY 10016, United States of America.

Library of Congress Cataloging-in-Publication Data
Names: Baron, Naomi S. author.
Title: How we read now : strategic choices for print, screen, and audio /
Naomi S. Baron.
Description: New York : Oxford University Press, 2021. |
Includes bibliographical references and index.
Identifiers: LCCN 2020044860 (print) | LCCN 2020044861 (ebook) |
ISBN 9780190084097 (hardback) | ISBN 9780190084110 (epub) |
ISBN 9780190084127
Subjects: LCSH: Reading—Technological innovations. | Computers and
literacy. | Reading comprehension. | Critical thinking.
Classification: LCC Z1033.E43 B369 2021 (print) | LCC Z1033.E43 (ebook) |
DDC 028/.90285—dc23
LC record available at https://lccn.loc.gov/2020044860
LC ebook record available at https://lccn.loc.gov/2020044861

DOI: 10.1093/oso/9780190084097.001.0001

1 3 5 7 9 8 6 4 2

Printed by LSC Communications, United States of America

For Freya

Contents

Foreword

"We have accumulated a massive collection of 'information' to which we may have 'access.' But this information, by being accessible, does not become knowledge."

Wendell Berry, *Our Only World* (2015)

The book you are about to read by the esteemed scholar, Naomi Baron, could not be more timely, more needed, or more worthy of all our efforts to understand the vast amount of information she brings to bear on "how we read now" in this moment of transition from a literacy-based culture to a digital, screen-based culture. She tackles some of the most prevalent questions raised today by parents, educators, and policy makers: What medium is best for learning? What are the pros and cons of reading books versus reading on screens? Are there valuable contributions to learning from audio and video mediums? Will literacy itself change? Will our young learn to read deeply, wisely, and well in a digital culture?

With deft objectivity Baron points the reader to the increased information on these issues *and their implications* for the development of the young of our species without forcing us to agree with any one perspective, including her own. In so doing, Baron propels the process which Wendell Berry worries will go missing with the current bombardment of information: the emergence of knowledge. Baron is helping us all construct that knowledge base, one book after another. The implications of her programmatic research apply not only to the young but also to every sector of our society, and indeed to the shaping and maintaining of a democratic society. This is what scholarship at its best does: It leads us from a synthesis of information, to a foundation of knowledge, to a leaping-off place where we, the readers, are best prepared to form our own judgments with as much wisdom as we can.

The last step takes no small effort on our part. Armed with the kind of knowledge Baron presents here, we all have a better chance of making wise decisions about the issues confronted in this book. Never have these questions been more front and center than now as we navigate an educational system forced to rely on digital resources to maintain the education of our young during a pandemic crisis and afterwards.

It is here that I will diverge slightly from the emulable objectivity found in this book's repository of information and knowledge to a perspective based on my work on the reading brain. Despite my continued belief in the transformational roles that digital media can play in disseminating knowledge and promoting learning during this crisis, my worries are undiminished (if anything, accelerated) about the threats to deeper forms of literacy that these technologies represent.

These concerns, which stem from my work as a cognitive neuroscientist, begin with the fact that learning to read isn't natural, despite what most humans mistakenly assume. Rather, reading is a cultural invention which requires the brain of every new reader to build a new circuit that is and *remains plastic* across the reader's development. The circuit of any reader is based on newly made connections among the neuronal networks for visual, language-based, cognitive, and also affective processes (Wolf, 2007, 2016, 2018). The reading circuit can be as basic or as complex as the reader's education and experiences, moving from the simplest of circuits in the young to the most elaborated of circuits in the older, expert reader. The *reading brain* is one of the most significant, epigenetic-based changes in modern history. Further, it is the scaffolding for developing many of our species' most complex intellectual skills, which make up the "deep reading processes" of expert readers, including many of our most important analogical, inferential, empathic, and critical analytical processes.

These deep reading processes generalize well beyond reading. When we learn to connect these processes over and over in our reading lives, we learn to think more deeply about everything. The key to the development and deployment of these processes, however, is time: time in years to form these processes; time in milliseconds to purposely allocate attention to them while reading. Nothing is a given, particularly when there are essential differences in how much time each medium encourages in the reader's allocation and quality of attention.

Herein lies the rub that Baron beautifully alerts us to in multiple ways. Every reading circuit will develop and/or atrophy according to the emphases of the medium or media used. If the dominant medium advantages processes that are fast, multi-task oriented, and well suited for large volumes of information, as is the digital medium, less attention and time will be allocated to slower, time-demanding cognitive and reflective functions, thereby compromising deep reading processes. Even if the latter processes previously shaped the expert reading brain through the medium of print, a plastic reading circuit will change as a result of the processes emphasized or deemphasized in the medium used most. The biological-cultural principle is this: Use or lose it. An expert reading circuit is not a permanent gift; rather, it is built and rebuilt by emphases in its environment and by the reader's *intention and purposes* for reading.

There are all too many statistics behind my worries, which Baron's book chronicles, but alongside far more positive trends than I knew before reading her book. My own most recent work concerns the need to build a "biliterate deep reading brain", capable of allocating attention to the more time-consuming deep reading processes across *any* medium (Wolf, 2018). Baron's new book gives me added incentive to develop this direction, based on the expanded knowledge she provides, and her always astute and often practical insights into this emerging body of research. Indeed, if anything could propel my hope that we will preserve the deep reading brain for the future of our children, it is the very expansion of our knowledge base about the cognitive, social, and emotional pros and cons of *each* medium which Baron gives us here.

In sum, Naomi Baron has given us a firmer foundation from which we can move forward more informed and more reflective about our goals for the future. In the process, it is my earnest hope that with this knowledge we will learn to preserve both the contemplative sanctuary perhaps best found through the pages of books, alongside the great increases of different forms of knowledge provided by screens of evolving variety.

Maryanne Wolf

Director, Center for Dyslexia, Diverse Learners, and Social Justice

University of California, Los Angeles

May 2020

REFERENCES

Berry, W. (2015). *Our Only World*. Berkeley, CA: Counterpoint, p. 11.

Wolf, M. (2007). *Proust and the Squid: The Story and Science of the Reading Brain*. New York, NY: HarperCollins.

Wolf, M. (2016). *Tales of Literacy for the 21st Century*. Oxford: Oxford University Press.

Wolf, M. (2018). *Reader, Come Home: The Reading Brain in a Digital World*. New York, NY: HarperCollins.

List of Figures and Tables

The New Great Debate in Reading

It was war.

Not what you would expect from normally mild-mannered educational researchers and teachers of young children. But that's what it was called at the time: the reading wars. The bone of contention was whether it's better to teach kids to read using a sound-based ("phonics") approach or to focus on meaning ("whole language"). Jeanne Chall's 1967 book *Learning to Read: The Great Debate* summed up the initial arguments. Decades later, opposing camps are still engaging in skirmishes, this time under the banners "science of learning" versus "balanced literacy".[1]

Now there's a new debate in the reading world, with a different battleground and broader array of players. In today's world awash in digital technology, the question on many people's minds is whether the medium on which we read matters. Given explosive growth of digital text—free on the internet or for sale as eBooks—we need to choose when to read in print or on a digital screen. And there's a third option. The massive surge in audio materials such as podcasts and audiobooks, along with audio-plus-video offerings from YouTube and TED Talks, means we can "read" with our ears as well.

Today's debate isn't just for reading experts. Let's say that

- you're a parent selecting a birthday book for your six-year-old child. Should you buy the print version or the eBook?
- you're a middle school principal worried whether students are reading carefully when they read digitally. What can you do to support their learning?

- you're a high school teacher finding your students are more likely to listen to an assigned podcast than to read the equivalent article. You wonder if it matters how they access content.
- you're a college student on a budget. Digital textbooks are cheaper but you believe you learn more from print. Are you just being nostalgic?
- you're a professional doing research. When does it make sense to read materials on a screen and when is it better to print them out?

How can you decide?

Each medium has its pros and cons. Print is familiar, has physical feel and smell, and is simple to personalize with annotations. It's also well suited for thinking through abstract concepts or reading long texts. Digital books are usually less expensive, highly convenient, and tailor-made for searching. Audio is both portable and easy to listen to while on a treadmill. Particularly if there's a good narrator, audio can stir imagination and help build empathy with fictional characters. Audio can also be an invaluable tool for those with limited vision or reading challenges stemming from dyslexia or ADHD.

Does medium matter? The question has no simple answer. What type of reading is it—a news story? a romance novel? one of Plato's dialogues? What is the reader's goal—to grab a quick piece of information? to kill time or relax? to analyze Shakespeare's *Macbeth*? What are your personal preferences—do you enjoy reading novels on an eReader or do you relish print? The list goes on.

Another vital issue is whether you're reading in your free time or because a teacher asked you to. We might tackle the same work for different reasons (*Moby Dick* over the summer, to prove to ourselves we can still read a long novel; *Moby Dick* in a college literature class on Melville).

Pragmatism also needs to figure in. What if you prefer to read in print but only have digital available—or vice versa? What about schools in which the medium chosen by the principal or regional administrator doesn't match what a teacher feels will most benefit students? These are pinch points for which the research we'll be talking about can help us work out compensatory strategies.

How We Read Now focuses on reading intended for learning, stretching from kindergarten to college and beyond. "Beyond" includes the rest of us no longer in school, in our lives as readers and as professionals. Although the majority of research I'll talk about and advice I'll offer is framed in language directed to the education world, most of the lessons learned are applicable to anyone.

We'll take into account real-world considerations that teachers and administrators, librarians and parents, and of course students need to balance for reading on one platform or another. Especially in the United States, cost is the 800-pound gorilla in the room. We'll weigh how much the educational move to digital is driven by price tag and how the open educational resources (OER) movement has surged in response. OERs are free to students and school systems (the good news) but are overwhelmingly digital. We'll also consider the likely effect of a pandemic such as COVID-19 on reading medium.

If money were no object, would print always be the best choice? No. Both digital text and audio have their own advantages. And pragmatically, digital reading and audio (plus video) are now major threads in the educational fabric and likely to remain so. The questions then become:

- When is each platform particularly effective for learning?
- What print learning strategies can be useful with digital media?

Recent years have seen considerable buzz about potential hazards of reading onscreen. (Similar debates about audio are likely waiting to happen.) Whether it's Nicholas Carr's provocative 2008 article "Is Google Making Us Stupid?", Susan Greenfield's cautionary 2015 book *Mind Change: How Digital Technologies Are Leaving Their Mark on Our Brains*, or Maryanne Wolf's 2018 invitation *Reader, Come Home: The Reading Brain in a Digital World*, journalists and scholars alike have been warning that online reading may not measure up in depth to reading in print. But do we really know? And does the difference matter?

The most reliable way to decide is to look at research. For more than 20 years, scholars have been designing experiments, distributing questionnaires, and interviewing readers (especially students) around the world. Some research compares comprehension results. Other studies gauge readers' attitudes. While most of the research we'll consider is about reading in print versus onscreen, we'll also look at studies on audio (and some video) learning, given the growing trend to replace text assignments with audio and video materials.

A word is in order about the notion of "reading" with audio. In this book's subtitle, *Strategic Choices for Print, Screen, and Audio*, you'll notice I fudged the language, not specifying what you do when you listen to audio. Should we talk about "reading" an audiobook? Maybe "reading with audio"? Audio scholars such as Iben Have and Birgitte Stougaard Pedersen[2] and Matthew Rubery[3] argue it's legitimate to speak of audio reading. For our purposes, let's not get hung up on terminology.

One other clarification is useful before we get started. When you see the words "reading" and "learning" juxtaposed, it's easy to think the discussion will include

learning to read. In its early stages, learning to read entails figuring out how to decode words: knowing how to pronounce them, recognizing their meaning. Later
stages advance to making sense of sentences, then paragraphs, and eventually issues
of complexity and nuance, from abstractions to inferences and metaphors, on to ap-
preciation of an author's selection of *le mot juste*.

All these are critical parts of education—but not what this book is about. *How
We Read Now* tackles the learning that takes place when we read (commonly dubbed
"reading to learn"). Think about how much you remember of a news article or podcast, whether you can reconstruct a story's plotline, if you followed the argument in a
political treatise. The more mature people's reading skills, the higher our expectations
for their learning from reading.

I'll emphasize reading to learn for several reasons. First, there already are several
excellent discussions considering smart use of digitally based books for young children, including those who haven't yet learned to read.[4] I will, though, summarize research on this age group, as well as offer some evidence-based strategies. Second, the
vast majority of research to date has been done with older students (middle school,
high school, and especially college-age), providing a more solid foundation for
evidence-based conclusions and concrete advice. And third, while we hope reading to
learn is pleasurable, explicitly reading for pleasure is a different field of research.[5] I will,
though, include findings about how pleasure reading predicts school-based learning.

Here's how we'll proceed. In Part I, we'll "size up reading", looking at what we
might mean by the words "reading" and "reader" (Chapter 1). Chapter 2 starts by
considering the different types of texts readers might encounter, then proceeding to
think about the physical structure of texts, along with why and where we read them.
We'll also introduce the critical question of how much our success in reading on a
particular platform is shaped by the technology itself and how much by the mindset
we bring to using that technology. Moving to Chapter 3, we explore whether print
reading is a legitimate standard against which to measure digital or audio.

Part II digs into questions about reading in print versus on digital screens.
Chapters 4 and 5 examine the current research here. Have no fear about getting
entangled in the weeds: I've tried hard to make the discussion user-friendly. We'll also
be clear about when researchers agree and where studies reach contrary conclusions.

You may wonder why print versus digital text deserves two chapters. One reason
is that here is where most research has been done. It's also critical to distinguish between reading a single text (Chapter 4) and reading multiple texts in tandem, especially multiple digital documents accessed through online searches (Chapter 5).
In middle schools and high schools—as well as in standardized testing—we find

increased emphasis on skills for finding, evaluating, and interpreting multiple texts online. We'll go on to ask whether the growing focus on multiple online documents is inexorably changing our conception of what it means to read.

Drawing upon what we learned in Chapters 4 and 5, Part II ends with strategies for nurturing students' learning when we ask them to read digitally (Chapter 6). Some of these suggestions are products of my own thinking, while others I've drawn from the broader research community.

Part III turns to reading with audio. Chapter 7 looks at what we know so far about listening for learning purposes. I say "so far" because compared with research on print versus screen reading, we understand far less about the pros and cons of substituting audio in place of text. While our focus is audio (think of audiobooks or podcasts), video creeps into some of the discussion, since the likes of YouTube and TED Talks are increasingly cropping up in student assignments. We'll also talk about possibilities for combining audio with text. Chapter 8 suggests strategies for making good educational use of audio, with some ideas about video as well. Because we'll have much less to say in Part III about video than about audio, I've signposted the difference by putting the word "video" in parentheses in the two chapter titles.

Part IV asks, "What's Next?" We begin by considering how print reading is being influenced by digital mindsets (Chapter 9). Chapter 10 opens with several paradoxes in the ways we compare reading in print versus onscreen, including in light of our educational goals. Unless we know what we want students to derive from reading, we can't make defensible decisions about the best way to support learning. The chapter concludes with recommendations for moving forward, based on the research and arguments we have explored in this book.

A couple of terminological clarifications may be useful. When we talk about reading text on digital screens, sometimes I'll speak of "digital reading" and other times of "reading onscreen". They mean the same thing. Similarly, when discussing students in higher education, I'll use the terms "college" and "university" interchangeably.

It's also useful to mention a stylistic conundrum I was faced with. This book is written with adult readers in mind. Educators (including parents) are the ones who will be contemplating the various arguments, summaries, and strategies. Yet these same teachers and parents will be giving advice, in turn, to their students and progeny, and hopefully using the strategies themselves. Depending on what made most stylistic sense, sometimes my comments are phrased as if I'm addressing students directly, while other times, the suggestions are overtly to teachers or parents. My hope is that this vacillation doesn't make for any confusion.

And one final organizational heads-up. It's common for textbooks to close each chapter with questions for students to think about in light of what they've just read. *How We Read Now* isn't a textbook. Its readers are teachers and librarians, policy makers and parents, and anyone else trying to understand the issues in the new Great Debate. You'll find no end-of-chapter questions. Instead, to help focus your reading, each of the four main parts of the book begins by identifying some major issues at stake that will be raised in the section ahead. What's more, each chapter opens with a list of the subheadings contained within, providing a roadmap to topics and order of discussion.

There's no test at the end. Instead, the measure of the book's value will be the understanding and pragmatic ideas you derive that can improve reading and learning experiences—your own and especially those of the next generations about whom we so very much care.

It's time to begin.

PART I   SIZING UP READING

WHAT'S
AT STAKE?

Here are some issues to be thinking about as you read
Part I:

- What different kinds of reading and readers
  are there?
- What does eye movement tell us about the reading
  process?
- How much are adults—and children—reading?
- Does it matter what types of reading children do?
- Do students complete the reading assignments
  we give?
- What strategies best help students learn when
  they read?
- Which print strategies make sense for digital
  reading? for audio?

CHAPTER 1   What Do We Mean by "Reading" and "Reader"?

You can read a stop sign, and you can read John Paul Sartre. You can read the help wanted ads, and you can read a haiku. You can read a Wikipedia article, and you can read the *Wall Street Journal*. All count as reading, but they mean different things. Knowing which meaning we're talking about matters in weighing the pros and cons of reading in print, on a screen, or with audio.

What Is "Reading"?

The standard approach for dividing up the possibilities is to talk about skimming (cruising through the text to get the gist), scanning (looking for specific information), and linear reading (reading all the way through). We might skim an article or a book's table of contents to decide if we want to read more (or read more carefully). With printed text, we scan if we're trying to locate a particular word, name, or date, though with digital, we make a beeline for the Search or Find function.

Linear reading has its own divisions. If we're thinking about the range of works a person reads, we might talk about extensive versus intensive reading. Extensive? Read a wide variety of books (or articles or stories). Intensive? Focus on a smaller number of works or topics, often in depth.

But even here we're being overly simplistic about linear reading. How many people start a piece and read to the end? In reality, many of us flip through sections or quit midstream. We have done so for centuries.[1] As we'll see in Chapter 3, the appealing belief that linear texts are all read in linear fashion is often more myth than truth.

Even when you read the entire text, you might go at it with different goals—and mindsets. Some works you traverse only once, moving along at a reasonably brisk pace. I like to call this "one-off reading". Think of mystery stories you pick up (in print, as eBooks, or as audiobooks) to occupy yourself on a long flight or on vacation.

The alternative is texts commanding sustained attention. In many cases, this means rereading. Think of a 12-year-old who especially enjoyed *Harry Potter and the Sorcerer's Stone* and has now read it five times. I have a friend who nostalgically rereads *Pride and Prejudice* every few years. And rereading scriptures goes without saying. A question to ponder: Are we as likely to re-listen to an audiobook as to re-read a text version? And another: Are we more likely to reread a print or digital version? Research shows that print is more likely to invite a second visit than audio or digital text.[2]

A different way of paying more attention is by focusing your mind intently. Years back, Reuben Brower, a professor of English at Amherst and then Harvard, developed an undergraduate literature course in which he taught students what he called "slow reading". What Brower had in mind was

> slowing down the process of reading to observe what is happening, in order to attend very closely to the words, their uses, and their meanings.[3]

Drawing on his background as a classicist, Brower wanted students to learn to focus on the words themselves, much as one does in translating Latin or Greek. Today there's a "slow reading" movement that encourages adopting a leisurely pace when reading for pleasure.[4] However, the two uses of the term are unrelated.

Brower's focus on words also lies at the heart of an Anglo-American literary movement called New Criticism, which flourished in the mid 20th century. In New Criticism, the goal in reading and analyzing literature was to view works (especially poetry) as self-contained—not invoking the writer's biography or the composition's historical context to discern meaning. The tool for accomplishing this task was called "close reading". The term applied explicitly to literary texts and more specifically to a theory of how to interpret them.

Despite its narrow origins, the phrase "close reading" has been co-opted to mean something much more familiar, namely paying close attention to a piece of writing. English professor John Guillory dubbed this more general sense "reading closely".[5] People have been reading closely for millennia, long before literary criticism emerged. Many college writing teachers talk about "critical reading", essentially meaning to read interactively by analyzing, interpreting, and challenging what the author is saying. If these processes sound vaguely familiar, it's because this is the kind of brain work underlying the amorphous—but wildly popular—idea of "critical thinking".

As concepts, "close reading", "reading closely", and "critical reading" inhabit similar mental space to that of another term now on many people's tongues: "deep reading". The phrase was introduced by literary scholar Sven Birkerts in his 1994 book *The Gutenberg Elegies*. Birkerts explained that deep reading is

> the slow and meditative possession of a book. We don't just read the words, we dream our lives in their vicinity.[6]

Over the years, Birkerts's phrase has gained increasing traction. A more recent (and concrete) definition is this one by reading specialists Maryanne Wolf and Mirit Barzillai:

> the array of sophisticated processes that propel comprehension and that include inferential and deductive reasoning, analogical skills, critical analysis, reflection, and insight.[7]

Paeons to deep reading come from many quarters, not just from educators and reading experts.[9]

"Given a reading diet of appropriate length and complexity, reading has the potential to foster mental focus, patience and discipline, offers emotional and aesthetic experiences, increases linguistic knowledge and enhances economic and personal well-being. Skimming texts doesn't bring such benefits."

Stavanger Declaration Concerning the Future of Reading[8]

Deep reading is thoughtful, typically slow, reflective reading. As we'll see, it is almost always associated with print. In the chapters ahead, we will revisit the notion of deep reading, asking how much of the reading being done meets these exacting standards, as well as whether screen reading and audio are suited to the task.

There's an antonym for deep reading, and that is "hyper reading". The idea was introduced by a communication professor, James Sosnoski, in the late 1990s to characterize what life online was doing to the way we read. Sosnoski defined hyper reading as "reader-directed, screen-based, computer-assisted reading" that entails "searching, skimming, hyperlinking, and extracting fragments from longer texts".[10] Sort of a brew of skimming and scanning on steroids.

Literature professor Katherine Hayles popularized the notion in her discussions of hyper attention and hyper reading. Her definition of hyper reading:

> A strategic response to an information-intensive environment, aiming to conserve attention by quickly identifying relevant information, so that only relatively few portions of a given text are actually read.[11]

Again, a version of skimming and scanning, but now with a twist: motivation. If you only read bits and pieces, you can conserve mental energy. In principle, you might apply this approach when reading either in print or onscreen. (With audio, you're locked into playing each word unless you fast-forward.) But in practice, it's digital technology that is most strongly driving the hyper reading train.

The word "hyper" reminds us of another dichotomy that's particularly relevant to digital reading, namely linear reading versus following hyperlinks. Those links can be a blessing or curse, in part depending on the type of reader. For accomplished readers with high levels of prior knowledge about the topic, links can unlock pathways to new ideas and understanding, while for struggling readers or those with lower familiarity with the subject, links may lead to mental mazes that stunt comprehension. In Chapter 5, we'll look at the research behind these conclusions.

As we start considering variables involved in reading, we'll see that medium can be critical in establishing a mindset for how we approach a text. Psychologists (first James Gibson, with later tweaks from Donald Norman) have talked about "affordances".[12] The term has come to mean the aspects of an object that make it useful. Handles are good for opening cabinets. Coats are good for keeping out the cold. Computers (and other digital tools) are good for searching, multitasking, and hyper reading. These devices don't force us to read quickly or selectively, but the technology is designed to enable—and entice—us to do so.

Finally, one more reading dichotomy: between reading a single text and drawing upon multiple documents. Those of us who grew up in the predigital age remember sitting with arrays of physical books before us as we wrote research papers. But today, those multiple items are often digital files or web pages. A growing area of research today is examining (and so will we) how students navigate their online reading across diverse sources.

To help keep all these terms straight, Figure 1.1 bundles them in one place.

Skimming [get the gist] vs. *scanning* [find something specific]
      vs. *linear reading* [read continuously]

Extensive reading [wide variety of topics] vs. *intensive reading*
      [narrower topics]

One-off reading [read once] vs. *rereading* [read again]

Close reading (à la New Criticism) [careful literary attention to
      text itself] vs. *close reading (in common parlance),
      reading closely, critical reading* [read analytically]

Deep reading [read analytically] vs. *hyper reading* [quick skimming, scanning,
      hyperlinking]

Linear reading [read continuously] vs. *hyperlinks* [follow online links]

Single text [read one document at a time] vs. *multiple documents* [read
      several documents in tandem]

NOTE: In contemporary practice, "close reading", "reading closely",
"critical reading", and "deep reading" are sometimes used interchangeably.

FIGURE 1.1 A Cornucopia of "Reading" Types

Literacies Old and New

Since we are talking about what we mean by reading, it's only natural to ask where the term "literacy" comes in. Back in the day, if we talked about literacy, we basically meant ability to read and write. (Let's leave out metaphoric extensions such as "visual literacy" or "digital literacy".) Yes, we might include spelling and punctuation (as part of writing) and vocabulary (a skill important in reading and writing, not to mention speaking). But essentially, all the discussion involved facility with handwritten, typed, or printed text.

In the early 1970s, that straightforward approach began to be cracked open.

Paulo Freire's plea for social justice in education, *Pedagogy of the Oppressed*, appeared in English in 1970. The Brazilian educator argued that the idea of literacy has to go beyond reading and writing words. Rather, we must see literacy as a tool for understanding how the world works—socially and culturally—to create inequalities.

About the same time, a cluster of linguists and educators in the United States started thinking about literacy in new ways. Scholars such as James Gee, Brian Street, Shirley Brice Heath, and Ron and Suzanne Scollon asked how learning to be literate is embedded in a sociocultural context. The new goal was to view literacy as the product of social practices.

By the 1990s, this socially based approach to literacy was gaining momentum. In 1994, a group of scholars who called themselves the New London Group (they met in New London, New Hampshire) began mapping out what a new literacy pedagogy should look like. They advocated replacing the unitary idea of "literacy" (with its normative approach to reading and writing) with the broader notion of "multiliteracies", which acknowledges linguistic diversity and its social, cultural, and political sources. The concept goes beyond writing to include spoken, gestural, and visual communication as well. More broadly, the multiliteracies approach emphasizes "how negotiating the multiple linguistic and cultural differences in our society is central to the pragmatics of the working, civic, and private lives of students".[13] Over time, the term "multiliteracies" was often supplanted by "new literacies".[14]

A fresh approach to literacy wasn't the only major educational shift in the late 20th and early 21st centuries. Even more visible was the explosion of digital technologies in the classroom. Proponents of new literacies, now including Julie Coiro and Donald Leu, began adapting the concept to encompass information and communication technologies (ICTs), including digital reading and the internet. The core argument is that with the coming of new digital tools, we need to consider the kinds of skills students must acquire to access and communicate information.[15]

How We Read Now looks at literacy (or literacies) through a wide lens, including print, digital screens, audio, and some video. But you won't find the full new literacies technology lineup, since that includes such activities as video games and video production, which go beyond our scope.

Physicality: The Role of Senses When We Read

Consider the physical act of reading. What senses are involved? Obviously, sight. But there's more to the story. The senses come into play not just for print reading but for reading on screens and listening as well.

> "Books are fundamentally multisensory objects."
>
> Charles Spence[16]

When reading text, the main focus is on the words (with a few exceptions, such as books filled with photographs or illustrated children's books). Yet we also "read" other features. With print, we notice how text is laid out on the page. We look at the cover. With digital screens, our visual sense has a more diminished role. Covers literally are not "at hand" (even if technically they exist), and the amount of text seen at a time is often at the user's discretion, not the designer's.

Our sense of touch also comes into play. Researchers remind us that tactile ("haptic") interaction with a print book is a critical component of traditional reading. We feel a book's heft, consider what kind of paper it's printed on. We physically hold the book (or magazine or newspaper), stick a finger between pages to mark our spot, use a thumb and forefinger as pincers to measure how much of a tome we've finished or have left to go. In the words of Anne Mangen,

> A text displayed on a screen and in a print book may *look* identical page
> by page, but the two texts differ in kinesthetic affordances.[17]

That is, the ways we use our hands to interact with text on screens and in print are not the same.

Touch isn't a variable we tend to think about with digital books. However, touch can be relevant here as well. Depending on the digital device, we might point and click with a mouse or move our fingers on a touchscreen. These interactions are meaningful for adults and perhaps especially for children.[18] In fact, consumer research shows that with touchscreens (compared with computers), people feel a greater sense of psychological ownership of what's on the screen.[19]

Physical texts often stimulate our olfactory sense. I used to think only readers of a certain age thought about a book's smell. Not so. In research with university students, I discovered a surprising number volunteering that what they liked most about reading in print was the smell of books.[20]

More broadly, reading is an embodied experience, meaning it entails more than just taking in and interpreting words. The physical circumstances in which we read are also part of reading. As Anežka Kuzmičová and her colleagues have documented, the medium on which people choose to do their reading is shaped by where they are in physical space.[21]

Then there is reading with our ears—with audiobooks, podcasts, and sometimes radio. While only one of our senses is involved, the listening process has nuanced possibilities beyond the words themselves. As audiobook aficionados remind us, the quality of the narrator can make a world of difference, for both understanding and enjoyment. Another factor is playing speed, which listeners can often control.

And let's not leave out video, which engages eyes and ears. While *How We Read Now* doesn't deal extensively with the role of video in learning, Chapters 7 and 8 offer some educational comparisons with print and audio.

Tracking the Reading Eye

While discussing physicality and reading, it's useful to take a closer look (no pun intended) at the "eyes" part. For more than a century, scientists have been studying how our eyes move when we read. Their answers provide a useful way to help identify skilled versus less skilled readers. Contemporary researchers also use eye-tracking technology to pinpoint potential differences between reading in print versus onscreen.

QUICK LESSON ON EYE MOVEMENT

When we read linear text, our eyes move across the page and then down to the next line. (For the sake of discussion, let's assume we're talking about reading an alphabetic script and one written from left to right.) Psychologists and reading specialists call such movements "saccades", coming from the French word for "jump" (*sauter*). Saccades come in three varieties: forward (progressive saccades), backward (regressive saccades), or down to the next line (line sweeps). The majority of saccades move forward, with only 10 to 15 percent typically going backward. Forward saccades vary in the amount of distance they travel (think of number of words jumped in one clip) and in the amount of time they take to do the traveling (on average, about 20 to 35 milliseconds, which is affected by how big the jump is).

Besides movement, there's another critical component: "fixations". Fixations are just what you imagine: The eyes stand still. It is during fixations that the eye actually reads. Fixations take up 90 to 95 percent of our reading time. These fixations vary in length—between 150 and 500 milliseconds, sometimes depending upon the kind of word we're reading. In general, we spend more time looking at content words (meaning nouns and verbs, plus adjectives and adverbs) than at function words (such as articles or prepositions).[22]

EYE MOVEMENT, READING SKILL, AND TEXT COMPLEXITY

We've known for years that reading skill can affect the length of eye fixations and use of saccades. Poorer readers tend to make more regressive saccades—that is, going back to what they just read. Moreover, those with reading challenges are prone to linger with longer fixations. Research comparing highly skilled versus average readers confirms that those with better skills use shorter fixations and fewer regressions.[23]

Once a text becomes complex, the picture shifts somewhat. The more difficult the text, the more regressive saccades readers make. Also, as we might anticipate, we fixate longer on unfamiliar words than on words we easily recognize.

EYE MOVEMENT AND READING MEDIUM

A natural question is whether our eyes move (and fixate) the same way when we read digitally as when we read print. Several initial studies indicated strong similarities across media.[24] Regressive saccades were about the same, though the number and length of fixations showed some variation. However, since each year we become increasingly practiced in reading digitally, it's conceivable that earlier variation in fixations across media might now be reduced.

Reading Report Cards

There's no debate that reading is a critical life skill in the 21st century. The evidence is also clear that the more exposure readers have to the written word, the better their overall language skills (including oral language, comprehension, word recognition, and spelling) through their years of formal schooling.[25] Amount of reading generally correlates with academic development.[26] It also turns out that the reading genre matters—an issue we'll address in Chapter 2.

WHAT ARE WE MEASURING?

The act of reading is multidimensional, and therefore so are ways of measuring it. For beginning readers, we focus on decoding skills (learning to read), while later the emphasis shifts to understanding and interpreting (reading to learn). We might also measure eye movement, reading speed, or how readers make sense of accoutrements to written text, such as tables, graphs, or illustrations.

Just now I mentioned reading for understanding and interpreting. To be successful, it surely helps to recognize the vocabulary and make sense of the syntax. But there's another component that often proves vital: prior knowledge of what the text is about. For this, please indulge me a quick story.

When my son was in high school, he (like millions of others) took the SAT, the standardized college entrance test administered by the College Board. A few months earlier, our family had vacationed in Scandinavia, where one stop was Uppsala, Sweden. Besides its university, the town is known as the home of Carl Linnaeus and his renowned botanic garden. Linnaeus, you'll recall, was the 18th-century botanist responsible for our Latinate system of classifying plants and animals. Today's Linnaean garden is a reconstructed version, but my family's tour was memorable nonetheless.

Back to the United States and on to the SAT Verbal. As luck had it, one of the passages my son encountered was about Linnaeus's garden. After a quicker-than-customary read, said son moved on to the questions, since he already had prior knowledge of the content. Prior knowledge can be a key factor in predicting not just how quickly readers progress through a text but how much comprehension they display.

Pause for a moment on the word "comprehension". What are we measuring? For several decades now, reading teachers and researchers have been emphasizing the importance of "reading for understanding", as the RAND Reading Study Group put it in their 2002 report. That report, plus another one, *Reading Next*, funded by the Carnegie Corporation of New York, addressed the concern that today's American middle and high school students are falling behind in comprehension skills.[27] The recommendation in both reports was for more explicit instruction to build comprehension skills.

What does comprehension entail? We include not just understanding the surface level of what a text says but being able to draw inferences based on what you read and to integrate new understanding with what you already know. (Notions such as reading closely and deep reading should be coming to mind.) In some cases, people include memory as part of comprehension, though typically this is a different dimension, particularly because a memory test might be conducted some time later than when the initial reading was done.

Tests measuring comprehension can vary widely, depending on design and audience. Are we talking about a standardized test for middle or high school students? About an experiment comparing reading in print versus on a digital screen? Looking ahead, we'll generally see two types of comprehension questions being used in formal experiments to measure reading:

- *Level of detail*: questions about the main idea in a passage versus about details (sometimes referred to as "key points")
- *Level of abstraction*: questions whose answers can be drawn directly from the passage versus those requiring students to make inferences

In addition, some of the research we'll be looking at has specialized measures of comprehension, such as when in the story an event took place or ability to integrate ideas drawn from multiple sources.

It's also vital to keep in mind the connection between comprehension and prior knowledge. Empirical evidence continues to show that students who already know about a topic (including relevant vocabulary and, of course, subject matter) tend to outscore those who don't on presumably content-neutral comprehension tests.[28]

Being clear about what we mean by comprehension will become particularly important when we look in Chapter 4 at research comparing reading single texts in print versus onscreen. As we'll see, there are crucial differences between surface versus more analytical types of comprehension.

Comprehension is also a vital issue when we talk in Chapter 5 about navigating multiple texts and using hyperlinks. Here, the issue of complexity involves not simply the difficulty level of words or how to make inferences but also knowing which pages (especially digital) to engage with and for how long.

READING VERSUS LISTENING

How do comprehension scores for listening stack up against those for reading text? Evidence continues to build that people with strong reading skills also do well on listening tests.[29] This relationship is evident from about age nine onwards. Before that, most children are still focusing on learning to decode writing, especially in languages such as English, where the rampant mismatches between spelling and pronunciation create special challenges. We'll have much more to say about reading versus listening in Chapters 7 and 8.

HOW MUCH ARE PEOPLE READING?

As recently as the 18th and 19th centuries, critics worried that a lot of reading (particularly of novels) was dangerous.[30] The problem? The new mass audience of readers might encounter vulgar materials, radical ideas, or unrealistic expectations for life's possibilities. People could also suffer exhaustion, given all there now was to read.

Women were assumed to be particularly vulnerable: By reading excessively, they might become barren or even go mad. Bashing female education more generally, the Victorian psychiatrist Thomas Clouston memorably concluded that women who spent time learning would seldom bear many children and

> only puny creatures at that, whom they cannot nurse, and who either die
> in youth or grow up to be feeble-minded folks.[31]

Mercifully, those sexist myths have been put to rest. Today the challenge isn't seen as too much reading but too little. In Chapter 3, we'll review the statistics.

Who Is the "Reader"?

There's no one-size-fits-all for talking about readers. The range of variables is vast—from age to gender to motivation, and much in between. Many of these differences are potentially relevant for thinking about when print, when digital screens, and when audio is the best platform for reading in an educational context.

Here are some of the factors to keep in mind.

AGE/GRADE/STAGE OF DEVELOPMENT

On the face of things, it might seem simple to divide up readers along a developmental timeline. But it's not. For starters, children don't begin school (and formal reading pedagogy) at the same age in different parts of the world. (In the United States, it's age six, but in Finland it's age seven, though the child's birth date can be another complicating factor.) High school doesn't end at the same age either. (In the United Kingdom, for instance, there are 13, rather than the American 12, years of schooling.) Confounding things further, terminology isn't consistent across countries. In the United States, "kindergarten" refers to the one year prior to beginning first grade. In Norway, the same word covers the entire range from ages one to five. And of course, a child's age doesn't necessarily correspond with reading level, regardless of grade placement.

Nonetheless, we need to start somewhere. The categories laid out in Figure 1.2, essentially following American educational divisions, are here simply as convenient guideposts.

	Age
Introducing words on paper or screen ("emerging literacy") (birth–kindergarten)	0 – c. 5
Learning to read (lower school) (1st – 5th grades)	c. 6 – c. 10
Reading to learn	
Middle school (6th – 8th grades)	c. 11 – c. 13
High school (9th – 12th grades)	c. 14 – c. 17
College and beyond	c. 18+

FIGURE 1.2 Educational Divisions in the United States

GENDER

On average, girls read more than boys (and once they're grown, women more than men). Whatever the reasons behind the discrepancies, the statistics continue bearing out this generalization.

Confirmation about gender differences in children's reading comes from many quarters, including in the United States, the United Kingdom, and cross-nationally.[32] Turning to adults in the U.S., multiple surveys tell the same story.[33]

Not surprisingly, girls' reading test scores are typically higher as well. Sampling the abundant evidence, first in the United States:

- On the 2017 NAEP (National Assessment of Educational Progress), girls outscored boys in both the fourth and eighth grades.[34]
- On the 2016 administration of both the PIRLS (Progress in International Reading Literacy Study) and the ePIRLS (a separate computer-based test), U.S. fourth-grade girls averaged higher scores.[35]

The same gender profile holds with international testing:

- On both the 2016 PIRLS and ePIRLS, international fourth-grade girls outperformed boys.[36]
- On the 2018 PISA (Programme for International Student Assessment), 15-year-old girls outperformed boys for the reading assessment in each of the countries and economies surveyed.[37]

REASON FOR READING

In talking about reading and readers, we can't ignore the question of *why* people are reading. The host of possible motivations includes:

- for pleasure
- to kill time
- to find something you are looking for
- to learn something you want to know
- because you are asked to read for a job or for schoolwork

We'll be focusing on school assignments.

MOTIVATION TO READ

Teachers and parents alike know that despite our best efforts, kids aren't always motivated to read. Among younger readers, there's evidence that if you let students choose their own reading, they are more likely to want to read.[38]

The same seems true of many in high school. As an eye-opening YouTube video posted by Heinemann Publishing reveals, students who confessed to doing almost none of the assigned reading became enthusiastic readers when allowed to make their own selections.[39] However, since at least some common works are required in most of our curricula, free choice isn't always an option.

What about technology? Will students who balk at reading print be more open to reading digitally? If so, maybe that's because digital reading is usually done on platforms with an internet connection to boatloads of alternatives to reading the text. Is the problem with reading print that students find it boring?

Yes, boring. That's what several college students reported in my own cross-national research.[40] When asked what they liked least about reading in print, their comments included "Just boring material and hard to read" and "It becomes boring sometimes". Responding to the same question in a different study, an even larger proportion of preteens and teenagers declared print to be boring.[41] No one in either survey wrote that reading on a screen was boring. In Chapter 10, we'll talk about why the discrepancy exists and why it matters.

Can digital texts or listening to audio motivate students to read? In the chapters ahead, we'll find some evidence for both.

MEDIUM PREFERENCE AND PREDICTED SUCCESS

Surveys of adults show that while most still favor reading print books, some prefer digital or audio.[42] A recent study conducted by *Library Journal* revealed some interesting generational issues. Table 1.1 summarizes preferences for print, eBooks, and audiobooks, by age cohort.

	Age 16–22	Age 23–38	Age 39–54	Age 55–73	Age 74–91
Prefer print	66.3%	66.1%	69.1%	57.3%	53.8%
Prefer eBooks	8.4%	12.4%	8.8%	11.8%	12.7%
Prefer audio	7.4%	7.6%	3.7%	2.8%	4.1%
No preference	17.9%	13.8%	18.5%	28.0%	29.5%

NOTE: Because of rounding, not all columns sum to 100%.

TABLE 1.1 *Library Journal* Study: Print, eBook, and Audio Preferences[43]

A striking finding was that two-thirds of readers from teenagers to those in their mid 50s preferred print. So much for the theory that younger generations, if given a choice, are leading the move away from print. By contrast, older users (age 55 to 91) had somewhat greater preference levels for eBooks than most of their juniors. More detailed questions in the study revealed that especially for the oldest cohort, the main lure of digital was adjustability of font size.

Finally, when asked their primary reason for specifically choosing hardback books (not paperback), cohorts age 16 to 54 said it was the smell and feel of such books. As we said earlier, the physical aspects of books can be a vital component of reading.

Children also have opinions about choice of reading medium. According to Scholastic's biannual *Kids & Family Reading* survey done in 2016, among children age 6 to 17,

- 45% said they preferred to read in print.
- 16% said they preferred eBooks.
- 38% said they had no preference.[44]

Some additional Scholastic statistics from a more recent report:

- 71% agreed that technology makes it easier to find books they would like to read.
- 70% who had listened to an audiobook agreed it encouraged them to read more.[45]

Does the medium on which people prefer reading influence how likely they are to learn when reading? Maybe. The answer is complex, partly because attitudes have been changing over the past decade or so. Earlier research showed that many college-age students said they preferred print, though their scores on print and digital reading were essentially the same. More recently, both younger and older students have been voicing a preference for digital, though their scores on more in-depth comprehension questions show they do better with paper.

A variant on the preference question involves prediction. Regardless of your preferences, you can predict how well you think you'll do answering questions when reading in print or on a digital device. (The same applies for listening to audio or watching a video versus reading.) Psychologists use the term "calibration" to measure how closely people's predictions correspond to actual test results. In the chapters to come, we'll see how accurate students' predictions are.

READING ABILITY

Finally, there's the longstanding issue of reading ability. Within the same classroom, schools commonly group younger readers by level. One basis for this practice is a clinical diagnosis such as dyslexia or ADHD. Another is if the student is a second-language learner. Or maybe the child is a less accomplished reader, with unknown etiology.

Some of the research on potential usefulness of digital screens or audio technologies as alternatives (or complements) to print has focused on younger students with reading challenges. In the chapters ahead, we'll look at how new technologies have the potential to foster both comprehension and motivation to read.

In this chapter, we've seen how nuanced the notions of "reading" and "reader" can be. There are no simple definitions for the terms and therefore no simple answer whether reading is best done in print, onscreen, or with audio. As they say in Italian, *depende*. In Chapter 2, we will see how the pros and cons of different reading media also depend on the kinds of texts we're talking about and on the types of research questions we ask.

CHAPTER 2   What Are You Reading?

Such a simple question: "What are you reading?" We ask it of friends, of children, of the stranger sitting beside us in an airport lounge. Usually we anticipate in return a book title or author's name, maybe followed by comments on whether it's a good read.

But the "what" question has other meanings that are relevant when giving advice on what reading medium—print, screen, or audio—is well suited to the content. One of those meanings relates to genre. We'll begin this chapter by laying out broad possibilities for types of content—and why they matter. Another "what" issue is more statistical: What reading media are people choosing?

From "what" questions we move to "how". One "how" concern is the extent to which conclusions about reading outcomes are shaped by testing contexts. Another is the way we physically interact with text, including when using digital technology. Finally, we need to think about how much our success when reading in print, on a digital screen, or with audio is influenced by the technology and how much by mental assumptions we make about reading platforms.

Genre

As language users, we can vary our words for denoting the same object: A canine friend is a dog, but potentially also a pooch or a pup, mutt or mongrel, Felix or Freya. However, when it comes to reading scientific studies, alternative terminology can be confusing. That's the case for research on reading in different modalities. Many reports specify the genre they are testing, but unfortunately, they don't always apply consistent labels.

The most basic genre distinction is between stories and information. However, the words used aren't always the same. Typically, researchers contrast "narrative" with "informational" text. But wait! Other authors talk about "narrative" versus "expository". And then you find those opposing "fiction" to "informational". The pairing is nearly always a dichotomy, even though technically, the terms don't always point to exactly the same kinds of writing.

Figure 2.1 is a crib sheet to help keep the various terms straight.

Terminology	Comments
Fiction vs. non-fiction	Imagined vs. factual
Narrative vs. informational	"Narrative" typically used for fiction, but can also refer to some non-fiction (such as biographies or reflective essays)
Expository	Typically used interchangeably with "informational", though more narrowly refers to description or explanation

FIGURE 2.1 Reading Genres Crib Sheet

We'll stick to the terms "narrative" versus "informational", except when the authors whose work we're discussing do otherwise.

Are "good" readers of narrative also "good" readers of informational text? Not necessarily. What's more, there's evidence that both children and adults tend to find informational text harder to read than narrative, given the seeking, integrating, and interpreting skills that making sense of informational texts may demand.[1]

Another genre question: Does medium matter? As we'll see in Chapter 4, there's evidence that medium is more relevant for informational reading than for narrative. A number of studies indicate little difference in comprehension scores between reading narrative text in print versus onscreen. However, for informational texts, print is more often the winner.

Obviously, just distinguishing between narrative and informational as reading genres will hardly suffice. Restricting ourselves to the fingers of one hand for narrative, we might talk about novels, short stories, plays, poems, and—why not—comic books. For the other hand (and informational reading), think of histories, political treatises, newspapers, feature stories, and scientific studies.

The issue of genre becomes yet more intriguing when we look at correspondences between genre types and matters ranging from gender patterns to reading scores. Start with gender. Linguists have observed for decades that statistically speaking, males and females gravitate to different language patterns in both their speech and writing. While men's language (again, statistically) tends to be more information-focused, women's speech and writing are commonly more social-interactive.[2]

It's hardly surprising, then, to find females more likely to be reading fiction, while males (again, statistically) more typically select nonfiction.[3] Overall, women read more than men.[4] However, according to Eurostat 2016, men are heavier newspaper readers than women, which fits with the "information" penchant.

Is it important that students read fiction? An analysis by John Jerrim and Gemma Moss argues "yes".[5] Using data from the international PISA test (for 15-year-olds) for 2009, the authors found what they called a substantial "fiction effect": Students who read fiction had higher reading scores than those who didn't. Checking whether reading magazines, newspapers, comics, or nonfiction gave a similar boost, the answer was "no". A different study, this time with 11- to 15-year-olds, concluded that "fiction book reading was the only reading habit to make a robust, unique contribution to the higher-level comprehension skill of inference-making".[6]

More data: In their study of German middle school students, Maximilian Pfost and his colleagues found that extracurricular reading of narrative texts, meaning fiction, correlated with reading comprehension and vocabulary development.[7] Adding to the story, Minna Torppa and her colleagues had this to say about the children they studied, ranging from age 7 to 16: Frequent leisure reading, especially of book-length works (genre not specified), correlated with better reading comprehension. Children who chose magazines, newspapers, or comics as their leisure reading didn't see an increase in their reading scores.[8]

Fiction (and books more generally) are known in the literary world as longform reading. Newspaper articles (and, to jump ahead, most websites) are shorter in length. If reading longer works contributes to better reading skills, what happens when the texts students choose to read on their own—or that we ask them to read,

> "Reading comprehension is promoted more strongly by leisure reading of books than other reading materials."
>
> Minna Torppa et al.[9]

especially online—are shorter? In later chapters, we'll see that research comparing reading platforms focuses on fairly short (sometimes very short) texts. It could turn out that if we increasingly ask students to read online, and the texts we have them read are short, we inadvertently wipe out the benefits of long reads.

Choosing a Reading Platform

It's easy to forget how recent some reading technologies are. While in the western world print is well into its sixth century, digital reading and modern audio options are relative newbies.

The concept of digital books can be dated to 1971, when Michael Hart, a graduate student at the University of Illinois, corralled some volunteers to type the text of classic works (which were out of copyright) into a mainframe computer. Anyone with access to the system could read the works for free. The venture—Project Gutenberg—continues to this day, though it has largely been supplanted by massive efforts from libraries, archives, and universities, not to mention Google.

Following several less-than-revolutionary commercial attempts to create eBook readers and eBooks, the real sea change came in November 2007, when Amazon introduced the Kindle and a first clutch of digital books. After several rapid-growth years of better hardware and more titles, eBooks seemed poised to challenge and potentially replace most print. The early 2010s saw triple-digit growth in eBook sales, year upon year.[10]

Then the music began to slow. Print sales, which had been taking a beating, became somewhat more stable. However, far and away the biggest winner of late has been audiobooks.

What are the numbers? Here are some sales figures. The data for print come from NPD BookScan (previously Nielsen BookScan), which tracks about 80 to 85 percent of all U.S. trade print books. The eBook and audiobook statistics come from the Association of American Publishers (AAP), which represents about 1,360 U.S. publishers of all three media. (Omitted from the AAP's numbers are small publishers and self-published books.) While admittedly not complete, the data in Table 2.1 offer a fair snapshot of three recent historical trends: reasonably steady-state for print, a decline in eBooks, and a surge of audio. In each case, the percentages represent gain or decline over the previous year.

	Print	eBooks	Audio Downloads
2019	−1.3%	−4.2%	+22.1%
2018	+1.3%	−3.6%	+37.1%
2017	+1.9%	−4.7%	+29.7%
2016	+3.3%	−16.9%	+24.7%

TABLE 2.1 Print Sales, eBook Sales, and Audio Downloads[11]

Fluctuation in print sales tends to reflect presence (or absence) of runaway bestsellers. For eBooks, earlier double-digit growth crested in 2013, followed by yearly declines since then. Audio is a growing market to be reckoned with, particularly impacting fiction sales of both print and eBooks.

Since *How We Read Now* focuses on reading in educational contexts, it's equally important to understand what's happening in the textbook industry. The most important thing to know? Textbooks cost too much. While I'll talk mostly about costs of college textbooks, price issues in K-12 are equally challenging.

Over the years, textbook costs have risen at an alarming rate. Between 1977 and 2015, they soared 1,041 percent.[12] The College Board estimated that for the 2018–2019 academic year, undergraduates should have budgeted about $1,200 for textbooks and related materials. In practice, many students didn't spend that much: Actual outlays for 2018–2019 averaged somewhere between about $200 to $500, depending on the survey you use.[13] Why the difference between budget estimates and expenditures? Students purchase used books (including earlier editions), rent books, share copies with classmates, borrow books from the library, or, in many cases, go without. Understandably, many faculty worry about textbook cost for students. A recent study found that 55 percent of faculty surveyed in the U.S. believed cost was the primary reason students didn't procure textbooks.[14] Notably, though, 37 percent believed the main reason was students thinking they didn't need the books.

The most significant move to address textbook cost has been creation of open educational resources (OERs). The OER movement, which is particularly active in the United States, creates digital resources—especially textbooks—that are freely downloadable and customizable. Perhaps the best-known OER project for university-level courses is OpenStax, a nonprofit initiative based at Rice University in Houston, Texas. OpenStax produces academically rigorous college textbooks in subjects ranging from macroeconomics to physics to U.S. history. There are dozens of other initiatives, including projects funded by the William and Flora Hewlett Foundation, New York

State's Open NYS, work of the Scholarly Publishing and Academic Resources Coalition (SPARC), and a bit of federal funding, thanks to Senator Dick Durbin's Affordable College Textbook Act.

The situation with OERs in K-12 education is a bit different. The first issue is that unlike in college, lower education (especially in lower school) commonly uses shorter modules rather than all-encompassing textbooks. A second consideration is that again in earlier grades, even if OER materials are accessed digitally by teachers, they tend to be printed out for students.[15]

A growing number of both module-sized and book-length works are available at no cost. Just a couple of the larger-scale initiatives include:

- EngageNY, an undertaking of the New York State Education Department offering pre-K through 12 English language arts and mathematics materials
- Utah Education Network, a project of the state of Utah, producing materials in the sciences (third grade through high school), English language arts (middle and high school), and mathematics (secondary level).

The OER website for the Utah Education Network also provides a valuable list of OER collections available elsewhere, including a link to OER Commons, which offers a treasure trove of possibilities.

Textbook publishers are painfully aware of both the cost challenge and competition from OERs. When college textbooks began appearing in digital versions, the pricing for digital was generally pegged lower than print, in part because of decreased production costs. Also competing for customers, at least in the U.S. market, is book rental—both of print and digital. In either case, the rental price is less than print or digital purchase. The rental alternative, which launched around 2008, has become huge. The rental share of the college textbook market has climbed to around 35 percent.[16] A 2019 survey by the National Association of College Stores found 44 percent of students polled said they had rented a book.[17]

The dollar differentials between purchase and rental speak for themselves. Consider these prices, pulled from Amazon's website in July 2019, for Robert J. Gordon's popular *Macroeconomics*, 12th edition:

New hardback purchase:	$177.00 (discounted from list price of $286.65)
eBook purchase:	$99.99
Print rental:	$20.99
eBook rental:	$69.99

Why does rental rather than purchase matter, besides to students' pocketbooks? Because when renting, students are guaranteed not to have the books in their possession when the course is over. Granted, many students sell their print books at the end of the term, and have done so for decades. However, if you have bought a book, there's the possibility you will keep it and even refer to it again. Good pedagogy suggests learning is cumulative and revisited, not one-off.

Meanwhile, with OERs becoming increasingly popular as antidotes to the crushing price of commercial textbooks (print or digital), textbook publishers started exploring alternative digital revenue streams. One has been the "value added" model, in which the publisher provides supplementary materials (for a small cost per student) that augment OERs with their zero price tag. From various corners of the publishing industry we hear reminders that professional expertise is worth paying for. This from David Anderson, as executive director of higher education at the Association of American Publishers:

> While there is a vast amount of free educational content available at our fingertips online, there is still a need for professionally researched and vetted materials produced by learning companies.[18]

Bluntly echoing the same sentiment was John Fallon, then chief executive officer of Pearson:

> If [the education community goes the open] route, it's not a free route. They will have to find a way to fund and sustain that approach. . . . Quality has to be paid for.[19]

A second strategy, which has been gaining traction, is to bundle access to multiple titles using a system called "inclusive access". Colleges sign on with the publisher to have titles available for students to download the first day of class. Payment is built into course fees, which students pay directly to the school. The school then pays the publisher. Pearson, McGraw-Hill Education, and Cengage have been leading the inclusive access charge.

To get a better sense of where pricing—and digital versus print publishing—might be heading, let's look at the textbook behemoth Pearson, whose sales for 2018 were more than $5 billion.[20] Whether you teach K-12 or are a college student, chances are you are using Pearson products. In case the name doesn't sound familiar, the company also owns Addison-Wesley, Prentice-Hall, and Scott Foresman. When Pearson makes a marketing decision, the whole educational publishing industry listens.

On July 16, 2019, Pearson spoke. Its print publishing is on the way out, replaced by a "digital first" policy. All future releases of textbooks in the United States will initially be published digitally. Print texts will still be around, but they will be updated less frequently. What's more, print will cost more to rent. In their announcement, estimates were about $40 for renting an eBook and around $60 for the print version.[21] As you surely noticed, the projected higher cost for print rental is the reverse of what comparative rental pricing patterns have been, even for Pearson. Why the shift? As Pearson's John Fallon proclaimed in the press release, "Our digital first model lowers prices for students and, over time, increases our revenues." For both buyer and seller, the move is essentially about money.

Money is clearly one parameter shaping how students (or, in the case of K-12, school systems) procure learning materials. But there's another factor that suddenly leapt into our consciousness in early 2020: global pandemic.

It all began, we think, with a bat that was butchered and sold at the Huanan Seafood Market in Wuhan, China. Bats are eaten in a number of countries, including parts of China. And bats carry viruses that, it turns out, can be deadly to humans. One of those viruses is what we now call SARS-CoV-2, causing the disease known as COVID-19. From there, a terrifying history unfolded: infections, deaths, cancellations of events, lockdown of geographic borders, economic unrest. And closure of schools, at least for in-person classes.

In March 2020, the growing response, especially in universities, was to move classes online. Stanford, Columbia, Princeton, and Harvard were among the first in the United States to make the switch, followed by scores of others. European universities did so as well. By that time in the term (at least in the United States), students had presumably already procured their course materials (print or digital). But the die had been cast for curricular planning going forward. If all courses could potentially be forced to go online, digital reading assignments—not print—made increasing sense.

As these events unfolded, I was reminded of our "warm-up exercise" in 2009, when the H1N1 virus threatened a pandemic and school closings. My university (and, I'm sure, many others) asked faculty to place as much course material as possible on the school's digital learning management system, in case in-person classes needed to be canceled. Abandoning the print books we had placed on library reserve or the print books we anticipated students would purchase or retrieve from library shelves later in the term, we rejiggered our syllabi. Instead of entire books, we substituted single chapters (following copyright law) that could be digitized and posted online. We looked for articles from journals to which our library had digital subscriptions. In short, the threat of disease helped launch a move from full-length print to piecemeal digital, a move that COVID-19 accelerated. The motivation in both cases was sudden practical necessity, not preferred pedagogical choice.

Beyond money and response to pandemics, a critical component in choosing a reading medium should be knowledge gleaned from research on how medium affects learning. For such research to be beneficial, it's vital to design experiments that tell us what we actually want to know. But successful research design is often not easy to achieve. To illustrate the challenge, I begin with a confession.

The Testing Challenge

As part of a larger study on print versus digital reading, I was interested in how much multitasking students do when using each medium. I already had self-reported data that indicated more multitasking when reading onscreen, but I wanted to document the process while it was happening. A graduate student (Mazneen Havewala) and I designed an experiment testing undergraduate psychology students, most of whom were fulfilling a course requirement by participating in studies of this kind.

We set up a room that had a computer with an internet connection, a place for students to set their mobile phones, and lots of potential distractors—intriguing pictures on the walls, colorful magazines on the table, Slinkies and Koosh balls to play with. Plus: video cameras to observe what was happening. There was no comprehension test afterwards and no time limit. We just wanted to observe whether college students were more prone to multitask in the computer condition than when reading print.

The experiment bombed. No sign of distraction or multitasking on either task. No ventures onto the internet, no checking their phones, no fingering the toys. Instead, the students were laser-focused on the reading task, as, in hindsight, I should have anticipated. Attentive students that they were, they simply followed instructions. You told me to read, so I did. The testing situation was radically different from settings in which undergraduates read when no one has a camera trained on them, such as sitting late at night in the library or sprawled out on their dorm sofa.

Why am I telling this story? Because we need to remember that test conditions are not the same as lived experience, and so formal testing situations may not be the best measures of learning. Sometimes they are better indicators of how well young people take tests. To be fair, tests can provide gross indicators of academic accomplishment, whether of content retention, mental agility, or more subtle thinking skills. However, it's vitally important we remain acutely aware of the distinction between learning and testing.

> *"Few tasks in life—and very few tasks in scholarship—actually depend on being able to read passages or solve math problems rapidly."*
>
> Howard Gardner[22]

A common testing variable is how long we give students to complete the task. Standardized tests such as the SAT are timed, in principle for good reason. (If not, some students might spend all day.) But we also know that exceptions are made to help students who legitimately need more time to complete the same work.

I often think about an op-ed in the *New York Times*, written by the Harvard psychologist Howard Gardner, back in 2002. Gardner argued that timed tests are poor indicators of what students actually know and what they are capable of.

Gardner is right. Our challenge as educators is that pragmatically, we need well-defined mechanisms for assessing learning. If we want to compare scores across students and countries, we need standardized measurements, one of which is time.

I stress the issue of time limits with testing for two reasons, both of which bring us squarely back to comparing reading in print versus digitally. Time issues have proven relevant in some of the research with university students we'll talk about in Chapter 4. When study participants are given fixed but ample time to read passages in print and digitally, comprehension scores are often comparable. However, when readers are under time pressure, they generally do better in print. Another issue with timing is what happens when readers can decide for themselves how much time to take ("self-regulation"). One study we'll mention showed that when students self-regulate, they tend to take less time with the digital task and do worse on comprehension.

Anecdotal evidence further suggests that if we're talking about linear text that happens to be in print, versus text that happens to be digital, readers tend to spend longer when reading print. In my own research, one student commented,

> It takes more time to read the same number of pages in print comparing to digital.[23]

Why the differential? Is the explanation that most of us initially learned reading skills and strategies using print, and we were told to read carefully? Do the physical characteristics of print shape our reading patterns? Do we have different assumptions about how we're "supposed" to read digitally? More broadly, how much do the ways we read digitally versus in print reflect technological issues and how much do they result from our mindsets? We'll tackle these issues as best we can with the research that's out there.

Handling Text

One reason for variation in how we read with different media is the ways in which we interact with them. In the last chapter, we talked about the role of touch as part of the reading experience. Here we focus on two other factors: how we move through a linear digital text and, for both print and digital reading, whether we annotate.

PAGING VERSUS SCROLLING

Before the development of the codex (what today we call books), longform writing was commonly done on scrolls. While we talk about the "books" of the Bible, those were later division names. Think of the Torah (the first five "books" of the Old Testament)—it's a scroll—or of the Dead Sea Scrolls. To read a scroll meant a lot of unwinding and rewinding—that is, scrolling. The codex (parchment pages, held together with a clasp) didn't start replacing scrolls until the first and second centuries AD.

The codex had many advantages over scrolls. You could write on both sides of a page. Books were easier to carry around and hold in your hands. You could find your place more quickly and focus attention on a particular span of words. True, with scrolls, it might be faster to skim and scan. The tradeoffs came down to what you wanted to accomplish when reading. In today's world of digital technology, the same tradeoff questions hold.

Assume for the moment we're talking about reading linear text, not navigating from site to site. If I'm reading on a computer, there are two basic modes for accessing subsequent lines of text. One, I can scroll down (with a touchpad, mouse, or scroll bar, or by depressing the "down" arrow). Two, I can "page" down, which, on my current Mac, means holding down the "fn" key and the "down" arrow simultaneously. (My old PC had distinct Page Up and Page Down keys.) The hitch with paging functions is that depending upon the format of the text you're reading, you might not get a full "page-worth" at a time.

If our goal in reading a text is to move quickly (say, checking if the piece is worth spending more time with or looking for something in particular when the Find function doesn't work), then scrolling is a blessing. However, what happens when the goal is to read more mindfully?

After nearly two millennia of reading distinct pages—and socializing subsequent generations to do so—it shouldn't surprise us that we tend to read more carefully when we read a page-worth of text than when we scroll. In Chapter 4, we'll review the research and possible explanations for the difference.

ANNOTATION

Let's shift gears now from moving between lines to how we insert ourselves into the discourse by annotating what we read. The simplest forms of annotation include underlining and highlighting, circling words, drawing arrows, and the like. Over the centuries, a more mentally engaging form of annotation has been marginalia, meaning writing your own comments in the margins.[24] If you can't write in the book, an alternative is, of course, taking notes separately.

In the next chapter, when we talk about longstanding advice for being a successful reader, we'll see annotation—especially marginalia—high on the list. Why? Because writing your own words facilitates active engagement with what you're reading. Annotation also slows down the reading process because you need to stop, think, and write rather than continually plowing ahead, sometimes with eyes glazed and mind elsewhere.

What happens when we read digitally? Do we annotate, especially by adding marginal notes of our own? Not nearly as much. The challenge of digital annotation has many faces. First, most software tools for doing digital annotation aren't as easy to use as an old-fashioned pen or pencil. (Surveys of students tell us this, over and again.) Second, many students aren't trained to do digital annotation, so it doesn't happen. Third, the literature on haptics indicates that physical manipulation of a handwriting tool—as opposed to a computer keyboard or touchpad—is a better aid to memory.[25]

But fourth, there's the question of attitude: Do we see digital text as meriting the slower, more careful reading that comes when you need to pause to annotate? Does the technology itself lead us to read in a particular way or is it our mindset?

Is It the Technology or What's in Our Head?

For more than a decade, writers, scholars, and educators have been debating the pros and cons of reading in print versus onscreen. However, over time, both the rhetoric and the research findings have been evolving:

- Phase 1: Asserting the equivalency claim
  Digital is just another medium for reading. As long as the content is the same, the "container" doesn't matter.
- Phase 2: Putting the claim to the test
  Some studies show equivalence in comprehension, though other studies show differences.

- Phase 3: Rethinking research design
    Maybe the original testing questions weren't sufficiently nuanced, and maybe
    we need a different research framework.

It's that last point—needing a different framework—that we have to talk about. The
framework I suggest contrasts external (physical) facts involved when we read versus
internal (mental) attitudes we bring to the reading experience.

EXTERNAL (PHYSICAL) ELEMENTS

Even diehard screen aficionados acknowledge physical traits that distinguish print
from digital reading. With print, there is the tangibility of the book itself and the
way we interact with it. This reading experience is then embedded in a material setting (where we read, how our body is positioned—the embodiment dimension).
Screens also have their external attributes: scrolling versus paging, screen and text
size, hyperlinks and navigation. One research challenge is that some of these external
features (especially hyperlinks and navigation) don't have print counterparts. And so
when we study them, we often can't make direct print-versus-digital comparisons.

How much do external attributes matter when we read? As we'll see in Chapter 4,
the answer is that especially for print, external issues matter a lot. Yet digital reading
proselytizers regularly muse that physical book huggers are simply being nostalgic
and unable to adapt to modern times.

Are they? To settle the point, psychologists and reading specialists have repeatedly
turned (our Phases 2 and 3) to empirical comparative research—which brings us to
the question of what's in our heads.

INTERNAL (MENTAL) ELEMENTS

When someone tells us that our fears (say, of little green men from Mars) are all in our
head, the implication is no, there are no such creatures; we only imagined them. There
is, of course, another sense of what's in our heads, and that is what we know. The latter
is a cognitive accomplishment, while the former is an assumption structure that can
be altered. Sometimes the two intersect.

Most of the research comparing print versus screen has looked at cognitive accomplishment. Typically, the tests are of comprehension at varying levels of sophistication. However, an alternative approach is to probe the extent to which a reader's
presuppositions come into play. The formal term in psychology for this dimension

is "metacognition", though we'll generally stick to the more ordinary language term "mindset".

The two meanings of "all in our head" come together in thought-provoking ways when we look at how we use technology—especially portable technology such as mobile phones—in our daily lives. It turns out that we really do behave differently, both socially and cognitively, when those devices are even passively on our minds.

Start with the social dimension. Let's say you're sitting with a friend at Starbucks, chatting. You both have your phones on the table but aren't using them. Just part of the furniture, right? No effect on the interaction? Wrong, as Shalini Misra and her colleagues showed.[26]

The researchers approached pairs of people entering a coffee shop, inviting them to take part in an experiment. When the participants had gathered up their food or drink, they were seated at tables. Some were asked to talk about a casual topic (specifically, their thoughts about plastic holiday trees), while others were directed to discuss something more personal (the most meaningful events over the past year). Observers made notes on what kinds of digital technologies (phones, laptops, or tablets) they had out on the table or held in their hands. When 10 minutes were up, participants was asked to complete a short survey that included psychological and social questions.

Among the most telling results:

- Conversations where no mobile technologies were present were rated as superior to those where technology was visibly available (even though not being used).
- In the absence of mobile technology, people rated their interlocutor as being more empathetic.
- For pairs who had a close relationship with each other, the presence of mobile technology drove their empathy level even lower than for pairs who weren't close.

In short, that phone in your hand or on the table, even when silent, can put a damper on face-to-face conversation, especially when you have strong ties to the person you're talking with.

Why? Another clever experiment, this time by Adrian Ward and his colleagues, offers some clues.[27] Ward's study set up three testing conditions in each of which participants were asked to complete two standard cognitive tasks, with their performance then scored. In the first condition, participants had their mobile phones placed face down on the desk during the testing. For the second condition, the phones had to be stowed in a pocket or bag. In the third condition, phones were left in another room before testing began. In all three cases, the phones were turned "completely on silent", meaning there would be no rings and no vibrations.

"The mere presence of [mobile phones] reduces available cognitive capacity."

Adrian Ward et al.[28]

Did proximity of the phone make a difference in testing outcome? You bet. The closer participants' phones were to them physically—even though silent—the worse the cognitive performance. Why?

The authors explain that the problem is limits on our cognitive capacity. Assume that each of us has a given amount of cognitive ability available at one time. If we divide up that quantity across multiple tasks (here, between working on the cognitive test and thinking about our phone), there's less cognitive power available for the task. Since the out-of-the-room condition yielded the best results, it's literally a case of "out of sight, out of mind", where the benefits are measurable. A further warning coming out of the study: The more participants reported being dependent on their mobile phones, the stronger the effects were of phone placement. Those heavily dependent were more likely to benefit on the tests from the phone being absent and more likely to have low scores when the phone was present.

All in our heads? Yes, in the senses of both cognition and personal assumptions. The important takeaway from this research is that given our real-world practices, experiences, and beliefs, we bring to our reading (and testing) an array of factors we can't check at the door.

Beginning in Chapter 4, we'll delve into research that confirms or refutes ideas about how we read using different media. But in preparation, we first need to take an honest look at whether print is a fair standard against which to measure reading in other media.

CHAPTER 3　Print Reading: A Gold Standard?

Ah, print! Depending on your age, it's likely you grew up largely or exclusively equating reading with printed text. Even if huge amounts of your reading are now on a screen (maybe augmented with audio), paper may still find a soft spot in your heart.

I value that spot. My house and office are overstuffed with bound volumes, and despite spending hours each day on a computer, I haven't managed to warm to leisure reading on a screen. But this book isn't about reading for pleasure, and it's not about me. It's about learning and objectivity—in this chapter, with regard to print. We need to assess not just how but also how much people are actually reading. We'll also benefit from thinking about tried-and-true strategies commonly cited as helping students become better readers of print, as well as asking the degree to which such strategies apply when reading becomes digital (either viewed on a screen or heard with your ears).

Why this heart-to-heart talk about print? Because often we romanticize print reading, instinctively leading us to judge reading onscreen as lacking. It makes little sense to obsess over whether reading digitally can measure up if we're not achieving presupposed—and sometimes unrealistic—standards based on print.

> "The way we do use digital media gets compared to the way we wish we used printed books: real apples with ideal oranges."
>
> Leah Price[1]

Anežka Kuzmičová makes the same point about reading print versus listening to audio: We tend to idealize how intently readers focus when reading hardcopy, when in fact the minds of print readers often wander, glossing over textual detail.[2]

How much are people reading these days? Let's have a look. We'll start with reading done of our own volition and then take on reading assigned to students.

Reading by Choice: What the Numbers Say

American educators and pollsters have long been tracking how much reading people do. Sometimes the metric is time per day, sometimes books per year. Many surveys target reading for pleasure overall, while others specify literary reading. Regardless of the yardstick, the core takeaway in each case is the same: In the United States, people are spending less time reading than before.

While most of our attention in this section is on reading patterns in the U.S., we need to remember that internationally, there's a lot of variation. In Norway, for instance, 88 percent of adults recently said they had read at least one book in the past year. By contrast, in the U.S., the figure was 73 percent, while in Italy it was closer to 42 percent.[3]

Why does it matter how much people read in general, especially for pleasure, when this book focuses on reading in educational settings? Because students who read for enjoyment are, statistically, better academic readers. Besides the evidence cited in Chapter 2, there's plenty more.[4]

Are young people these days avid readers in their free time? Even moderate or occasional readers? And what about their older siblings, parents, and grandparents?

We might start with a season, namely summer, when, in principle, students have time for leisure reading. Don't count on it happening. Scholastic's discussion of summer reading in its *Kids & Family Reading Report*, 7th edition, has some troubling statistics, including the trend over time. Table 3.1 summarizes a few highlights.

	Percent of children reading *zero* books over the summer	
	2016	**2018**
Age 9–11	7%	14%
Age 15–17	22%	32%

TABLE 3.1 Summer Reading Patterns[5]

Yes, you read that correctly: Among 15- to 17-year-olds, one-third read *no* books over the summer of 2018. Two years earlier, the proportion of missing-in-action readers was only one-fifth. The 9- to 11-year-old cohort had a somewhat better showing, but the percentage of summer non-book-readers still doubled between 2016 and 2018.

As U.S. children move from lower to middle to high school, their overall amount of pleasure reading (on average) declines. Consider these statistics from the most recent Common Sense Media survey of tweens (8- to 12-year-olds) and teenagers on frequency of pleasure reading:[6]

	Tweens	Teens
Enjoy reading a lot	38%	24%
Read daily for pleasure	35%	24%
Read for pleasure less than once a week or never	22%	32%

Given this pattern, further slides year-on-year, especially among older students, should trigger alarm bells about how teenagers on the cusp of high school graduation will look upon reading in the next phase of their education.

Move now to statistics for a broader age range, this time courtesy of the Bureau of Labor Statistics (part of the U.S. Department of Labor). The Bureau's annual American Time Use Survey includes self-reports on how much time people spend reading.[7] The first survey was done in 2003 (reported in 2004). The most recent data (as of my writing) were collected in 2018 and published in 2019.[8]

Begin with the big picture. The amount of leisure reading people are doing in America is going south:

	Some leisure reading on a given day	Minutes of leisure reading per day
2004	28%	23 minutes
2018	19%	16 minutes

How much reading people do isn't evenly distributed. While females in the 2018 survey averaged a bit over 17 minutes of daily pleasure reading, the average for males was barely 14 minutes.

Age also matters. Not surprisingly, the most avid pleasure readers in the latest survey were age 75 and above—48 minutes a day—with those age 65 to 74 not far behind (almost 37 minutes). It's the averages at the other end of the age spectrum that are concerning:

- Age 15 to 19:   7.2 minutes
- Age 20 to 24:   6.6 minutes
- Age 25 to 34:   6.0 minutes

Declines in reading, especially for teenagers and younger adults, aren't unique to the United States. A study by the Dutch Reading Foundation confirmed a similar pattern, shown here over a five-year span:[9]

- Age 13 to 19:   2013: 23 minutes
                          2018: 14 minutes
- Age 20 to 34:   2013: 17 minutes
                          2018: 13 minutes

Understandably, adolescents and young adults often have hectic lives, but these numbers—especially for the U.S.—are sobering. I don't know if reading social media online was included in the estimates. If so, the findings are even more worrisome.

What's more, the American survey for 2018 found that all three younger age cohorts managed to fit in at least two hours of television-watching daily.

U.S. results from the Bureau of Labor Statistics aren't an anomaly. The National Endowment for the Arts, Gallup, and the Pew Research Center all confirm this general profile, including a decline in leisure reading over time.[10]

What about students in college? The 2007 report of the National Endowment for the Arts (*To Read or Not to Read: A Question of National Consequence*) concluded that in 2005, 39 percent of college freshmen reported reading nothing for pleasure in a week. Another 26 percent read for less than an hour. Only 35 percent did more than an hour of weekly pleasure reading.

Findings from some studies are a bit rosier. For instance, Kouider Mokhtari and his colleagues reported that undergraduates in their research averaged 5.7 hours a week of leisure reading, though this paled before more than 12 weekly hours of internet use (which tally presumably excluded reading substantial linear text online).[11] SuHua Huang and her colleagues found a similar imbalance: 4.2 hours a week for leisure reading, but nearly 9 on the internet.[12]

Why such discrepancies between studies on pleasure reading? It's likely that differences in research methodology, which kinds of students were sampled, and the extent to which digital technologies were pervasive at the time (and whether online reading of substantial text was counted in the tallies) all played potential roles. What matters isn't absolute numbers but trends.

These patterns have been documented in other countries. Take findings from a Japanese study of more than 10,000 students, undertaken by the National Federation of University Co-Operative Associations.[13] In 2017,

- 53.1% of students didn't read books at all.
- The number of non-readers was up 18.6% over the past five years.
- Among humanities majors, 48.6% didn't read for pleasure.

OK. College students are busy. Maybe they would read more for pleasure if they had time. We'd like to believe that at least they are doing the reading assigned for schoolwork.

Are Students Doing the Reading We Assign?

Those of us who teach in high school or college are often filled with optimism as we prepare course syllabi for the semester ahead. We labor to identify books, chapters, articles, or online postings that we hope will enhance our students' understanding, develop their analytical abilities, and even offer enjoyment. But for this to occur, students need to do the reading.

Are they? Not so much.

Threaten them with quizzes, and the needle typically moves to the right. But trust students to read what you've assigned without such a stick, and you're often in for a rude awakening.

For nearly 40 years, this reality has led researchers to try quantifying how much of the reading is being completed in time for the class for which it's assigned or by the end of the term. A complementary approach is looking at the number of hours per week students are reading for schoolwork. Nearly all the answers about "reading compliance" have come from student self-reporting. Admittedly, self-reports are notoriously inaccurate. However, a good reason for taking them seriously is their consistency, especially over the past 20 years.[14]

The go-to study repeatedly cited is Colin Burchfield and John Sappington's comparison of reading completion rates over time.[15] The authors asked students in university psychology classes, ranging from lower-level undergraduate to graduate courses, how much of the assigned reading they did. Back in 1981, the overall finding was more than 80 percent. By 1997, the average was closer to 20 percent.

Twenty percent? Are you kidding? Sadly, not. A spate of other research on university students has reported numbers in the same range: 28 percent, 27 percent, and 25 percent.[16] In another study—this one polling more than 18,000 seniors from 45 U.S. colleges and universities, Amy Ribera and Rong (Lotus) Wang found only 21 percent saying they usually completed all their assigned course reading, presumably by the end of the semester.[17]

What if you ask, instead, how many hours per week students are reading for school assignments? Here's what some researchers found when surveying U.S. college students:

10.9 hours/week
7.7 hours/week[18]

The latter number is close to figures reported by the National Survey of Student Engagement (NSSE) for their 2019 college survey:[19]

First-year students: 6.4 hours/week
Seniors: 7.1 hours/week

Hours college seniors spent on academic reading: 7.1 per week

NSSE 2019

To contextualize: The NSSE also asks students how many hours, in a typical seven-day week, they estimate spending overall preparing for class, where preparation includes "studying, reading, writing, doing homework or lab work, analyzing data, rehearsing, and other academic activities". (Time spent in class was not included. In the United States, for full-time undergraduates, the number of class hours typically ranges from 12 to 17 weekly.) Here are the responses for preparation time:

First-year students: 14.4 hours/week
Seniors: 15.0 hours/week

Aren't these numbers low? Many of us remember having done far more reading (and studying in general) when we were in college. Perhaps our recollections aren't off-base. A 2010 study by Philip Babcock and Mindy Marks cited earlier research showing that in 1961, U.S. college students were averaging 24 hours per week studying. When you add in hours spent in class, that made college a roughly 35- to 40-hour-per-week full-time endeavor. True, not all "studying" entails reading, but it's highly likely that more than seven hours a week were devoted to reading.

What changed? For starters, far more people are in college now than 40 or 50 years ago, and they come from increasingly diverse backgrounds. A large proportion have part-time or full-time employment, reducing hours available for school work. Add in the dramatic growth of internships (which can consume 20 hours a week or more), throw in time spent on sports, volunteering, and of course social media, and time left for academics shrinks even further.

Is it only American students who aren't doing much academic reading? The story here is complicated. In countries where university grades are determined by a single examination at the end of a course of study, the norm among students is to do all the reading just prior to the exam, not incrementally before the class for which it's assigned. I learned this reality the hard way when teaching a master's-level class in Italy in spring 2019. My colleagues had cautioned me not to expect students to do much homework, so I paced the syllabus with short amounts of reading that I asked students to complete before the class in which we'd be discussing it. It soon became clear that practically no one was doing the assignments. When I questioned them—a bright group, most of whom seemed eager to learn—they diplomatically informed me that my request for pacing the reading was an alien concept.

Some countries or universities set expectations for the number of hours per week students should be reading (or studying more generally). In the United Kingdom, Helen St Clair-Thompson and her colleagues report that college students said they were reading an average of 14.1 hours per week.[20] While this is high compared with American practices, the authors write that according to university guidelines, students should have been spending at least 25 hours weekly, either reading or otherwise using learning materials.

Interesting, this U.K. expectation is fairly close to the official standard for U.S. colleges and universities.[21] According to accreditation standards, students are expected to spend two hours doing outside preparation (typically reading and otherwise studying) for each in-class hour. If students have 15 hours per week of class, 30 hours of preparation are expected. Thirty is a far cry from the roughly 15 hours total that the NSSE report tells us American students are actually devoting to studying.

Why are so many students completing so little assigned reading? The primary reason they offer is lack of time.[22] However, another rationale is not believing that doing the reading is necessary to succeed in the course. Students (at least in the U.S.) regularly complain when the assigned reading isn't discussed in class or doesn't appear on an examination. Kylie Baier and her colleagues reported in 2011 that almost 32 percent of the students they surveyed believed they could earn an "A" grade in the class without doing the reading.

The U.S.–Norway Faculty Study

We've been looking at students' self-reports on how much academic reading they do. An alternative approach is to survey faculty practices, along with faculty perceptions of student compliance. Is the problem only that students aren't reading what we assign? Maybe we've cut back on our assignments, at least in part because students weren't doing the reading. Anecdotally, many of us who teach know we've reduced the reading in our courses, though I couldn't find any formal studies confirming this reduction. It also seemed important to gauge whether today's university professors feel that digital technologies are reshaping academic course assignments or student reading patterns.

I undertook to find out. My partner-in-crime was Anne Mangen, a reading expert at the University of Stavanger in Norway. Because we had access to faculty members in both the United States and Norway, we also were able to explore whether national context shaped faculty practices or perceptions. The study was limited to these two countries simply for convenience, not because of prior hypotheses about national similarities or differences. We hope colleagues in other parts of the world take up our invitation to gather data from their own institutions to see how our findings compare with theirs.

We designed an online questionnaire for faculty in the U.S. (at American University, my home base) and in Norway (at the University of Stavanger, the

University of Oslo, and the University of Bergen). At American University, 78 faculty members completed the survey. In Norway, the number was 71.

Participants all taught in the humanities and social sciences, areas that commonly include what we used to call "reading courses"—that is, courses traditionally assigning a sizable amount of reading. Disciplines we drew on included English literature, communication and media studies, comparative literature, education, history, international studies, philosophy, political science, and sociology. Since this was a relatively small and somewhat informal study (no random sample of participants, no matched set of courses between countries), our modest goal was to identify trends.

When doing cross-national research, we need to be mindful of diverse country practices that can make direct comparisons difficult. One of our challenges was defining what counted as a course. In the United States, the average course at most universities potentially earns students three academic credits. Norway's system follows the Bologna Process, an educational agreement among 48 European countries designed to make university curricula in Europe more compatible with each other. For our purposes, the U.S. questionnaire asked faculty how much reading they assign for a 3-credit undergraduate course, while the Norwegian version asked about assignments for a 10-ECTS course (ECTS standing for European Credit Transfer and Accumulation System).

We also needed to think about differences in curricular decision-making. In the United States, especially in private colleges and universities, professors have considerable latitude in selecting not just subject matter but also how much reading to assign. By contrast, Norway has national reading assignment guidelines, partially adapted for different universities, subject matters, and types of reading. As a rule of thumb, Norwegian students in the humanities and social sciences are expected to read about 800 to 1,000 pages in a 10-ECTS one-semester course. For literature courses where students read novels, the numbers are a bit higher.

After gathering general demographic information, the survey began by asking participants the following questions, both about a typical introductory course they offered and then about a typical advanced-level course:

- How many entire books do you ask students to read for the entire semester?
- About how many pages of reading do you assign for the entire semester? (Page ranges were provided from which to choose.)

The next inquiries probed faculty perceptions about how much of the reading they believed students were doing (reading compliance). Again, we asked about both introductory and advanced courses. Our questions were:

- What percent of assigned reading do you think your students do before class?
- What percent of assigned reading do you think your students do by the end of the semester?

A third set of questions concerned whether participants had made changes to their reading assignments over the past 5 to 10 years regarding amount or level of complexity, and, if so, why. The "why" options included:

- Students weren't doing all the reading, so I reduced the amount.
- Students weren't understanding the reading, so I substituted less difficult reading.
- Instead of having students read so much, I substitute more audio materials (such as podcasts).
- Instead of having students read so much, I substitute more video materials (such as YouTube videos, TED Talks, or movies).
- Other (please describe)

The last group of questions explored whether participants thought digital technologies were affecting student reading. We specifically asked if respondents agreed or disagreed with these statements:

- Digital technologies may be leading students to do less academic reading than before.
- Digital technologies may be leading students to do more shallow reading than before.

The online survey concluded with a place to offer additional comments. Besides the online survey, we conducted in-depth face-to-face interviews with several people who had completed the survey.

Here's what we found.[23]

AMOUNT OF READING ASSIGNED

Norwegian faculty participants reported assigning more books, especially at the introductory level. Yet overall numbers are still low:

	U.S.	Norway
Introductory course	1.7 books	2.8 books
Advanced course	2.3 books	2.8 books

Remember these are only averages. Among history faculty in the United States, responses spanned from 0 books to 8, both for introductory and advanced courses. In Norway, the range for history faculty was from 0 to 3 (introductory) and 1 to 4 (advanced).

For assigned pages of reading per course, again the level was higher in Norway. Here are the responses for assigning more than 600 pages per semester:

	U.S.	Norway
Introductory course	53.0%	72.7%
Advanced course	64.3%	75.7%

The higher Norwegian numbers (both for books and pages) likely reflect, at least in part, Norwegian regulations. Judging by the additional remarks from several of the U.S. participants, another factor may be that advanced students in the United States are often asked to find their own reading materials for doing research papers, and those books and pages don't count as faculty assignments.

In their additional remarks, a few people commented that either their students—or they themselves—sought ways of reducing required reading. One U.S. respondent said,

> Students come to expect more films and alternatives to reading and are disappointed when a class is more reading-heavy.

Several Norwegian participants were concerned that depth of understanding was being compromised by regulations. For instance,

> The amount of literature and pages to read—that is not my decision. . . . But—I reduce the number of pages in a way—I focus on something "that must be learned" in depth.

HOW MUCH OF ASSIGNED READING DO FACULTY THINK STUDENTS ARE DOING?

Let's begin with faculty estimates of what percentage of the assigned reading they thought their students (as a whole) complete before the class for which the reading was assigned. For both introductory and advanced courses, the averages were higher for the United States:

	U.S.	Norway
Completed before class		
Introductory course	53.8%	31.4%
Advanced course	63.0%	41.6%

However, for estimated completion by the end of the semester, results for the two countries were nearly identical, for both introductory and advanced courses:

	U.S.	Norway
Completed by end of semester		
Introductory course	65.0%	65.7%
Advanced course	72.8%	72.3%

Why were the Norwegian "before class" estimates so low compared with the American ones? It could be that in the United States, academic assessment is typically interlaced throughout the term, putting pressure on students to read at more regular intervals. Or maybe American students are pulling the wool over their teacher's eyes.

Participants acknowledged that student completion of reading assignments is not a new problem. What's more, students make strategic choices about what to read. A U.S. faculty member wrote that threat of a quiz on the material was a "compelling reason" to do the assigned reading. A participant in Norway reported that students strategize what they must do to pass the course.

HAVE FACULTY CHANGED THEIR READING ASSIGNMENTS IN RECENT YEARS?

Not everyone in the survey reported altering their reading assignments in recent years. Forty-seven U.S. respondents said they had, compared with 27 in Norway. Accordingly, when we ran statistics on shifts in reading assignments (seen in the percentages below), we only included participants who had made changes.

In both countries, more than 40 percent of respondents said they now assign less reading than in the past. A critical factor driving this reduction was faculty perception that students weren't completing what had been assigned (the response of one-third of respondents in both countries). We also asked whether faculty were now assigning less difficult reading because students weren't understanding the texts. While almost 20 percent of U.S. respondents said "yes", the number in Norway was a whopping 56 percent. Although we can't be certain about the reason for this discrepancy, our hunch is that the large enrollment growth in Norwegian universities in recent years brought with it less academic selectivity.

Our last two questions considered whether professors were now assigning more audio or video materials in place of written texts. Here's what the respondents said:

	U.S.	Norway
More audio materials	14.9%	8.0%
More video materials	31.9%	24.0%

Given how easy it is to access audio and video these days, it's not surprising that both (especially video) are making curricular inroads. However, the trend is larger in the United States.

Participants were invited to indicate other kinds of changes they've made over the years and why. Among the U.S. responses:

"I used to include supplemental reading for essays. I don't anymore."
"Students struggle to read and analyze scholarly literature thus I have reduced the amount so we can improve critical reading skills."

Norwegian replies included:

"Instead of having students read so much, I let them do work/tasks in class."
"The variation of students is bigger so the better students contribute to some more difficult texts, while the not so good students is a reason for having more of the easier texts as an average."

DO FACULTY BELIEVE DIGITAL TECHNOLOGY AFFECTS STUDENT READING?

Are digital technologies seen as impacting the amount or effectiveness of student academic reading? The answer from our faculty participants was "yes" for almost 88 percent in the United States and 73 percent in Norway. For those answering "yes", we asked two follow-up questions:

	U.S.	Norway
Do you think digital technologies are leading students to do less academic reading than before?	62.0%	64.0%
Do you think digital technologies are leading students to do more shallow reading than before?	82.0%	80.0%

Less academic reading. More shallow reading. And near-identical perceptions across the two countries. The numbers—especially for depth of reading—should give us serious pause.

But there is more to tell—both positive and negative. These are some of the additional U.S. comments about digital technologies:

Positive: "They're exposed to more academic readings than before, I believe."
           "Digital technology has improved my students' critical reading skills."
           "Easier access, lower cost."
Negative: "Digital technologies shatter their ability to concentrate for long periods of time."
           "I don't think students retain information when they read online because they aren't always taking notes or interacting with the text."
           "They read more quickly these days. They miss a lot."

And some Norwegian responses, again both positive and negative:

Positive: "Digital technologies are fantastic for the access they provide to primary sources."
           "May also lead some students to read more."
Negative: "Digital technologies reduce their ability to concentrate."
           "Easy distraction."
           "Digitization has a negative effect on the focus and concentration, the deep reading of large amounts of text."

As the range of faculty comments suggests, the effects of digital technology on student reading aren't seen as all good or bad. However, we cannot ignore the sobering statistic that four out of five respondents in both countries perceived that these technologies were leading to shallower student reading.

GENERAL CHANGES IN STUDENT READING PRACTICES

The additional responses yielded yet more insightful comments. One U.S. participant was concerned that "Except the very best students: students do less of the reading than before. And they are less capable of reading for main arguments". Norwegian faculty participants addressed a host of issues:

Speed: "They read too quickly."

Genre: "My students read less narrative than before."

Attention span: "I experience students' attention span as shorter than before."

Complexity: "Students' expectations in making complicated stuff more accessible increases. I cannot conceive of a student reading Kant's *Critique of Pure Reason*."

The fact that such comments cover a wide swath of concerns tells us this: Many faculty members sense that digital technology is not simply an alternative container for the same reading content as print, but rather a platform that can shape what and how students read.

THE COST FACTOR

Differences in the price of higher education in the United States versus Norway are huge. In America, students (or their families) are responsible for footing what is often a very sizeable bill, while in Norway, taxes fund everything but a small registration fee. Accordingly, the price of textbooks is a much larger burden in the U.S. than in Norway. Nonetheless, faculty members in both countries were mindful of textbook cost. U.S. participants stressed the importance of locating free sources:

"I cannot in good conscience ask my students to pay the outrageous cost of books. I use web available material and academic journal articles."

"Most of us have reduced books and turned to free online content to help students with costs."

In Norway, in addition to reliance on digitally available resources, a common model was creation of a print compendium of selected book chapters. As one Norwegian respondent noted,

"I don't think the cost has become more of an issue during the past few years; however, we do have the compendium precisely so that students don't have to buy all these books from which the chapters are taken."

In the United States, print compendia were popular in the 1980s and 1990s. However, because of copyright challenges, the model has largely been abandoned in favor of libraries securing copyright clearance and mounting selected materials online.

SHIFTING STUDENT PROFILE

Participants commented on other changes impacting student reading. Several involved time pressure stemming from employment:

U.S.:   "Students do more paid work so have less time to read."

Norway: "They work more, and this trend has increased over the last ten years. . . . They are registered as full-time students now, too, but in practice they are not."

Another type of comment—specifically from the United States—related to a declining national focus on liberal arts education: "There is a greater emphasis on practicality now. It comes from the administration and from students. It's impossible to justify 'longform' reading in an environment that is anti–liberal arts."

Finally, there's the issue of student academic preparation. We already saw that many faculty members have reduced reading complexity because their students weren't understanding the assigned texts. As one Norwegian interviewee noted, "Mass education has brought much more variation into the student population in terms of reading qualifications".

Our faculty study reinforced anecdotal impressions about student academic reading, at least in university courses. The first is that students aren't "doing the reading", and their faculty notice. The second is that in response, many professors are reducing the amount they assign, choosing simpler texts, or substituting audio or particularly video materials. The third is that at least some professors feel that digital technology is leading to diminished reading: in amount, in depth, or both.

This last finding reminds us how important it is to weigh carefully the pros and cons of reading onscreen. If those who teach are concerned that digital reading may be detrimental to the learning enterprise, and if students have similar concerns, how do we handle the challenge? We'll tackle this question in Chapter 6.

Tried-and-True Reading Strategies

Parents and educators are rightly concerned about how much (or little) young people are reading. Proactively, we think about strategies to help students—when they do read—to benefit most from the experience. To this end, there have long been educational "gold standards" for reading productively.[24] Let's have a brief look at some of the suggestions commonly bubbling to the top. We'll then ask how applicable these practices are as models for digital reading and audio. We'll end with a more daunting question: How effective are the strategies even when reading print?

TRADITIONAL STRATEGIES FOR READING PRINT

I've grouped a dozen such strategies (Figure 3.1) into three categories: those involving "just" reading, those enlisting some form of writing, and those requiring some form of review or testing. Yes, there are more tactics (including those involving mental inference, analysis, and synthesis). And of course, not everything listed is appropriate for every age student. But at least this array gets us started.

Strategy	Comments
Reading activities	
Prereading	Scanning through the text before doing a careful read
Pacing reading	Knowing when to skim, scan, or read more mindfully
Rereading	Often when reviewing for a test; might include reviewing annotations or separate notes (see below)
Writing-as-you-read activities	
Annotating text	
Marginalia	Specifically, writing comments in the margins
Highlighting	Very common
Underlining	Very common
Writing separately	
Taking notes	Becoming less common
Copying passages	Increasingly rare
Response activities	
Listing keywords	Typically teacher-driven
Summarizing	Typically teacher-driven
Answering questions	For example, questions at the ends of textbook chapters
Taking a quiz	Quizzes embedded in chapters

FIGURE 3.1 School-Based Strategies for Reading Print

All these ideas are familiar, but a couple of observations are still in order. First, copying passages may seem very old school: Isn't this what our great-grandparents did in grammar school? But before you dismiss the practice, consider these words from the eloquent writer Nicholson Baker:

Reading is fast, but handwriting is slow—it retards thought's due process, it consumes scupperfuls of time, it pushes every competing utterance away—and that is its great virtue, in fact, over mere underlining, and even over an efficient retyping of the passage.[25]

While underlining and highlighting (the tools of choice for the vast majority of students—and many of the rest of us) let you cruise text at 90 miles an hour, actually writing out the words that matter puts on the brakes so your mind has time to think.

The last strategy in the list—taking a quiz—is not what you'd expect to find on a list of reading strategies. Quizzes as part of the reading process are more typically a feature of adaptive learning textbooks, which are generally digital (though print versions exist). Why include quizzes here? At the end of this chapter, we'll have the answer.

DO PRINT STRATEGIES APPLY TO DIGITAL READING?

When new technologies arise, we commonly look to their predecessors for ideas going forward. A familiar example is early printing in the West. Compare an original Gutenberg Bible with the Great Bible of Mainz, both produced in the 1450s. Viewing the two together (which used to be possible in the Great Hall of the U.S. Library of Congress), you'd be hard-pressed to tell that Gutenberg's was printed and the Great Bible of Mainz written entirely by hand. Both volumes are of similar size and have vellum pages. Both are written in Gothic (blackletter) textura script, and both are heavily illustrated and rubricated (those large red letters) manually.

What do 15th-century Bibles have to do with reading strategies? Those first printed books remind us that it took another several hundred years for printing to come into its own, with its particular conventions for production and use—including (eventually) standardized spelling. Digital reading is still in its comparative infancy. At this early stage, it's reasonable to look back to print-reading strategies when thinking about reading onscreen, especially for reading linear text. After all, if we believe the content in print and on a digital screen is meant to be the same (again, with linear text) and that the reading goals are identical, print-reading strategies should be directly applicable when reading digitally. For digital reading that is nonlinear (such as using hyperlinks or navigating across multiple online sites), the reading goals are different and, presumably, so will the reading strategies be.

Assume for the moment that students who score well on standard print-based reading tests make use of at least some of the strategies we laid out in Figure 3.1. The question then becomes: Will scores on print-based reading tests also predict results for digital reading?

The answer is generally "yes", as illustrated by reading results from the 2012 PISA (Programme for International Student Assessment) test of 15-year-olds. That administration had both a print and digital version, and results showed a high correlation between scores on the two tests.[26] Importantly, though, the structure of the tests was different. With the print version, students read individual linear texts, while the online version included multiple texts. Researchers analyzing the PISA results found much more variation in digital scores across countries, probably due in part to students' differing levels of computer skills.

DO PRINT STRATEGIES APPLY TO READING WITH AUDIO?

Reading and listening are both forms of language. In literate societies, children develop listening skills before learning to decode text. However, listening and reading share most of the same linguistic DNA. To be successful in either, you need knowledge of vocabulary, morphology (essentially, word formation), and syntax (combining words to make sentences). It also helps to understand the language's sound system, as well as common types of composition (such as poetry versus prose).

Educators working with younger children have been asking how much skills in listening are good predictors of reading ability, or vice versa. A spate of studies indicates a strong relationship between listening comprehension and reading comprehension.[27] Evidence from second- and third-graders suggests that the strongest point of mutual prediction is vocabulary.[28]

Predictive power is relevant because we're interested in potential transferability of print-reading strategies to reading with audio. Understandably, since reading text is visual and listening is done with our ears, many of the reading strategies we presented in Figure 3.1 don't apply. Figure 3.2 identifies text strategies that might or might not make sense for audio.

We're left with a short list, composed of writing-as-you-listen and response activities. All could potentially be useful (with caveats we'll discuss in a moment). The real question, of course, is whether students do take notes, list keywords, or summarize while listening to audio (or, for that matter, watching a video). Without explicit training and direction, the chances are lower than when reading with a physical text in hand. Copying passages, answering questions, or taking quizzes? Even less likely. Yet if audio (or video) is to become a larger-scale learning medium, we will need to crank up expectations and instruction.

Strategy	Viability for Audio
Reading activities	
Prereading	No
Pacing reading	No
Rereading	Unlikely
Writing-as-you-read (listen) activities	
Annotating text	No
Writing separately	
Taking notes	Yes
Copying passages	Possible (transcription)
Response activities	
Listing keywords	Yes
Summarizing	Yes
Answering questions	Potentially
Taking a quiz	Potentially

FIGURE 3.2 Which Text Strategies Are Viable for Audio?

DO TRADITIONAL STRATEGIES REALLY WORK?

As digital screens and audio increasingly become alternatives to print reading, it seems reasonable to draw upon tools long used for guiding student reading in print. Annotating, identifying keywords, and summarizing are among the techniques we'll see in the chapters ahead being advocated by researchers.

But do the strategies work—even with print? What a question, you might ask. Yes, there's evidence these strategies can be beneficial, especially when the techniques slow down the reading and when students review their annotations. However, educational psychologists have been questioning the efficacy of some of these tried-and-true print-reading strategies.

An important article in 2013 by psychologist John Dunlosky and his colleagues reviewed student reading and study strategies.[29] The issue? Many of those tried-and-true reading and study techniques are not particularly effective when it comes to sustained learning—in Dunlosky's words,

> especially if students want to retain their learning and understanding of content well after the exam is over—obviously an important educational goal.[30]

Which reading and study strategies work best and which are less successful? The authors' review of the research literature examined the effectiveness of 10 learning techniques. Here, we'll zero in on those we included in Figure 3.1:

Highly useful:	Practice testing (on our list called "Taking a quiz")
Less useful:	Rereading
	Highlighting and underlining
	Summarizing

> "More than 100 years of research has revealed that taking practice tests (versus merely rereading the material to be learned) can substantially boost student learning."
>
> John Dunlosky[31]

The authors stress that actively engaging with what you know—and don't know—is an excellent way to increase learning. In a reading (or classroom) context, this approach typically entails low-stakes or no-stakes testing. If the textbook you're reading doesn't provide built-in quizzes, at the very least you can ask yourself, "Could I explain that concept to another person?" Then try doing so, even if the listener is imaginary.

What's the issue with rereading, highlighting, or summarizing? The research literature reviewed by Dunlosky and his colleagues doesn't suggest they're useless but rather that they are not as effective as other strategies. Take rereading. While a second read may help with recall of main ideas, it's less effective in improving memory for details.

What about highlighting and underlining? The main problem is that these are generally mentally passive activities. As with food at a Thanksgiving buffet, we often help ourselves to more than we can consume (for food) or make good sense of (for the texts we mark up). There's some (though not conclusive) evidence that students remember more of a text if they are limited in how much they may highlight or underline, rather than being given free rein. Why? Because when you're restricted in how much you're allowed to mark, you need to engage in active mental processing to select what is most important.

And summarizing? Isn't that a form of quizzing yourself—which should make it a successful strategy? Summarizing isn't a unitary technique. It might entail writing a sentence or two or an entire paragraph. It could be done in writing or orally. And it might happen with or without the original text present. Not surprisingly, the better the quality of the summary, the more beneficial for learning. In principle, summarizing can be a valuable pedagogical technique. The problem is that many students aren't trained how to construct an effective summary, and so the technique is often not particularly effective.

No one is suggesting that teachers or students abandon any of these reading and study strategies. Rather, the takeaway message is that we can't assume any of the strategies listed in Figure 3.1 will automatically improve reading and learning, either for print or when reading digitally or with audio. Effective strategies are those that actively involve our minds. The challenge is to support such engagement.

In Chapters 1, 2, and 3, we have laid the groundwork for thinking about both reading in general and reading using different media. We've also hinted at some research findings regarding the pluses and minuses of using print, digital screens, or audio. Now it's time to delve into that research.

PART II   READING IN PRINT VERSUS ONSCREEN

WHAT'S
AT STAKE?

Here are some issues to be thinking about as you read Part II:

- What do students say about the pros and cons of reading onscreen?
- Does genre or text length affect performance with digital or print reading?
- Is formal testing a fair indicator of how students read independently?
- How is use of social media shaping students' onscreen academic reading?
- How important is mindset in the way we comprehend digital text?
- Are students better at estimating performance with print or digital reading?
- What special skills should we teach for using multiple online documents?

CHAPTER 4   What Research Tells Us: Single Texts

Digital text is the most common alternative to reading in print. In principle, a downloaded eBook invites our exclusive attention. However, when we go online, we often access more than one text in tandem. As we'll see in this chapter and the next one, the ways in which readers approach single versus multiple texts—whether in print or onscreen—tend to be quite different. So, too, are the questions that researchers ask.

We begin our foray into the research by looking at reading single texts. It's useful to divide the discussion into two parts, since questions relevant for talking about young children are quite different from those appropriate for school-age readers. We'll take the youngest first.

Young Children and Digital Books

ARGUING AT CROSS-PURPOSES?

Do you believe that young kids (say, from birth to age five or six) should be firmly rooted in the world of print? Or are you worried you're depriving children of a valuable opportunity if you deny them access to digital reading?

Parents are torn. Studies from multiple English-speaking countries show the majority of parents continue to prefer print for their toddlers and preschoolers.[1] Yet by nixing digital offerings, mothers and fathers worry their kids will be left behind—in enjoyment, learning, or preparation for primary school, where children might be handed a tablet their first day.

As I thought about the dilemma and read conflicting research, I began asking myself, was the debate missing the point? Just as many adults choose print for some purposes and digital for others, were there solid arguments for when digital is appropriate for young children and when to stick with print? Sensing the answer was "yes", I began thinking about . . . food.

> *"Parents' different reading strategies with print and digital books may be related to their strong preference for children's print books."*
>
> Natalia Kucirkova[2]

Food? Indeed. We've likely all seen the traditional food pyramid (now reconfigured as MyPlate). While the proportions of what goes where change over time, the pyramid (or plate) concept reminds us that a balanced diet has multiple components. Lots of fruits, vegetables, and grains? You bet. But you also need some oil and salt. Meat, poultry, and fish? Optional, but if you're vegetarian, figure out how to compensate elsewhere in your diet.

Back to children—and books. We start with infants (birth to roughly two years of age). Experts agree that when it comes to book-reading, physical books are an obvious choice. However, particularly over the last few years, even print-loving pediatricians are identifying sound reasons for letting kids younger than two have some access to touchscreens. As early childhood specialists Natalia Kucirkova and Barry Zuckerman argue, touchscreens potentially foster vocabulary development, contribute to fine motor control and hand/eye coordination, and facilitate communication when, say, Skyping grandparents or sharing family photos onscreen.[3]

What about the next phases of early childhood—and materials that count as books (print or digital)? For a meaningful answer, we need to start with the purpose of reading: What are parents looking to accomplish when they sit with their child and a book, or when children are ensconced with books on their own? We can think about reading with toddlers and preschoolers through three perspectives:

- The social side
- The linguistic and cognitive side
- The engagement side

Keep in mind, though, that while it may be convenient for research purposes to distinguish these three approaches, in actual practice they are interwoven.[4]

THREE SIDES OF READING WITH YOUNG CHILDREN

The Social Side

Years ago, the psychologist Jerome Bruner argued that children begin learning to talk not as a standalone enterprise but as a linguistic overlay atop social interaction with caregivers.[5] Similarly, much of the reading we do with young children is as much about being together and sharing experiences as about the books themselves. In fact, joint reading is one of the tools recommended by pediatricians to foster bonding between parent and child.

Among academics, the term "dialogic talk" describes conversation with infants and toddlers that takes place around reading. (With infants, understandably, the adult generally needs to uphold both sides of the conversation.) Yes, you read the book, but you ask questions and connect what the book is about to experiences in the child's own world: "Look at that elephant! Remember the elephant we saw at the zoo yesterday?" Such conversational give and take spontaneously takes place in many households, but other times the practice benefits from being structured and modeled for parents.

Decades ago, most of the research I did was on child language acquisition. At the time, linguists were starting to recognize that not all children learn language the same way. Among the reasons is cultural context. For instance, middle-class infants in the United States tend to start using words earlier than kids living in societies where parents aren't constantly pointing out names for things, as in, "Peter, there's a fish. It's a fish. Can you say 'fish'?" Take the Tsimané, an Amazonian tribe in Bolivia, where mothers average less than one minute a day directly talking with babies—about one-tenth the amount in the U.S.[6] But regardless of the cultural parenting patterns, all these children learn to talk.

The same cultural issue extends to dialogic talk around books with young children. In many literate societies in which children grow up to be accomplished readers, interactive reading with infants and toddlers isn't part of the social landscape. My husband, who's from a highly literary family in India and learned to read by himself around age four, reminds me of this difference.

Debate over print versus digital books for young children often revolves around the assumption that print encourages dialogic talk more than digital does. (More on that in a moment.) But is this difference inevitable? Recent initiatives, in both Norway and the United States, suggest productive ways of building dialogue into the ways we read digital books with young children.[7]

What's also often missing from the discussion is that the role of books with young children extends beyond child–caregiver bonding. We need to think more broadly about goals, including which platform best supports them.

The Linguistic and Cognitive Side

Before children are able to read on their own, there is much they absorb in the presence of books. Those books could be read by an adult or, in the case of digital books, through voice activation. In either case, young children might come to pair picture, written word, and spoken word with an object (such as that elephant). They also might learn about cause and effect through following a storyline.

We know that children's linguistic development is bolstered by the richness of language used around them. Particularly in social contexts where young children aren't hearing a lot of vocabulary and more complex syntax, it's useful to harness additional tools to enhance kids' learning opportunities. *Sesame Street* is a resoundingly successful example of good modeling for children and adults alike. (While watching with my toddler son, I learned the word "puce" from an episode in the 1980s, where Maria went shopping for shoes.)

With the coming of digital books and apps, it's hardly surprising that educators and parents want to know how these materials measure up against print when it comes to language-based learning. As we'll see, many researchers are investigating this issue.

The Engagement Side

You've seen those parents—or been one. You're at a restaurant, and that two-year-old at the next table won't stop crying. In desperation, Dad fetches his iPhone, pulls up a cartoon video, plants the phone in front of the miserable toddler, and voilà! Peace is restored.

There's no question that digital technologies can be engaging. In debates between those for and against handing digital books to young children, the "con" side points to research showing children tend to focus on the device more than on the storyline or the parents trying to read with their child. All true. Does that mean such engagement is wholly negative? And how does it relate to broader senses of engagement, including cognitive or physical interaction?

As Natalia Kucirkova and Teresa Cremin eloquently argue in their book *Children Reading for Pleasure in the Digital Age*, the act of reading (or being read to) is most beneficial when it includes activity on the child's part. Importantly, this activity involves constructing meaning from what's being read, but it might also entail patting fuzzy surfaces or opening windows in a print book, or perhaps selecting music or exploring an image in a digital work.

Researchers have begun unpacking the varied functions print or digital books might serve for young children, particularly in the eyes of parents. Roxanne Etta surveyed more than 2,000 parents of preschoolers, asking when print or digital was more appropriate. While print was typically judged best for social experience with a child, eBooks were commonly used for entertainment or, in Etta's term, babysitting.[8] As the quality of eBooks continues to improve, and as parents learn ways of incorporating dialogic talk with children while using digital materials, we'll see whether these patterns shift.

WHAT COUNTS AS A DIGITAL BOOK?

Before getting into the research, let's clarify what we mean by "digital books" for kids. At a basic level, we're talking about books (or, for that matter, apps) that replicate the written and graphic materials you'd find in a print book, but are accessed on a digital device (typically a tablet, but potentially a computer, eReader, or mobile phone). In essence, a PDF or EPUB file.

By contrast, an enhanced digital book (or app) incorporates one or more of the add-ons that make digital reading potentially different from print: animation and sound, hotspots and games. As we'll see, the type of enhancement proves critical in determining if digital books for young children are a good move.

WHAT THE RESEARCH SAYS

The Social Side

A number of studies have compared adult–child conversation when reading a print versus a digital storybook. In some cases, it has been a simple digital book, but other times enhanced. (As we'll see, the distinction matters.) Consider two investigations that generated considerable attention. Early research by Julia Parish-Morris and her colleagues focused on three-year-olds. A more recent analysis by Tiffany Munzer and her colleagues looked at toddlers.[9]

The upshot? Both research teams concluded that reading a print book with an adult produced more parent–child conversation than when reading a digital book. With the digital book, talk tended to focus on the technology. Here's what Parish-Morris and her colleagues concluded:

> the behaviors characteristic of a dialogic reading style—a style of story-book reading shown to be predictive of improved later literacy skills—is diminished in the case of [digital] books.[10]

Other research with preschoolers also reports more conversational interaction between adult and child with print books.[11] Returning to toddlers, Munzer and her group offered this advice:

> Given the decreased quantity of parent-child verbalizations and quality of interactions occurring with the electronic books that we studied, pediatricians may wish to recommend print books over electronic books with distracting features for parent-toddler shared reading.[12]

It's not surprising to hear that reading a print (rather than digital) book with a young child is likely the best way for parent and child to share conversation centering around the content of the book. But does this mean digital books have no rightful place in young children's lives? Hardly. To see why, pause for a moment over that phrase "distracting features" in the second quotation. What distracts young children from human dialogue is often what attracts them to the digital device in the first place. Such distraction may not generally nurture dialogic communication, but is it productive for anything else, such as linguistic or cognitive development?

The Linguistic and Cognitive Side

In thinking about the question, keep in mind the difference between basic and enhanced digital books. Basic digital books offer fewer distractions than enhanced books (say, with hotspots or music). Early empirical evidence for the distinction came from work at the Joan Ganz Cooney Center.[13] Researchers compared what happened when parents and their three- to six-year-olds read together one of three kinds of books: a print book, a basic eBook, and an enhanced eBook. Activities of both adults and children that connected to the book's content (such as labeling, pointing, and elaborating items in the story) were fairly similar for print and basic digital books. However, for the enhanced digital book, there was less activity related to the content of the book, again from both adults and children. So maybe what we need to focus on is those enhancements.

It turns out that some enhancements boost learning while others don't. Researchers distinguish between multimedia features "that include story congruent animations, sounds, voices or music" and features such as "built-in games or activities requiring children to shift their attention away from the story content".[14] You might think of hotspots and games that aren't congruent with the storyline as acting like online hyperlinks, leading you away from the main text. Yes, the linked material is in some way connected, but without strong mental discipline, it's easy to lose track of what you were initially reading.

The key issue here is relevance. If the enhancement is relevant to the storyline (or at least doesn't detract), the digital feature has either a neutral or beneficial effect. If not, the enhancement gets in the way of potential learning. This division makes intuitive sense. It also dovetails with what we know about adult multitasking: If you're at your computer and working on X (like writing a technical report) but then shift your attention to Y (say, buying plane tickets for an upcoming vacation), it takes time to get your mind wrapped back around that report.

Which are the educational winners and losers in digital software for young children? We'll review some of the evidence in a minute, but first, here's the scorecard:

☺: animations
    sounds (including background music)
☹: most hotspots
    games

You would think that designers of children's eBooks and apps would have consulted with educational psychologists or reading specialists before cramming in digital bells and whistles that children find engaging but end up detracting from the "educational" part of "educational software". Apparently not. In a review of popular apps, websites, and eBooks that claimed to focus on developing literacy in young children, Lisa Guernsey and her colleagues found that for the eBooks,

- 75% had hotspots, but only 20% of these related to literacy development.
- 65% had games or other activities, but only 25% of these were related to literacy activities.[15]

More recent reviews of children's eBooks and apps aren't more encouraging.[16] The good news is that a number of researchers are working to design more learning-focused digital materials.[17]

Now for some of the evidence on enhanced eBooks and learning. I'll begin with the caveat that not all studies reach the same conclusions. However, seen collectively, there's evidence that at least sometimes, enhanced eBooks—done right—are on par with or even edge out print. We'll focus on the two measures most often used: story comprehension and vocabulary development.

One role that adults have typically played when reading to young children is "scaffolding" the story. By scaffolding we mean building a conceptual structure on which the child can hang new learning or understanding. Think of talking in advance about some of the new words in the story or asking children to relate something in the story to a similar experience in their own lives. A question on researchers' (and of course parents') minds is whether well-done enhanced eBooks can play this role in the absence of adults.

Investigators in the Netherlands reviewed the findings of 29 previous studies, involving more than 1,200 children, ranging in age from 3 to 11, to gauge vocabulary learning and story comprehension. The question was how smartly done multimedia ("enhanced") eBooks stacked up against print, specifically with or without an adult present for support. The conclusion? With an adult providing support, the amount of learning with multimedia eBooks was on par with learning from print. However, when an adult wasn't present, children's vocabulary and comprehension were actually better with eBooks that were enhanced with animation, background music, or relevant sound effects.[18]

Before banishing all the adults to Starbucks, again keep in mind that not all research draws the same conclusions. Another study, this time in Turkey but involving some of the same authors, worked with four- to six-year-olds. They used only enhanced eBooks—that is, no print comparison—and no adult support condition. Children "read" the stories by listening to a recorded narrative. The goal was to see what difference visual versus auditory enhancements made for vocabulary or story comprehension. While the visual enhancements seemed to boost story comprehension, the auditory add-ons had a negative effect on understanding vocabulary.[19] Yet another study, this time with four- and five-year-olds in the United States, compared how much information children remembered from a story on an eBook when they "read" by themselves using recorded narration (supplied by the publisher) versus when a parent read to them in person. While the children remembered a fair amount when reading by themselves (and listening to the audio), they remembered more when the text was read by a parent.[20]

The good news seems to be that solid learning can take place with well-done enhanced eBooks, even without adults present. But we still have much to learn about what enhancements are best suited for which kinds of learning, which ages, and perhaps even which personalities.

There's one more point we need to emphasize, this time about culture. The whole discussion of using books for vocabulary development or boosting measurable story comprehension presupposes a model of early childrearing that emphasizes quantifiable educational milestones. An alternative view is that young children should be encouraged to explore and discover rather than be instructed. In the United States, the first model has tended to predominate. (Think of flashcards marketed for preschoolers, picturing famous art objects.) The second model, which is more characteristic of traditional societies and the original progressive education movement, would as soon use such flashcards as a vegan would eat bacon.

Our aim here is not to advocate for a particular approach. It's to recognize that adults' goals for young children's experience with books may vary.

The Engagement Side

Try this experiment: Standing in front of a two-year-old, hold a brightly colored pinwheel in one hand and a grayish lump of clay in the other. Do we even need to talk about which one the child will likely go for? Just so, it's easy to predict that many toddlers and preschoolers find electronic books (especially enhanced ones) attention-grabbing.

You can hardly blame children. I'm reminded of the old song, from 1919, that cautioned how alluring the wider world had become to American soldiers returning from World War I:

> "How ya gonna keep 'em down on the farm
> After they've seen Paree'?"

For a real-life example of how eBooks can be like Paris to young children, here's a telling observation from Parish-Morris and her colleagues about when happened when they pilot tested their initial study design:

> Pilot children who were assigned to read [electronic books] first [then] resisted reading traditional books afterward, which would have made it impossible to counterbalance reading order in a within-subjects design.[21]

The authors had planned to give children both print and digital books ("within-subjects design"), where half of the children would first get the print and half the digital. However, because of the pilot test results, the researchers ended up giving one group of children only print and a different group only digital ("between-subjects design"), since they worried that after children had "seen Paree'" (the digital), they wouldn't attend to the print.

Yet the engagement issue is more nuanced, especially if the digital book doesn't have distracting interactive features. A more recent study of 17- to 26-month-olds by Gabrielle Strouse and Patricia Ganea, comparing eBooks with print, found that toddlers reading the eBooks paid closer attention, made themselves more "available" for reading, and offered more comments that related to the content of the book.[22]

Stepping back from all the details, here's what we've learned about the pros and cons of using print or digital books with young children:

- *Identify your main goal* when reading with a young child. If it's social dialogue (and all the personal and educational richness that entails), go for print. If it's high engagement with the book itself, digital might be a reasonable choice.
- *Not all digital books (or apps) are equal.* The best ones have enhancements that contribute to the story content, not distract.
- *There's no definitive answer* whether young children learn better (as measured by story comprehension or vocabulary acquisition) from print or digital. Opportunities for learning vary across book content, adult–child relationships, culture, and children's personalities. Age may also be an issue, though chronology isn't always a good yardstick. A 36-month-old could developmentally be more like a toddler or a preschooler.[23]

The issues at stake with reading in print versus onscreen change considerably as children get older.

Research with School-Age Readers

"School-age" covers a wide swath of learners. We could mean kids in lower school (roughly age 6 to 10), middle school (typically age 11 to 13), or high school (generally age 14 to 17), with a year's leeway for each group, in each direction. The next stage is college or university. (Again, we'll use these terms interchangeably.)

When it comes to research comparing reading in print versus with single digital documents, there are fewer studies with children below college age. Conversely, for studies involving multiple digital texts and online navigation—the subject of our next chapter—most of the research is with middle and high school students.

Why the abundance of print versus single digital document studies with college students? Partially because, at least in the United States, there are fewer hurdles researchers need to clear to get projects approved if participants are above the age of consent. What's more, since researchers generally work in higher education settings, a ready pool of participants awaits them. And why the paucity of studies with college students involving multiple texts? I'll wager it's because online navigation isn't a skill commonly taught in college. The assumption is students already know how.

In Chapters 1 and 2, we considered a slew of dimensions regarding reading, readers, and texts. The research we're about to talk about focuses on a number of these issues, summarized in Figure 4.1.

Is it the test?	User perception vs. experiment
	Type of experimental questions
	Speed: reading time, time pressure
Is it the text?	Text length
	Genre
Is it the technology?	Affordances of print vs. digital
	Digital paging vs. scrolling
	Adapting text display
Is it all in our heads?	Metacognition ("mindset")
	Prediction vs. success ("calibration") and
	preferences
	Motivation

FIGURE 4.1 Issues for Comparing Print Versus Onscreen (Single Texts)

Obviously, individual studies don't address all these issues. What look like contradictory findings sometimes result from authors generalizing conclusions to all print versus digital reading without considering that their results might only apply to specific conditions. I'm not faulting the researchers. You can't control for everything. But recognizing that comparing research findings is sometimes comparing apples with oranges can help explain why two well-conducted experiments might reach opposite conclusions.

Several other issues aren't in Figure 4.1 but are important to keep in mind. One is readers' experience with digital devices. People who had never used an eBook but were then tested on one might have a different comfort level than regular Kindle readers. Another issue (sometimes overlapping with the first) is when the study was conducted. As the general population gains increasing familiarity with reading onscreen, it's plausible that attitudes, performance, or both are shifting. Indeed, there's evidence of such change, though not always in the direction we might anticipate.

We'll see shortly that contemporary students are more likely to assume they'll perform better after reading digitally. (They are largely wrong, but we'll get to that story.) Similarly, we'll find that newer studies more often report a print advantage for comprehension than earlier ones.

IS IT THE TEST?

The kinds of answers you get in any study depend heavily on the questions you ask and the variables you control for. This caveat applies in spades when asking whether reading platform matters for learning.

User Perception Versus Experiment

To oversimplify a bit, there are basically two kinds of studies comparing reading in print versus reading onscreen. The first probes what users themselves report to be the pros and cons of each reading medium. The second has study participants read linear passages in print or on a digital device, and then assesses something cognitive, typically comprehension.

Let's begin with user perception studies. There have been dozens by now, but I'll talk about three. Two involved university students (undergraduate and graduate), while the third polled secondary school students. Here's an overview of how the research was organized:

University studies
    Baron, Calixte, and Havewala (2017)
        Ages 18 to 26
        429 participants
        Five countries (United States, Japan, Germany, Slovakia, and India)
        Data collected spring 2013 to spring 2015
    Mizrachi, Salaz, Kurbanoglu, and Boustany (2018)
        Two-thirds between ages 18 and 24
        More than 10,000 participants
        21 countries
        Data collected from 2014 to 2016
  Secondary school study
    Tyo-Dickerson, Mangen, Baron, and Hakemulder (2019)
        Ages 11 to 19
        212 participants

International School of Stavanger (Norway)
Data collected spring 2019

Although the survey questions weren't exactly the same in all three studies, the questions addressed closely related cognitive issues. The results? Highly similar across all three studies. Here are responses to specific questions about concentration, learning, and remembering. The percentages are based on everyone who answered the question:

Q : With which medium is it easiest for you to concentrate or focus?
A: Print

Baron et al. university study:	92%
Mizrachi et al. university study:	82%
Secondary school study:	85%

Q : With which medium is it easiest for you to learn?
A: Print

Secondary school study:	71%

Q : With which medium do you remember more?
A: Print

Mizrachi et al. university study:	72%

The numbers speak for themselves. When it comes to overall learning (including concentrating and remembering), students felt print was the better medium.

A related pair of questions in the first and third studies asked about multitasking:

Q : Do you multitask (very often or sometimes) when reading?
A:

	Baron et al. (university)	**Tyo-Dickerson et al. (secondary school)**
Digitally	67%	46%
In print	41%	23%

Students (both university and secondary school) were more likely to multitask when reading digitally. While I'm not sure why multitasking was higher for the university students (in both formats), I have two hunches. The first is that in the university study, students may have counted listening to music as a form of multitasking. In the study with secondary school students, the question explicitly excluded music as a type of multitasking. The second hunch is that university students tend to have more reasons to multitask, whether with social media, reading news updates, making restaurant reservations, or shopping for shoes. Incidentally, if you look just at the U.S. students in the university study, you find much higher levels of multitasking when reading digitally (85 percent), compared with only 26 percent when reading print.

All three studies invited participants to answer open-ended questions. The first university study and the secondary school study, in both of which I was directly involved, asked what students liked most and liked least about reading in print versus digitally.[24]

Let's zero in on responses about concentration, focus, and distraction. A heads-up on the percentages: Since not everyone responded to every question, the calculations are based on students who did answer.

> What do you like <u>most</u> about reading in print?
>   Percentage of comments about ability to concentrate or lack of distraction
>   Baron et al. university study: 7%
>   Secondary school study: 29%
> What do you like <u>least</u> about reading digitally?
>   Percentage of comments about distraction or inability to concentrate
>   Baron et al. university study: 21%
>   Secondary school study: 47%

In answering these open-ended questions, students could have talked about anything—and did. They praised the smell of print and protested that print kills trees. They enjoyed the convenience of digital but complained it causes eye strain. What's striking is the very substantial number of participants—especially in middle school and high school—who felt that digital technology compromised their ability to focus on reading. Turning once more to just the U.S. university students, 43 percent (double the number for all five countries combined) complained that what they liked least about reading digitally was distraction or inability to concentrate.

Taking these open-ended answers together with the earlier percentages about concentrating, learning, remembering, and multitasking, the handwriting is on the wall—from the student perspective—about the educational benefits of reading in print. Granted, this perception doesn't always match up with students' pragmatic choices. But it's vital to be aware of what learners themselves have to say.

In the faculty survey we talked about in Chapter 3, recall that many professors felt that digital technologies were leading their students to read more shallowly. Connecting the dots between the student and faculty perception studies, a contributing factor could be all that multitasking that happens when reading on digital devices. A related cause may be the non-academic reading students are doing online.

A number of researchers suggest that poorer comprehension when reading digitally is evidence for a "shallowing hypothesis", meaning that when reading on a digital device, people expend less mental effort than when reading print.[25] One major driver of shallow reading is the vast amounts of time young people are spending on digital social media, which requires relatively low mental effort. Several studies have found that heavy users of social media have lower reading comprehension scores.[26]

Let's move now from student perceptions to formal testing. It's here that the bulk of research lies. The rest of this chapter focuses on findings from experimental studies. Most of the discussion is divided up in terms of the categories in Figure 4.1.

But first, the big picture. Several meta-analyses (that is, research reviewing results from multiple studies) reached the same conclusion: Comprehension was better when reading in print than reading onscreen.[27] Not every individual study found print to be superior. Sometimes comprehension was comparable in both media. But very rarely was it better when reading digitally.

To figure out when medium matters (and when it doesn't), we need a finer-toothed comb. Researchers looking to explain the source of experimental results distinguish between two kinds of factors: "medium effects" (the impact relating to the reading medium itself, such as digital scrolling versus paging) and "moderator effects" (other variables, such as reading speed and genre). We'll now look at some of the specifics.

Types of Experimental Questions

Start by comparing results of research done in the late 2000s and early 2010s with more recent studies. An important difference jumps out. Earlier testing often showed comparable results for reading in print versus onscreen.[28] Now, that's less often the case. Are students getting worse at reading onscreen, as they spend increasingly more time on digital media (the shallowing hypothesis)? Alternatively, are the kinds of questions researchers are asking these days more nuanced? While the first hypothesis may be somewhat responsible, I suspect another chunk of the explanation is the questions.

Most studies comparing reading in print versus digitally follow a similar design. The best analogue is the verbal section of a standardized test, such as the SAT. The reading passages are commonly between about 250 and 750 words—think one to three pages. After reading the selection (in print or on a digital device), it's time to answer comprehension questions.

But what kind of questions? Here's where more recent studies have gotten interesting. Two chief distinctions now being made are between (1) answers to concrete versus abstract questions and (2) memory for the main idea versus key points. Take the difference between a concrete question (one whose answer, like a pebble on the beach, can easily be picked up) versus a question whose answer calls for abstract reasoning or inference-making. Geoff Kaufman and Mary Flanagan explored whether reading medium was relevant for each type of question. The answer was "yes". Participants did better using print for more abstract questions requiring them to make inferences. But there was an important additional component to the study. If participants first engaged with an activity involving abstract reasoning and then did the reading task, their digital performance on abstract questions improved.[29]

Now for the second distinction—memory for the main idea in a passage versus remembering key points (which entails more detailed recall of the text). Lauren Singer (now Singer Trakhman) and Patricia Alexander tested undergraduates' ability to answer questions after reading print or digital texts. For questions simply asking about the main point of a passage, results were essentially the same for both platforms. However, when the questions involved a more focused reading of the text (here, being able to identify key points), print proved superior. A subsequent study by Singer Trakhman and her colleagues confirmed the same pattern.[30]

> *"Are students willing to give up detailed understanding of the text read in order to have the ease offered by digital texts?"*
>
> Lauren Singer and Patricia Alexander[31]

This finding is intriguingly reminiscent of a result reported by Parish-Morris and her colleagues in studying three-year-olds:

[W]hile children reading [digital] books performed similarly to children reading traditional books in character and event identification tasks (superficial information), they had a harder time understanding higher level aspects of story structure and story details (deeper story structure) [when reading digital books].[32]

I was amazed by how similar the findings were for two radically different age groups. I suspect that in both cases, one of the culprits with digital is the assumption that careful reading isn't as strongly called for as with print. I keep harkening back to what an undergraduate wrote in one of my studies regarding what he liked least about reading in print:

It takes me longer because I read more carefully.

Speed: Reading Time, Time Pressure

Assuming the text is identical, do you read print and digital material at the same rate? Some people read onscreen more quickly—because they feel that they can skim or hyper read. Others are slower with digital reading—maybe because they're juggling reading the text with multitasking. If you warn people in an experiment that there will be a test afterwards, it's reasonable to predict they will read both print and digital at the same rate. In fact, that's what Virginia Clinton's meta-analysis found.[33]

Yet choices of reading speed are sometimes more nuanced. When people read in natural settings, they don't behave the same way as in a classroom or laboratory. It also turns out that if you experimentally manipulate time allocated for reading, you detect some important differences in the way adults read—and comprehend—in the two media.

Take an experiment that Rakefet Ackerman and Morris Goldsmith did in Israel. When undergraduates were asked to read longish texts (1,000 to 1,200 words) in print or digitally and given a fixed amount of time, their comprehension results were comparable in both media. However, when students were handed the same task but allowed to choose how long to spend, two things happened when reading digitally: They took less time, and they did worse on the comprehension test.[34]

As we've already reminded ourselves, not every study yields the same results. In subsequent research, Rakefet Ackerman and Tirza Lauterman found that students who were allowed to choose their own timing performed comparably with paper and screens, and spent the same amount of time with each medium. One explanation offered for the difference between this result and the earlier one: Students in the first study expressed a preference for reading in print, but the preference wasn't as strong for those in the second.[35]

More recently (this time in the United States), Singer Trakhman and her colleagues found undergraduates reading faster and scoring worse on comprehension when using a computer screen than with print.[36] More confirming evidence comes from younger children, grades one through six. The kids—especially in the earlier grades—tended to read faster and make more errors with digital than with print.[37]

> "There is something about reading digitally that seemingly increases the speed at which students move through the text and this processing time translates into reduced comprehension."
>
> Lauren Singer Trakhman et al.[38]

It shouldn't surprise us to find that faster reading onscreen leads to poorer comprehension. Psychologists have long talked about the speed–accuracy tradeoff.[39] But why read digital texts more quickly than print? We don't know for sure, though we'll look at some hypotheses later in this chapter. Until then, mull over this idea from Wolfgang Lenhard and his colleagues:

> [W]hen time pressure is high and task complexity is low, some kind of "computer gaming mode" might be induced in the test-taker in a computerized condition. In simple computer games, speed is typically more important in winning the game than accuracy.[40]

Food for thought.

Speed figures into another type of experiment that has been done with university students: putting the squeeze on study participants, not allowing quite enough time for the task. Several Israeli studies confirm that when you constrict reading time, students do worse with digital than with print. It appears that with print, students applied additional mental effort.[41]

Why should we care about experiments that put the screws on students regarding time? Because that's the educational world so many live in. In Chapter 2, we contended that timed tests may not be the best indicators of what people know or can figure out. But as long as society insists on such tests, it's essential to understand the potential effects of medium on test-taking. If you're under time pressure, digital test administration is likely not your friend.

IS IT THE TEXT?

Think now about the kinds of texts researchers use to compare success when reading in print versus onscreen. We'll focus on two dimensions that might influence the outcomes: length and genre.

Length

All three of the user preferences studies we talked about earlier asked students which medium they would select if the text were short or long. "Long" and "short" are squishy terms, but taken as antonyms, participants from a host of studies have seemed to understand the contrast. Responses for "short" are sometimes mixed, but the choice for "long" is clear: print.

Q: Which medium do you prefer when reading long texts for schoolwork?
A: Print
    Baron et al. university study: 86%

Mizrachi et al. university study: 73%

Secondary school study: 59%

(another 19% had no preference)

For the two studies with university students, the question required an answer of print or digital. For the study with secondary school participants, students had three choices: print, digital, or no preference. Nonetheless, almost 60 percent of these middle and high schoolers explicitly chose print.

Experimental studies that control for text length show parallel results. In their review of the literature, Singer and Alexander found that with short texts (meaning fewer than 500 words), comprehension scores tended to be comparable for print and digital reading. However, when the texts were long (500 words or more), comprehension was consistently better with print.[42] Less clear is the extent to which this superiority of print was a function of length itself or partially resulted from the fact that longer digital texts may have required scrolling, while the print reading involved page turns. We'll have more to say a bit later about paging versus scrolling.

Genre

In Chapter 2 we talked about text genre, distinguishing between narrative (commonly fiction) and informational. As educators and parents, we encourage children to read both. Studies of print versus digital reading have tended to use informational texts, and for understandable reasons. Most reading passages in tests are fairly short, which means relatively few narrative texts (even short stories) qualify. And if you're going to be asking comprehension questions, informational texts are a natural.

That said, there have been some studies involving narrative texts (or contrasting narrative and informational). We'll start with the comparative studies, then turn to just narrative.

Results comparing adult comprehension on narrative versus informational texts are mixed. Some studies report comparable results for the two genres—with both print and digital media.[43] That is, no evidence of genre mattering. But not all researchers agree. Two meta-analyses concluded that while comprehension was better in print for informational texts, there was no medium difference for narrative.[44]

What should we make of apparently conflicting findings regarding genre? I'll wager the answer mostly lies with the kinds of questions asked—an issue we've already talked about. Support for this hunch comes from an inventive study that Anne Mangen and her colleagues did on reading a short story either in print or digitally.[45]

This research differed from traditional comprehension experiments in two ways. First, the text that participants were given (either in a print version or on a Kindle) was genuinely long: 28 pages (taking about an hour to read). And second, participants were asked to respond to two different types of questions. One set comprised normal comprehension queries. On these, participants did equally well on both reading platforms. However, the other set asked about place and time issues: where in the story an event took place and when in the chronological flow of events. On these questions, participants did better with print. The authors conclude that the physical properties of a print book—you manually turn the pages, you tangibly see how much you have read and how much is left to go—offer sensorimotor cues helping readers orient spatially and temporally in the story.

After reading Mangen et al.'s study (which involved adults), I once again found myself harkening back to the research Parish-Morris and her colleagues did with three-year-olds. It turned out that print was the medium in which children did best with questions about chronological order of events. For character and event identification, the kids did equally well with both media, echoing the findings of Mangen and her colleagues.[46] It seems very likely that the physicality of a print narrative—for both young children and adults—helps us remember what happened when and where.

IS IT THE TECHNOLOGY?

Affordances of Print Versus Digital

In Chapter 1 we introduced the idea of affordances, meaning what an object (or here, technology) might be good for. Computers (and other digital tools) are useful for searching, multitasking, and hyper reading. Print books are well suited to long, detailed reads.

Obviously, both print and digital texts have a slew of other affordances. In two of the user perception studies we've talked about, secondary school and university students shared with us the affordances that most mattered to them through answers to questions about what they liked most about reading in print and most about digital reading. Here's some of what they said:[47]

> **Like most about reading in print**
> - Emotional/Aesthetic
>   "The memories of every individual copy of a printed book" (secondary school)
>   "You can relax and it becomes a sort of ritual" (secondary school)
>   "It feels more authentic" (secondary school)
>   "The calmness of diving into the book" (secondary school)

"I like the smell of paper" (university)

"Able to feel that I am actually reading" (university)

- Physical

"You get to feel the book getting thicker with what you have read" (secondary school)

"It is easy to skip back through the book" (secondary school)

"I can feel the paper in my hands, and just the touch and feel of it makes me focus more" (secondary school)

"Easier to highlight pages, write notes" (university)

"Physically turning the pages" (university)

- Cognitive

"I don't get distracted" (secondary school)

"Reading in print gives you more of a feeling for the characters and the story for me personally than digital books do" (secondary school)

"More concentration" (university)

"Feel like the content sticks in the heard more easily" (university)

- Convenience

"Being able to take my book everywhere I go" (secondary school)

"It's just easier for me to read it I guess" (secondary school)

"Able to refer to multiple books simultaneously" (university)

"The text is properly visible while sitting or lying" (university)

Like most about reading digitally

- Emotional/Aesthetic

"It can be a bit more entertaining" (secondary school)

"For pleasure only" (university)

"It is fun when the content is short" (university)

- Physical

"It looks shorter to read on" (secondary school)

"It's easy to scroll through" (secondary school)

"The documents are saved in the memory so you can't lose them" (secondary school)

"You can look up something right away if you don't understand it" (university)

"Able to enlarge the character size" (university)

- Cognitive

"It keeps me awake" (secondary school)

"It's very easy to organize and keep in order" (secondary school)

"Sometimes they have videos or images to help you understand" (secondary
   school)
"I can multitask while I'm reading" (university)
"That I can do research at the same time" (university)
- Convenience/Access
"You can find so many more things on a digital device than on paper" (secondary
   school)
"It is often easy to access and easy to just bring around" (secondary school)
"Accessible everywhere" (university)
- Resources (Ecological and Monetary)
"Print . . . is bad for the environment using too much paper" (secondary
   school)
"Saves the environment" (university)
"It saves printing money" (university)

While these student responses seem neatly categorized, it's important to remember that users are sometimes conflicted, particularly between beliefs about how
they learn best and pragmatic considerations, such as cost, convenience, or the environment. Here's what one respondent wrote as an additional comment in one of my
early pilot studies:

> While I prefer reading things in Hard copy, I can't bring myself to
> print out online material simply for the environmental considerations.
> However, I highly, highly prefer things in Hard copy—just to clarify.[48]

This response closely mirrors a student's observation in Diane Mizrachi and Alicia
Salaz's qualitative analysis of their large-scale international study:

*"We . . . see a schism
in which many students
must consciously decide
between better learning
tools or better economics
and convenience."*

Diane Mizrachi and Alicia
                    Salaz[50]

I retain more information if I read the
material in print but I use the time spent
in trains and buses to read and revise
using electronic copies.[49]

Such comments reveal how at least some students
feel about print versus digital reading platforms and,
by extension, their impact on enjoyment, learning, or
overall study habits. But there are also experimental

measures of the effects of reading technology affordances, particularly for digital platforms. We'll look at two of these: scrolling and adapting text size.

Digital Paging Versus Scrolling

We just saw one student's comment about the digital advantage of being able to scroll through a text. Scrolling is a blessing if you're looking for something in particular or scanning to decide if the text is worth your time. But what about when you are reading to learn, especially if there's a test at the end?

More than a decade ago, some Swedish researchers argued that scrolling when reading long texts on a digital screen increases the amount of cognitive effort readers need to expend, leading to lower test results.[51] Other investigators have offered additional confirmation, though stressing that more research is needed.[52]

What's the challenge with scrolling instead of seeing a whole page of digital text at a time? The problem, as Gertrude Stein might have said, is there's no "there" there. Scrolling offers no markers of beginnings or endings, while the confines of a defined page give readers a sense of geographic place, even if it's only virtual.

Reading while scrolling reminds us of a larger cognitive issue when trying to make sense of information that isn't neatly bounded. As we'll see in Chapter 6, psychologists talk about the benefits of constructing "concept maps" of information encountered in diverse places. The material might be drawn from a single linear document or from multiple documents when navigating online.

The cognitive challenge of scrolling seems to be more pronounced for some readers. There's evidence, for example, that readers with low levels of working memory capacity (that is, using short-term memory to deal with limited amounts of information) are more negatively affected by scrolling than those with higher levels of working memory.[53] Since working memory levels tend to be associated with general intelligence, having to scroll through digital documents may also be detrimental to children with other educational challenges.

Most experiments restrict digital texts to one page or explicitly use page turns to avoid getting into possible complications from scrolling. Were I the betting sort, I'd put money on future research establishing definitively that students (and the rest of us) focus more clearly when reading fixed pages (and "paging" from one to the next) than when scrolling through a document.

Adapting Text Display

In the user perception studies we talked about, a number of students commented on the digital advantage of being able to adjust text size. Many of us, particularly of a certain age, share the sentiment. But the issue here isn't personal preference or comfort but learning. For some students, particularly those with learning challenges, digital adjustment of font size, along with spacing on the screen, can be educationally important adaptations.

Even before the proliferation of digital devices, psychologists and reading specialists were studying the potential usefulness of adjusting spacing between letters, words, and lines in texts for younger children, especially those with reading challenges. The technical term for the issue is "visual crowding".

Who benefits? And for what kind of spacing: within words? between words? between lines? Not all researchers agree on the details. For example, a study of Dutch children with dyslexia (compared with non-dyslexics) found both groups of kids (about age 9 or 10) did better at reading sentences when letters and words were spaced out than with normal spacing. An Israeli study of younger children concluded that first-graders were better at reading long words when the letters were spaced out. However, with the third-graders they tested, only kids with lower reading ability were helped by additional spacing. Then there's an American study of adults with dyslexia. The authors argue that some—though not all—dyslexics have problems with visual crowding. For people in the study, reading speed was faster when spacing between letters, words, and lines was increased.[54]

Spacing isn't the only kind of digital adaptation available. We've already mentioned font size. Changes in font size obviously affect how much text is visible at one time on a screen. But so does screen size. Many of us complain about reading on mobile phones because, compared with a computer or even a tablet, relatively few words fit on the screen. And with a phone, outside of contexts like eBook apps, you have no choice but to scroll.

However, recalling the words of the Roman poet Lucretius, one man's poison is another man's meat. For some readers with learning challenges, there are advantages of restricting the amount of text encountered at one time. A study with high school dyslexics compared reading on a small screen eReader (an iPod Touch) with reading on a larger digital device (an iPad). Students performed better with the smaller screen, including faster reading speed, fewer eye fixations, and fewer backwards (regressive) saccades.[55]

IS IT ALL IN OUR HEADS?

We've been talking about possible explanations for outcomes when students read onscreen or in print. We looked at whether the sort of research questions you pose influences results, whether genre or length of text is an issue, and whether the technology itself leads us to read in particular ways.

But what if a crucial element is what's going on in our minds when we approach print or a digital screen? We've already hinted at the importance of user attitudes and presuppositions. A bevy of researchers—some predating the digital reading revolution, some in the thick of it—have much useful to say here.

Metacognition ("Mindset")

Psychologists use the word "metacognition" to talk about the way we keep track of thought processes and allocate cognitive resources. It's through metacognition that we decide how to approach a mental task. To recast the idea in ordinary language, we'll use the term "mindset".

In the context of this chapter, mindset plays out in two ways. The first is whether you think the task at hand will be easy or difficult. If you anticipate it will be easy, you might not invest too much effort, because you assume you'll do well. The second involves prediction: How well do you think you will do (or just did) on, say, a comprehension test? Social scientists talk about "calibration", which is the difference between predicted and actual success. We'll have more to say about calibration in the next section.

How do you decide whether a task will be easy or difficult? One way is gauging your prior knowledge. If you already know the essence of what you'll be asked to do or read, you might reasonably assume you will ace a subsequent test.

That's not always how the world works. Back in graduate school, I had a roommate from France who was in the United States to do her Ph.D. in American history. When it came time to take the required language exams for her degree, she breezed through the French test—and failed. This super-smart woman had assumed the test required little mental effort, and so she neglected to check her work before waltzing out of the exam room.

There's a technical term in educational psychology, "AIME", meaning "amount of invested mental effort". The notion dates back to the 1980s, when Gavriel Salomon was curious how children judged the amount of effort needed to understand a film watched on television versus when reading a comparable text. The sixth-graders he tested felt they would do better with the TV film, which they also thought would take less effort. Indeed, they seemed to expend less mental energy with the TV version, since they performed better when reading print.[56] Fast-forward to the 2010s. Using the same notion of AIME, researchers at the University of Michigan studied how undergraduates undertook digital searches, using either the Web or the university's online library system. Students worked harder when searching the library site (and found more productive results) than with the Web, which they had judged to require less mental effort.[57]

We've already seen the "effort" issue in action for how college students approach digital versus print reading. Remember the finding of Ackerman and Goldsmith that when free to decide how much time to spend reading digital and print material, students read digital faster but did worse on the comprehension test? Study participants weren't looking to get lower scores with digital reading. Rather, they seemed to assume they could do just fine reading faster onscreen than in print. Why the assumption?

Rakefet Ackerman and her colleagues have written extensively about the role of metacognition in explaining many of their research findings. Although mindset is hard to measure accurately, it appears to be quite real in shaping the way children and adults alike tend to approach online reading. Maybe the cause is the gobs of time we spend online (when not in testing situations), often doing some version of hyper reading. Maybe digital reading in a testing context reminds us of the other things we might be doing with digital devices but aren't. Think of the studies by Misra and by Ward and their colleagues we talked about in Chapter 2, showing that social behavior and cognitive performance decline when a mobile phone is within hailing distance.

Predictions and Preferences

One aspect of mindset about which we have considerable data is calibration—that is, the degree to which research participants accurately judge how they will do (or just did) on something like a comprehension exam. Our question is whether students are more likely to predict better performance when reading in print or digitally. We mentioned earlier that in a number of studies from the early 2010s, university students (and in some cases, older adults) predicted they had done better with print, although their performance in both media was essentially equivalent.

But times are changing. Multiple studies now show that students are more likely to overestimate their performance when reading onscreen than when using print. Evidence comes from across the educational spectrum, from lower school to college.[58] A number of researchers suggest the reason for the prediction mismatch is that students believe it will be easy to understand the digital text and therefore don't try as hard.[59]

One question I haven't seen many researchers address head-on is why, over time, students' calibration patterns have largely changed. About 10 years ago readers were predicting they would do better (or did better) with print. Why are so many now assuming better performance when reading onscreen? I suspect multiple causes. The first is that today's students have far more experience reading on digital devices than a decade ago, and therefore assume they're good at it. The second is that teachers and administrators have been shifting reading assignments from print to digital, often giving students little choice but to read digitally. Should we be surprised that students believe authority figures when they say that reading digitally is a fine way to learn?

As digital reading has become the norm—in everyday life and in school—we need to remind ourselves about students' preferences and the reasons behind them when it comes to learning. In my own research, almost 87 percent of university students said that if cost were the same, they would prefer print for academic reading. Even more (92 percent) said they concentrated better with print. In the study of secondary school students, 85 percent indicated they concentrated better with print.[60]

What about experimental studies that examine both medium preferences and text comprehension? Keep in mind that these studies differ from the user perception research in a crucial way. While the user perception research asked about academic reading and learning in general, these experiments confronted students with short reading passages followed by an SAT-style comprehension test. It's quite possible that the same students prefer print for overall school reading but favor digital in an experimental setting that is all about short reading and immediate testing. Relevantly, in the university perception study, while 86 percent preferred print for long texts, that number dropped to barely 40 percent for short ones.

Having set the context, let's see what some of the research shows.

Students' own preferred reading medium has some interesting relationships to test results. One study with university students found that when participants used their preferred reading medium, they were better at predicting how well they would do on the comprehension test.[61] Another study added a novel twist by having students use learning strategies (here, doing a practice test or generating keywords) before taking the "real" test. Students who preferred digital reading (but not those preferring print) improved their performance in the digital condition after doing a practice test. Generation of keywords before testing was also more useful for those preferring digital.[62]

Consider now a study of fifth- and sixth-graders where the kids predicted better digital success but actually had higher scores with print. The children were also asked their reading preference. In fact, they were asked twice: before the experiment and then afterwards (though students hadn't yet seen their test results). Before the experiment, 61 percent said they would rather read on the computer. That number dropped to 57 percent after the test.[63]

The authors raise the possibility that at least some children became aware of the benefits of print after encountering a test requiring substantial mental effort. Like closing the barn door after the horse has bolted. When I read this analysis, I thought about a parallel realization among college students listening to a podcast or reading the same material in print.[64] We'll return to the story in Chapter 7.

Motivation

When choosing a technology for reading, we've seen that individual mindset can play a role in the medium we prefer, how fast we read, and how well we think we'll do if tested. There's one more "it's in our heads" issue to raise, and that's motivation. If you're not being made to read, do you choose to? And can the reading medium make a difference?

At the beginning of this chapter, we saw that digital texts prove especially engaging to young children. They are hardly alone. A variety of studies have shown that digital screens can be a motivator to read, especially for males, struggling readers, or reluctant readers.[65] When we get to Chapter 7, we'll see that digital audio can also be a motivator for reluctant readers.

Key Takeaways About Reading Single Texts in Print Versus Onscreen

This has been a long chapter, with lots of topics and a wealth of detail. Let's summarize the main lessons learned about print versus digital reading involving single texts. The summary is organized in terms of the two age groups and then the strengths of each medium, along with a few caveats about digital. We'll distinguish between the findings we can be pretty certain about and those that are probable but backed by less conclusive evidence at this point.

Young Children
Print strengths
    For sure: social interaction
    Probably: vocabulary, comprehension
Digital strengths (caveat: simple digital or smart use of enhancements)
    For sure: engagement
    Probably: vocabulary, comprehension

School-Age Readers
Print strengths with single texts
    For sure: concentration
                    comprehension under time pressure

deeper level of understanding (abstractions, inferences, key
    points)

preference for reading longer texts

memory for where, when in a story

ease of annotation

Digital strengths with single texts

For sure: cost/convenience/accessibility

adaptability of type size, character spacing

search tools available

can save own comments in file for future reference

Probably: surface understanding (concrete issues, main idea)

motivation to read

Digital factors to consider

For sure: overestimate comprehension

tendency to read quickly and shallowly

Probably   paging vs. scrolling: better comprehension with paging

narrative vs. informational: comprehension with digital
    generally better for narrative than for informational text,
    but depends on type of questions asked

Now on to Chapter 5 and navigating your way with multiple texts.

CHAPTER 5   What Research Tells Us: Multiple Texts

Inventions sometimes have effects their creators didn't anticipate. That's true in the world at large and with technology.

The Trail of Unintended Consequences

Take aspirin. It's a synthetic version of salicylic acid, a substance found in willow bark and used for millennia as a pain remedy. An engineered pill reached the market in 1900. But not until the 1970s did scientists recognize its added power to reduce inflammation—and so help protect against coronary artery disease, heart attacks, and strokes.[1]

Some unintended consequences are less welcome. Take kudzu. Part of the pea family, kudzu arrived in the United States in 1876 as an ornamental plant. In the 1930s and 1940s, the government encouraged the planting of kudzu in the South to combat soil erosion.[2] That it did—and then some. Today if you drive along a Georgia highway, you might believe you're in the production set for a creepy movie, seeing trees totally enveloped in the invasive vine.

What about technological innovations? We know that spending hours at a computer keyboard contributes to back problems and carpel tunnel syndrome.[3] But how about the internet itself?

The internet's origins can be traced back to 1958, the height of the Cold War. The U.S. government worried that vital communications could be crippled in the event of a Russian nuclear attack. The response: develop a computer network, known as ARPAnet (Advanced Research Projects Agency Network), which would decentralize communications, freeing them from dependence on vulnerable telephone lines.[4] Over time, ARPAnet morphed into the internet, and the rest, as they say, is history. While the U.S. government still relies on the internet, so do billions of others.

The internet has led to positive and negative unintended consequences. Teamed with the World Wide Web, the network allows us to unearth seemingly infinite troves of information. But it has also enabled a vast cadre of online actors to mine our searches for commercial ends. With social networking, we can rekindle friendships, meet new people, share our agonies and ecstasies, and gather news. But social networking gobbles huge amounts of our time and has the power to propagate fake news and upend the democratic process.

Coupled with ubiquitous personal computing devices driven by increasingly sophisticated software, the internet also makes it possible to read in new ways. We can click on hyperlinks, transporting us to related pages. Given the processing speed of today's devices, we easily hop between sites, leaving behind digital breadcrumbs should we need to retrace our steps. With the internet, we can access multiple documents in short order—and potentially read them. The questions before us are what kind of reading we are doing with multiple online texts, plus what consequences might there be—intended or otherwise, positive or negative.

This chapter explores the biggest consequence, which is the need to locate and navigate across sites, and then judge and make sense of what we encounter. We'll look at effects on school pedagogy of this need to navigate, at concomitant changes in standardized testing, and at potential transformation in our understanding of what it means to read.

The Digital Turn in Schools

How did locating, reading, and evaluating multiple online documents come to play such a major role in teaching and testing of reading, particularly in middle and high school education? I suspect this move—unintended consequences—wasn't an overt goal. Instead, it followed the inexorable logic of a shift to digital learning, coupled with astronomical growth in material that's available online.

The year 1977 was seminal for computing in education. Three personal computers—the Apple II, the Commodore PET, and the TRS-80—were introduced to a small but curious public. A year later, Apple won a contract from MECC (the Minnesota Education Computing Consortium) to provide 500 computers to Minnesota schools. Jump to the early 1980s, when Steve Jobs managed to offer "a free Apple IIe system to every eligible elementary and secondary school in California".[5] Other manufactures' machines would follow, into tens of thousands of classrooms.

If this was the hardware (with loadable software) revolution, the next move was equally dramatic: going online, first with desktop machines, and then with laptops and tablets. The rush was on to capitalize on all that content in cyberspace. Students needed to learn how to find sources and then make productive use of their discoveries.

Running in parallel were other digital developments. One was to shift modules, courses, and eventually entire degree programs online. Expansion of online education is well known in higher education, where two of the strongest motivating factors have been addressing physical distance and cost (especially an issue in U.S. community colleges and public four-year institutions).

The United States has seen growing moves to ensure that younger students know how to study online. As of 2018, five states—Alabama, Arkansas, Florida, Michigan, and Virginia—had laws requiring that every student take at least one course online before high school graduation.[6] The European Union has also been striving to strengthen students' digital skills, though not specifically through online courses. In early 2018, the European Commission launched a Digital Education Action plan, warning that "Europe will lose its competitiveness if education fails to provide digital competences to Europeans of all ages".[7] As a result of the COVID-19 pandemic, when schools were closed and instruction moved online for millions of students, we can expect online learning requirements to become the new normal.

A second development has been increasing replacement of print textbooks with digital materials. We already told much of the story in Chapter 2.[8] As print textbook prices continued to rise, so did growth of the eBook market. Universities began assigning digital books, both to save students money and to facilitate online courses.

The net result—of computers (or tablets) in the classroom, of online courses, of digital learning materials, and of the multitudinous resources available on the internet—has been to foreground the role of cyberspace in education. With all those resources, it seems foolhardy to limit students to encountering only one document at a time.

Navigating Online Navigation

What's so novel about readers using multiple texts? The answer, of course, is nothing. Scholars have long consulted more than one source. What has changed is the ease with which cumulative—or comparative—reading can be done.

WHAT'S OLD IS NEW

Transport yourself back to England in the 1300s. You're a monk wanting to read several works by Aristotle, whose writings reached the West in Latin translation fairly recently. Let's hope you have a good horse or are an intrepid walker, since the texts you seek may only reside at monastic libraries in far-flung parts of the country.

Fast-forward two centuries. The printing press, which arrived in London in 1476, gradually enabled such readers to stay home. In the words of the historian of the book Elizabeth Eisenstein, "To consult different books it was no longer so essential to be a wandering scholar".[9] Comparative scholarship became more do-able, now that you could spread out multiple works before you simultaneously. This "spread out" model of reading and research is familiar to many of us from student days, when we surrounded ourselves with print materials along with handwritten notes. A lot of us still do.

One virtue of this physical array has always been, as Eisenstein said about the print revolution, that "[c]ontradictions become more visible".[10] Remember that word "contradictions", since it plays a prominent role in the story of reading multiple digital texts in educational settings.

Next stop is the 20th century. For several hundred years now, people have been using multiple documents to investigate topics that interest them. But in the interim, another development was unfolding in the education world, namely the rise of textbooks.[11] Now, if you wanted to learn, say, American history, you could turn to a single bound book that covered a sizeable time span and included a continuous narrative, maybe complemented by maps, graphs, or reproductions of original documents. Such textbooks became an integral part of the educational landscape.

Now zoom ahead to the present. Yes, there are still textbooks, though increasingly we expect students to gather information by going online to multiple sources, often reached by clicking through hyperlinks. What's more, we ask students not only to use and make sense of multiple online documents but also to navigate the internet to find their own sources. (A bit later in the chapter, we'll get to how using multiple online sources compares with juggling multiple print materials.)

Before getting to the nuts and bolts of how the process works, it helps to have some historical context for the notion of navigation.

FROM SHIPS TO HYPERLINKS

These days everyone talks about "navigating" online. But what do we mean? Obviously, the word is a metaphoric extension of something to do with ships. The noun "navigation" derives from Latin, meaning the action of traveling by ship. When the term entered English in the 16th century, it only referred to going by water. Later the verb form "navigate" was extended to balloons, aircraft, and finally, in the mid 1970s, to computers. When you "navigated" using a computer back then, it was generally within a database.

To understand how we got from there to today's ubiquitous online navigation, we need to start with an essay written in 1945 by the engineer and inventor Vannevar Bush. Intriguingly entitled "As We May Think", the article was intended as a rallying cry to scientists to figure out how to make our collective stores of knowledge available to everyone. Bush's proposal was to build a new machine he dubbed "memex", which would enable users to establish links between documents stored on microfilm. Although the device was never created, it inspired the thinking of technology icon Ted Nelson, who, in the mid 1960s, coined the term "hypertext". Nelson's vision was partially implemented in a system he called XANADU (recalling the idyllic spot made famous in Coleridge's poem "Kubla Khan"). Similar to Bush's memex, XANADU was intended to build a linking system for a repository of the world's knowledge.

Segue now to linking systems—hyperlinks—that have actually been constructed. Computer scientist Ben Shneiderman, along with then-graduate-student Dan Ostroff, gets the honors for creating functioning document-internal hyperlinks. Work began in the early 1980s. By the late 1980s, the notion of forging links within a document or database was generating considerable interest. One well-known venture was the Apple Macintosh HyperCard, launched in 1987.[12] This same hyperlink principle would enable users to go from maneuvering within a single document to searching broader horizons.

In 1989, Tim Berners-Lee, an engineer and computer scientist, drafted a proposal to CERN, the European Organization for Nuclear Research, located in Switzerland. Berners-Lee sought to use Shneiderman's notion of hyperlinks to craft a system that linked computer-based information sources located around the world. Think about the initials "HTTP" in all those URL addresses we use. They stand for "Hypertext Transfer Protocol". By the end of 1989, a prototype system existed, and the World Wide Web was born.

It took another half-dozen years before search engines became the powerful navigational tools we take for granted today. There was Gopher in 1991 (developed at the University of Minnesota, and named after the school's mascot), Mosaic in 1993 (dreamt up at the University of Illinois), and Google (created at Stanford and officially born on September 27, 1998). People around the world have been busy searching online ever since.

But what does it mean to search—and what do you do with what you find?

SEARCH, SCRUTINIZE, SYNTHESIZE

When people in education talk about wanting students to learn how to navigate online, they actually have three activities in mind:

- Gathering sources by moving from site to site
- Assessing the credibility of sources, plus resolving contradictions
- Making sense of what you have found

"Navigation", "evaluation", and "integration" are the terms you'll find in academic research articles.[13] But to make things more intuitive, we'll refer to the trio as "search", "scrutinize", and "synthesize". While the tripartite framework (by whatever names) is apt for analyzing use of multiple documents online, you'll recognize all three elements as also applicable when using multiple print sources.

Search

Say you're about to undertake online research on whether eating eggs is good or bad for your health. Since your search palette is potentially the entire Web, you need to:

- Choose your search terms
- Lay out a search path (what to look at when)
- Decide how long to spend on each site, including whether to skim, scan, or read entirely

When you're looking at a particular site, you also need to:

- Figure out which internal hyperlinks to follow and which to ignore

These aren't the only steps involved in successful searching, but they're a good start.[14]

Becoming a good navigator isn't a simple task. As I write these words, I can't help thinking of the country music ballad "The Gambler", where the late Kenny Rogers counseled that in playing cards, you need to know when to hold, fold, walk away, or run. Too often, even experienced internet users don't know when to keep reading or move on. It's no surprise that students don't either.

Scrutinize

You've located a number of online sites talking about the virtues or evils of eating eggs. Among your finds are information from the Mayo Clinic, *Time* magazine, *JAMA* (the *Journal of the American Medical Association*), and the American Egg Board, along with half-a-dozen YouTube videos weighing in pro and con. Here are some of the issues you now need to grapple with:

- Where conclusions on the sites differ, how do you decide which ones are more trustworthy?
  - How might you go about vetting different sources?
  - If a source (say, an online news page) cites someone's research, do you need to check the original yourself?
  - Does your prior knowledge of the subject come into play? What about personal biases?
- Is your judgment swayed by how professional the site looks?

You'll notice that the first issue targets the possibility of contradiction between sources. Dealing with online contradiction is a major part of both school pedagogy and researcher interest. Granted, learning how to adjudicate inconsistencies is vital in so much of our lives—from weighing testimony in a court of law to deciding which politician to trust. When reading, inconsistencies might surface between texts, but also within a single document. However, as I'll counsel later in this chapter, we don't want to reduce all mindful reading to managing contradictions.

Synthesize

Now that you've located your materials and made at least a first pass about which ones to trust, you need to make sense of the assemblage. Your task will likely include:

- Integrating what you found with your prior knowledge about the subject
- Synthesizing the findings into a coherent discussion
- Interpreting the results—that is, drawing a conclusion based on evidence

All these steps should sound familiar from the kinds of research projects we have long assigned to students—or undertaken ourselves.

COMPARISONS WITH READING PRINT

Chapter 4 compared reading single texts in print versus onscreen. While the reading media were different, the words were the same. Equally importantly, in all the research we discussed there, documents were provided by the experimenter. Students didn't need to seek out texts on their own. In this chapter, our focus is on how students find, read, judge, and make sense of multiple documents online. But since reading a single print document and reading multiple texts online both entail reading, some obvious questions are:

- What's similar and what's different about the two kinds of reading?
- Does skill in print reading predict success in online reading with multiple documents?

A number of researchers have tackled the comparative question. They agree that print (single text) and online (multiple texts) share a number of important aspects. For instance, Julie Coiro and Elizabeth Dobler identify the ability to:

- Draw upon prior knowledge of the topic
- Use inferential reasoning strategies
- Connect the different components of the reading, including knowing when to reread and how to evaluate what you have read[15]

Peter Afflerbach and Byeong-Young Cho list:

- Identifying and learning text content
- Monitoring strategies (such as establishing goals, overseeing progress, and identifying challenges)
- Evaluation strategies (such as judging the accuracy of information, looking for evidence to support claims, and judging the suitability of the text to the reader's goals)[16]

What distinguishes successful negotiation online from traditional (print) reading competencies? Largely it's the search process (knowing how to navigate efficiently), combined with some scrutiny skills (knowing which sites to trust). Because these are additional skills, many researchers argue that internet reading is harder than reading in print.[17]

As I thought about this conclusion, I understood what the authors had in mind, since the contrast they were drawing was between working with multiple online documents (that students had to identify on their own) and reading a single printed text (provided by the teacher). However, not all our print reading on a topic is restricted to single documents. What's more, when doing research using print, you need to find—and evaluate—your sources, just as you do online. However, regarding evaluation, most print materials have traditionally gone through prior vetting, in principle making scrutiny less of an issue than with online postings.

Imagine yourself in the library stacks, encountering multiple physical volumes as you try to determine which books are most relevant to your research on the dissolution of the Soviet Union. You need to decide which books to pull off the shelves, which authors (or presses) you recognize (perhaps lending them greater credence), when to just scan the tables of contents, and when to delve into a particular chapter. You might get waylaid by a book with an attractive cover one shelf down, though the book is tangential to your topic. And because you went to the library stacks rather than accessing a full shelf list or subject catalogue, you might end up missing the most crucial book, since it was checked out.

Yes, I know that today research is heavily done online. And yes, navigating multiple documents digitally doesn't correspond exactly to unearthing multiple works in print. Empirical comparative research here would be useful. Realistically, though, the main roadblock to designing such an experiment is that fewer and fewer students are being taught how to identify and evaluate multiple print sources.

What the Research Shows About Multiple Documents

What do researchers say about online search, scrutiny, and synthesis? Since the fundamental purpose of pedagogical research is to improve education, many of the studies we're about to look at combine experiments with recommendations for teaching online multi-document skills to students. We'll save up those explicit recommendations for Chapter 6.

Please keep one terminological point in mind about the studies we're about to discuss. These days, when many researchers talk about "reading online" or "digital reading", they specifically mean "reading multiple documents online". That is, they are referring to searching for documents, judging their veracity, and synthesizing findings across texts. They aren't referring to reading single texts that happen to be accessible digitally. It's important to keep straight the two kinds of reading scenarios.

SOME OF THE FINDINGS

An abundance of research is now exploring how students search, scrutinize, and synthesize multiple online documents.[18] Because the driving goal in this book is to compare reading platforms, not analyze details of multiple source online reading, please take these findings as representative, not comprehensive.

Search

These are some main takeaways from research involving navigation (search) skills:

- Younger children (around middle school) tend to base hyperlink selections on superficial cues such as highlighted keywords.[19]
- Navigation skills increase with age.[20]
- Strong visuospatial working memory (that is, ability to harness short-term memory for information presented visually) correlates with shorter time looking at irrelevant content.[21]
- Print comprehension skills are a good predictor of identifying relevant online sources.[22]
- However, good navigation skills can help compensate for weaker print reading skills when it comes to overall performance on digital tests.[23]

In Chapter 1, we talked about growing use of eye-tracking technology to study how people read, both with print and onscreen. In Spain, Ladislao Salmerón and his colleagues are harnessing eye-tracking tools to better understand how students do online searching. When students navigate online, they need to minimize time spent looking at irrelevant information in hyperlinks, while devoting more time to pertinent information.[24] The researchers had an interesting question: Could you use videos of the eye movements of skilled versus less skilled searchers to train students to be more successful navigators? Trying out the technique with ninth-graders, the investigators found that students who watched the training videos improved their online reading comprehension and spent more time reading relevant pages.[25] The technique may not be practical on a large scale. However, the study reminds us that searching is a skill that can be improved through overt teaching.

Another important factor is how much confidence users have in search engines. A study done in 2005 found that 72 percent of internet users age 18 to 29 said internet engines were "fair and unbiased".[26] A few years later, Eszter Hargittai and her colleagues put such confidence to the test. After posing search tasks to about 100 undergraduates, the experimenters sat with the students during the search process, as the students talked through their thinking. Behind the scenes, the researchers were doing screen captures on every site visited.

How did the students select which sites to visit? More than one-quarter choose the first hit the search engine turned up, indicating "considerable trust" in the search engine. But "trust" didn't lead to "verify". Although 10 percent of the students mentioned something about the site's author or credentials, the screen capture history revealed that no one actually checked out any of these qualifications.[27]

Scrutinize

Clearly, students need guidance in selecting sites. But there are also challenges specific to scrutiny of the sites they choose:

- *Students need training* to determine whether information on a website is credible. Assessing a site's trustworthiness is more of a problem than students—and sometimes educators—recognize.
- *Many of the criteria students use* (such as the aesthetics of the site) have little to do with credibility.
- *In the age of rampant fake news*, developing assessment skills is especially important.
- *Assessment of factual accuracy isn't the only problem.* Students' judgments may also be influenced by ideological preconceptions and level of psychosocial development.

Learning how to judge the trustworthiness of sources has long been an educational goal, predating the digital revolution. Many of us remember being taught as children, "Don't believe everything you read", back when that reading was exclusively in print. But the challenge has magnified with the explosion of online information, social media posts, and fake news.

A major project by the Stanford History Education Group, led by Sam Wineburg (whose prior work we'll encounter in a moment), assessed what they call "civic online reasoning"—that is, students' ability to judge the credibility of online sources, particularly relating to identifying fake news. The core competencies researchers identified for civic online reasoning involved students' ability to answer three questions about what they read online:

- Who is behind the information?
- What is the evidence?
- What do other sources say?

The project cast a wide net—in 12 different U.S. states, including 405 students in middle school, 348 in high school, and 141 in college. In each case, students were asked to read and evaluate the trustworthiness of online information by providing explanations for their assessments. Performance was scored as being at the Beginning, Emerging, or Mastery level.[28]

The results were sobering. Among the most glaring findings were that students:

- Had troubling distinguishing advertisements from news articles
- Struggled to determine the real source of information they encountered
- Provided personal opinions rather than following hyperlinks to evaluate veracity of claims
- Judged veracity on such bases as a site's aesthetics or professional look, or the quality of audio or graphics

Troublingly, even college students didn't demonstrate much "Mastery". Other research confirms that university students sometimes rely on ease of use or visual aesthetics, not credentials of the authors, to judge reliability of websites.[29] And a study with undergraduate and graduate students found students spending a mere 2 to 3 seconds on websites before rendering judgments of credibility. Not exactly enough time for reflection.[30]

"Civic online reasoning is necessary for students to be informed participants in civic life. . . . Our results suggest that students are not prepared to navigate the maelstrom of information online."

Sarah McGrew et al.[31]

There are, though, even more challenges students face in scrutinizing online material, particularly when it comes to recognizing fake news. An often overlooked—though critical—variable is the biases and presuppositions we bring to what we read. Such beliefs run the gamut from politics to race or religion. What counts as a fact in someone's mind might be judged not by evidence (think civic reasoning) but by a person's entrenched prior beliefs.

In analyzing why fake news works, H. James Garrett reminds us that many people accept information that bolsters their views while dismissing data that challenge their position.[32] Such confirmation bias can surface at any age. Or, as aptly phrased by Avner Segall and his colleagues,

> Students, like adults, may be motivated to learn, but they also avoid learning, affirm preconceived ideas, refuse knowledge, and defend themselves psychologically against evidence, news, or facts that trouble their assumptions and understandings of self, other, and the world more broadly.[33]

"Civic action, political knowledge, and engaged participation are influenced by much more than the ability to evaluate evidence; they are influenced by the psychical investments we have in those issues."

H. James Garrett[34]

Finally, one more factor to consider when it comes to scrutinizing material read online: brain development. Ellen Middaugh wonders why adolescents, so many of whom have been taught strategies for assessing credibility of news and information, are still prone to making judgment mistakes. Part of the answer, she argues, is that teenagers are still developing mentally and emotionally. Ability to think about a problem from multiple perspectives remains a work in progress. Sensationalism online (a common attribute of fake news) can be highly attractive. If the material whose credibility students are asked to verify is seen as boring and unrelated to their lives, their motivation for engaging in serious assessment may be low.[35] We can all hope these challenges diminish with the maturation process.

Synthesize

There's considerable overlap between the synthesis skills called for when reading online documents and the kind of mental reasoning we encourage when using tangible materials. The main difference is that when working online, you need to keep in your head the content of what you unearthed during your online journey, along with where those sources were, in case you need to consult them again.

Research findings about synthesis when working with online documents will come as no surprise:

- Prior relevant knowledge seems to aid in the synthesis process.[36]
- Readers' levels of verbal working memory (that is, ability to harness short-term memory for information presented as words) may impact their success in synthesizing information across multiple sources. Since navigating between sites increases cognitive demands, such navigation may exceed some users' working memory capacity.[37]

In principle, readers can harness various tools for keeping track of the pieces, including making notes (digital or handwritten) as they go. We'll talk in Chapter 6 about options.

THE MEANING OF "MULTIPLE"

Given today's push in education for training students to function online, it's no surprise that current research involving multiple documents has focused on digital sources (commonly text, but also graphics, audio, and video).[38] However, interest in the ways students interpret multiple documents predates the digital revolution.

A classic study is Sam Wineburg's 1991 comparison of how high school seniors versus professional historians make sense of historical documents (all hard copy) that contain contradictory information. Students displayed limited ability to assess the trustworthiness of sources or to determine the validity of competing claims to truth. In Wineburg's words, "high school students can know a lot of history but still have little idea of how historical knowledge is constructed".[39] Three decades later, students confront the same challenges, whether in print or online.

Another way of looking at multiple texts has been to compare sense-making using the same information broken up into several sources as opposed to incorporated within a single document (such as a textbook chapter). Studies have included print materials and, more recently, online texts.

First, print-based. Again focusing on history, Jennifer Wiley and James Voss asked undergraduates to use multiple individual sources or a textbook chapter containing the same material for two writing exercises: a historical chronology (with names and dates) and an essay explaining causal or explanatory relationships. Results on the chronological writing task were comparable with the textbook chapter and individual sources. However, when asked to produce an argument, students did better when using separate documents.[40]

Additional research with undergraduates offers confirming evidence. Several studies focused on science-based topics, with emphasis on handling conflicting information.[41] While some investigations used print materials and others digital, all documents were provided (that is, no search was involved). The crux of their findings? Better performance with multiple documents:

> [B]y reading multiple documents, readers are stimulated to fill in coherence gaps between documents by connecting different pieces of information, which in turn helped them identify and mentally represent conflicting information.[42]

With multiple documents, students needed to do more mental heavy lifting to figure out how the pieces fit together.

What does using a single text versus multiple sources (especially with physical texts) have to do with print versus digital reading? One crucial answer involves look and feel.

If you're working with multiple physical documents, each one has distinguishing characteristics: an oversized atlas, a handwritten letter, a tabloid newspaper. When reading a textbook chapter, the presentation looks homogeneous throughout—same page size, same type fonts, same writing style. Analogously, now think about a fundamental sensory difference between reading in print versus online. Print documents have noticeable "fingerprints". It's not any old book but a book with a broken spine. It's not any old periodical but a *Time* magazine issue with the Dalai Lama on the cover. We mentally tag not just "print" but a collection of specific attributes. By contrast, while websites may be visually distinctive in their graphics and layout, there is a sameness in the way we access and manipulate them.

We'll return to the importance of distinctiveness later in the chapter.

THE MEDIUM QUESTION: PRINT OR ONLINE?

Let's turn now to research comparing multiple texts in print versus online. The pickings are slim, but let's see what we can learn.

Mônica Macedo-Rouet and her colleagues compared how undergraduates worked with multiple print or digital documents dealing with abortion issues. In both cases, there was a main document accompanied by auxiliary materials (some texts, some graphics). While the print materials were distinct documents, the online condition used hyperlinked materials. The central issues (for our purposes) were how students did on a comprehension test and whether students perceived the print or digital condition to require more cognitive effort.

For comprehension questions about the main document, students scored about the same whether reading in print or online. However, scores on the auxiliary materials were much better with print. When asked how much effort they felt was entailed in doing the reading, students were far more likely to report the hypertext (digital) version to be particularly mentally burdensome, though their scores didn't reflect this cognitive exertion.[43]

Another study, this time by Emily Peterson and Patricia Alexander, analyzed how undergraduates developed PowerPoint presentations, using either print or digital sources. The authors remind us that in the American education system, the Common Core Standards include a requirement (to be met through 11th- and 12th-grade English language arts classes) that students be able to "synthesize information from a range of sources . . . integrating information into a coherent understanding".[44] The PowerPoint task was a clever way of confirming how well students who had now graduated from high school met this goal.

Peterson and Alexander provided students with 16 sources about Alzheimer's disease, 8 in print and 8 digital, including such items as a textbook, a newspaper piece, an article from a scientific journal, and a graph. Unlike many other multi-document studies, there were no contradictions or controversies in the sources. Students were asked to draw upon whichever materials they wished in creating their presentation.

Overall, students spent more time using the print resources than the digital ones. Participants were also more likely to transform the print materials (for instance, paraphrasing or drawing inferences rather than copying directly). However, many of these medium differences disappeared when the researchers factored in students' prior knowledge about Alzheimer's. Students with higher prior knowledge used more sources (both print and digital), incorporated more digital sources into their

PowerPoint presentations, and performed more content transformations with print, compared with those who initially knew less about Alzheimer's.[45]

Drawing inferences on your own (rather than copying) is surely a skill we want to foster. Yet we see once again that prior knowledge can be at least as important as reading medium.

A third study, here by Natalia Latini and her colleagues, combined reading platform (print or digital) with purpose (reading for pleasure or in preparation for an exam). This time the multiple texts contained conflicting positions on the effects of social media. Undergraduates were given written comprehension tests, which measured their ability to draw inferences. The main takeaway for us is that when students were reading as if preparing for an exam, using print materials led to longer written responses and to a more integrated understanding of the issues (that is, comprehension).[46]

At this point you may be asking, "Haven't I already seen research findings that more sophisticated or mentally focused tasks seem to benefit from using print?" Indeed you have, in Chapter 4, where we compared reading single texts in print or onscreen.

PREDICTORS OF SUCCESS WITH MULTIPLE TEXTS ONLINE

The ultimate goal of all these studies is to bolster students' learning when reading digitally. To the extent we can identify predictors of success, we're a step ahead.

Several predictive factors stand out: level of print reading comprehension, amount of prior knowledge about the reading topic, and level of working memory capacity. There are others we haven't talked about (including students' beliefs about whether knowledge is fixed or evolving),[47] but we'll include just one more here: time spent on the internet reading informational material versus accessing social media sites.

Print Reading Comprehension
Given the overlaps between skills needed for reading print and negotiating meaning with multiple online texts, it's not surprising that print reading comprehension predicts success in reading multiple documents online. In Chapter 3, we mentioned that on the international PISA test of 15-year-olds, higher print comprehension scores predicted better navigational paths, which in turn predicted stronger online performance.

Other research confirms this predictive power. Looking at seventh-graders in the United States, Julie Coiro found a positive correlation between offline (print) reading comprehension and comprehension when reading online.[48] Ladislao Salmerón and his colleagues probed the online behavior of Spanish 7th- to 10th-graders, concluding that print reading skills were accurate predictors of internet reading comprehension. In essence, print skills are transferable.[49]

The Spanish studies also asked more specifically if print reading was a good indicator of skillful online navigation (what we've called "search"). Navigation skills contribute to comprehension, but there are also distinct navigational behaviors that need to be nurtured, such as search speed and efficiency. The researchers concluded that while efficient online navigation skills are predicted by level of print comprehension,

> navigation should be learned and practiced in Internet instructional settings specifically, as students may not get the necessary proficiency just by practicing comprehension with print media.[50]

Prior Knowledge

Back in Chapter 1, I recounted the anecdote of how my family's fortuitous visit to Carl Linnaeus's botanic garden in Uppsala, Sweden, helped my son ace a section of the SAT Verbal. Throughout this chapter, we've seen repeated evidence that prior knowledge can boost comprehension scores, whether the texts are in print or digital.

The challenge is how to level the playing field among students from disparate backgrounds and with varied acquaintance with the content we throw at them on standardized tests. Assessment organizations such as the Educational Testing Service have long grappled with this dilemma. There's no easy solution, but we need to remain mindful of the consequences when evaluating student performance.

Working Memory

Twice in this chapter we've invoked the notion of working memory—first to report that strong visuospatial working memory predicts shorter time spent with irrelevant online content, and then to see that higher levels of verbal working memory may enhance ability to synthesize multiple online sources. Without getting into the weeds, let's talk for a minute about what working memory is and why it's so relevant when dealing with multiple documents online.

Psychologists distinguish between short-term and long-term memory. The terms mean what you would think: memories held for a brief period of time (such as directions for reaching a particular building) versus for longer stretches (such as, one hopes, the declension of German pronouns). Short-term memories can, of course, transfer to longer-term storage. Working memory encompasses the content of short-term memory but adds in the "working" part, meaning it includes not just the memories themselves but the apparatus for storage (albeit briefly) and manipulation.

We've mentioned a couple of times that a major challenge of maneuvering among multiple documents online is their evanescence. They visually disappear when you go on to the next site. Unless you take notes or can view multiple sites on your screen simultaneously, it's easy to lose track of what you've just read. Here's where people with strong working memory capacities (for words, images, or both) can have an advantage. In Chapter 6, we'll talk about tools assisting students in "mapping" the content they encounter, helping them to keep track of their online journeys as well as to connect the dots between the stops.

Informational Versus Social Media Use

An area of research we haven't talked about yet is whether students' independent multi-text online reading involves informational material or social media. Some fascinating studies with adolescents show that while their amount of experience doing informational searching online predicted success on comprehension-based internet tasks, time spent using social media did not.[51] A further study with teenagers concluded that heavy use of social media correlated with poor ability to evaluate online sites (what we've called "scrutiny").[52]

There's a logic to these results. Doing online information searches (and reading the results) usually draws more upon our cognitive resources than spending time on social networking sites. The first tends to be a form of work and the second, of entertainment and socializing. What's more, we can think of experience doing online information searches as a form of prior knowledge—here, knowledge of how to use a tool for understanding and evaluating online sites.

Revisiting the Content Versus Container Debate

In Chapter 2, we mentioned a distinction between "content" (here, meaning written text) and "container" (for our purposes, print versus digital). But even within the categories "print" or "digital", we have options. For digital, think of desktops, laptops, eReaders, tablets, and mobile phones. What about for print?

The majority of studies we've looked at comparing print versus digital reading used either individual sheets of paper for the print condition or, depending on the amount of text, a handmade booklet that was bound or joined with a staple. Attempts to make booklets look more or less like physical books have varied. However, students weren't given an actual book.

A clever study by Ladislao Salmerón, Laura Gil, and Ivar Bråten asked if verisimilitude mattered.[53] That is, what would happen if readers were given authentic print materials (such as real books) in contrast to duplicated pages? I'm introducing this study here because the experiment dealt with multiple documents (our topic here in Chapter 5), all of which appeared in print. However, you can imagine the relevance of the question for reading single print or digital documents (the domain of Chapter 4). The study focused on authenticity of reading materials but has implications for two other aspects of the reading experience: how physically distinctive the texts are and the role our senses play in reading.

AUTHENTICITY

Here are the basics of the experiment. Undergraduates (plus a few master's-degree students) were given one of two sets of source materials dealing with climate change. The first set contained original materials (a printed textbook, a hardcopy newspaper, a popular science magazine), while the second set consisted of printout versions of the relevant texts. After doing the readings, students were instructed to write an argumentative essay about climate change and then asked to list all the information they remembered from the sources, including author, document type (such as magazine or newspaper), publisher, and date of publication.

Students using authentic materials remembered more specifics, incorporated more information about those sources into their essays, and wrote more coherent essays than students using printouts. The question is why. The authors suggest two interconnected explanations: distinctiveness and our sense of touch.

DISTINCTIVENESS AND PHYSICAL SENSES

A bit earlier in this chapter we talked about differences between reading the same information in one document as opposed to using multiple documents. We saw that engaging with multiple components tended to yield better outcomes, perhaps because more cognitive work was involved in putting the pieces together but also because of the distinctiveness of the pieces. In the authenticity study, Salmerón and his colleagues argue that the visual distinctiveness of authentic documents (including their covers and size) helped make the source material more salient and therefore better remembered. By contrast, the printouts essentially all looked alike.

Besides their visual properties, the authentic documents also differed in tactile ways. They didn't all weigh the same or have the same feel to the touch. And readers likely held them differently (think about a textbook you might set on a desk versus a magazine you could hold in the air versus a newspaper you might need to fold). As students from the perception studies we talked about in Chapter 4 told us, touch matters when reading print.

The Long Arm of Online Navigation

We began this chapter by talking about unintended consequences. With an invention—be it aspirin or the internet—we find new uses but may also encounter challenges we hadn't anticipated. Let's reflect on two unintended consequences of the proliferation of multisource reading online, especially in educational settings. One is our approach to standardized testing. The other is our sense of what it means to read.

WHAT STANDARDIZED TESTING NOW TESTS

We spoke a bit in Chapters 1 and 2 about standardized testing. Besides transitioning from paper and pencil to online, what's being tested is evolving as well. One essential change, particularly in middle school and high school testing, has been to incorporate online multi-source use. Two important questions we need ask:

- How do scores on the paper versus online tests compare?
- What aspects of reading are being maintained, excluded, or given less prominence now that testing includes multiple online documents?

Do students score as well on digital testing as on paper counterparts when the questions are the same? Earlier data were mixed,[54] but more recent studies indicate students seem to do better with paper. In Norway, Anne Mangen and her colleagues found that 10th-graders who used paper-based standardized tests outperformed classmates given the digital version.[55] Confirming data keep coming from:

- 5th-graders in Norway
- 4th- through 10th-graders in New Zealand
- 3rd- through 8th-graders in the United States[56]

Especially troubling in the U.S. was that the difference between print and computer administration hit some students harder than others. The negative effects were "stronger for students at the bottom of the achievement distribution, for English language learners, and for special education students".[57] The first Norway study we just mentioned (with 10th-graders) showed a comparable pattern: Students with lower basic reading skills were more negatively impacted by reading digitally.[58] It goes without saying that we need to be especially mindful of unintended consequences of testing mode for more vulnerable students.

Another important finding is that the kind of response format used in the tests further shapes differences between paper-based and digitally based assessment. In the PIRLS and ePIRLS administered in 2016, some items called for multiple-choice answers while others asked students to write out ("construct") their responses. Looking at the Norwegian subset of the 2016 test, Katrin Schulz-Heidorf and Hildegunn Støle discovered that the fifth-grade students did significantly better on the more cognitively demanding "constructed responses" when answering on the paper test. By contrast, they performed slightly better on the less demanding multiple-choice questions in the digital version.[59]

One other research result, this time involving gender, needs mentioning. In analyzing results from a specially designed test for Norwegian 5th graders, Hildegunn Støle and her colleagues revealed a worrisome pattern. The girls in the study who had the highest overall level of reading achievement suffered the most in terms of low scores when assessed digitally. The authors caution that moving testing from paper to screen may have the unexpected consequence of disadvantaging the strongest female readers.[60] If these results are replicated elsewhere, we have genuine reason for concern about accuracy—and fairness—of digital testing.

But as we've said, the transformation in testing isn't just in the platform used. It's also in what is being tested. Increasingly, students are given multiple documents to navigate, assess, and integrate. The argument for the shift is this: Since school activities now involve searching, scrutinizing, and synthesizing multiple texts online, we need to measure students' levels of accomplishment in these areas. Here's the way the creators of the 2018 PISA test put it:

> Although the ability to comprehend and interpret extended pieces of continuous texts—including literary texts—remains valuable, success will also require the deployment of complex information-processing strategies, including the analysis, integration and interpretation of relevant information from multiple text (or information) sources.[61]

The shift in school-based standardized testing from paper to screen, and from single-document digital to multi-document digital, has been phased (and is still ongoing). Let's follow the trajectories of the PIRLS and the PISA.[62]

The PIRLS (the international test for fourth-graders) has been given every five years since 2001. The exam was designed to assess, in balanced amounts, both reading for literary experience and reading to acquire and use information. The most recent administration (as I write this chapter) was in 2016. However, in that year, test designers introduced a supplementary exam, dubbed the ePIRLS, which assessed "how well students can read information in an online environment that consists of content tabs, navigation bars, graphic icons, links, and scroll bars".[63] Importantly, all the reading on the ePIRLS involved informational texts.

Since most students took both the traditional PIRLS (single-text literary and informational readings) and the ePIRLS, it's possible to compare performance on both parts. Overall, students in some countries did better on the PIRLS and in other countries on the ePIRLS, perhaps reflecting the extent to which computers were regularly used in their classrooms.[64]

Plans are well under way for the next administration of the PIRLS in 2021. The new "digitalPIRLS" will include the content of the 2016 ePIRLS, along with both literary and informational questions from the PIRLS. The entire test will be digital. The PIRLS component will require some scrolling and will incorporate graphical elements, especially for informational passages. Students in half the countries will take the new digitalPIRLS, while those in the other half will take the traditional paper-format PIRLS. We'll need to wait and see how the results compare.[65]

What about the digital shift with the PISA, the international test for 15-year-olds? Begun in 2000, the exam is administered every three years, though a different subject (reading, mathematics, or science) receives special attention in each cycle. An emphasis was placed on reading in 2009 and 2018.

Here's what happened between then and now. As with the PIRLS, a separate reading test was created to measure proficiency with multiple online texts. The new ePISA was first given in 2009. As with the ePIRLS, only informational texts were included. Reading results from the 2012 PISA and ePISA were analyzed extensively. Since many students took both the regular PISA (containing individual literary and informational readings) and the ePISA, we can compare outcomes. Generally, there was a strong correlation between print (PISA) and digital (ePISA) scores, though individual testing jurisdictions showed considerable variation. Overall, students with low print reading scores also had low digital scores.[66]

For the 2018 PISA administration, a different framework was developed for measuring student accomplishment in reading. The new test was composed of two kinds of materials. "Fixed" texts included words, diagrams, pictures, tables, graphs, and even comic strips, all of which were static documents. "Dynamic" texts, as the name implies, required students to do something, such as estimate how much information might lie behind a hyperlink, navigate across pages, or synthesize information from multiple sites.[67] Similar to the design of the 2021 digitalPIRLS, the 2018 PISA rolled traditional linear reading and online reading (here, PISA plus ePISA) into a single bundle, but now all tested via computer.

Main results for the 2018 PISA were released in December 2019. However, at the time I wrote this chapter, there weren't analyses comparing performance on fixed versus dynamic texts, or specifically performance on linear reading. As the nature of testing and pedagogy continues to shift, it will be instructive to examine these findings.

IS ONLINE NAVIGATION CHANGING WHAT IT MEANS TO READ?

If you're into crystal balls, the future of standardized testing looks digital—both for PDF equivalents of paper-based testing and the growing incorporation of multi-document, navigational reading. Some consequences of this move can be anticipated, including potential cost savings (on the positive side) and foreseeable disadvantages (on the negative) for students with reading challenges or those with more restricted experience using computers and the internet.

What about other possible outcomes?

In Chapter 4, we used four questions to scaffold conversation about reading single texts on paper or onscreen: Is it the test? Is it the text? Is it the technology? Is it all in our heads? We've already addressed the test issue. But the other three queries are also well suited to helping us think about possible unintended consequences of shifts in the way standardized testing is being done, especially for students in middle school and high school.[68]

Is It the Text?
Two factors stand out here: text length and genre. Creators of the digital reading revolution—or, for that matter, of the internet—didn't set out to replace long texts with short ones or to support informational reading over literature or essays. Yet both trends have been creeping into how we read online. Since so much of our reading these days is internet based, technology is nudging us to keep the text short and to spend growing amounts of time reading fact (at least, ostensibly so), not fiction.

Understandably, classroom content is being reflected in what we ask on standardized tests. The feedback loop gets completed by the extent to which (let's admit it) we all too often teach to the test. If you're designing a digital test (whether with single or multiple documents), it's hard to imagine asking students to read the equivalent of an entire short story or book chapter. To be fair, paper-based testing hasn't generally included lengthy texts either. However, the digital screen inherently favors shorter writing.[69]

As the notion of reading is now seen by teachers and test designers to include working with multiple digital documents, the move away from literary texts to information seems inexorable. Yes, literature students might be asked to compare multiple texts—say, Shakespeare's *King Lear* with Sophocles' *Oedipus Rex*—but not on a standardized test. The new digitalPIRLS and most recent PISA do include some narrative passages. But with the growing push to assess students' abilities to navigate and weigh the legitimacy of various sources, informational texts end up reducing time available for literary works.

Should we care? You bet.

Recall what we saw in Chapter 2 about the benefits of reading literature. Here's a recap:

- Among middle schoolers, extracurricular reading of fiction correlated positively with reading comprehension and vocabulary development.
- Among 11- to 15-year-olds, "fiction book reading was the only reading habit to make a robust, unique contribution to the higher-level comprehension skill of inference-making".
- Among 15-year-olds, students who read fiction had higher reading scores on the PISA than those who didn't.

When it comes to long versus short reading, regardless of genre,

- Among 7- to 16-year-olds, frequent leisure reading, especially of book-length works, correlated with better reading comprehension.[70]

Since we've also seen that good reading comprehension tends to be a strong predictor of success in reading multiple documents online, the evidence doubly suggests we should think hard before letting long—and especially literary—reading get demoted in school reading programs.

Is It the Technology?

Two technology issues may have unintended consequences when it comes to reading multiple documents online. The first involves scrolling, a problem we talked about in Chapter 4. If you don't have fixed pages in front of you—in this case, for multiple texts—it's challenging to form a mental picture of the whole. And without such a picture, it's hard to comprehend and integrate what you have read.

The second issue is digital skills. Results from the ePISA suggest that in countries where students have limited school-based experience with computers, lower scores on the test might reflect cross-national inequity in digital opportunities rather than lower cognitive achievement.

Is It All in Our Heads?

In Chapter 4, we talked about the shallowing hypothesis, which argues we tend to read online materials more superficially than we do print. When it comes to doing online searches, we saw earlier in this chapter that in one study, university students devoted no more than 2 or 3 seconds to a site before judging its worthiness for the task at hand.

In reviewing the current state of digital standardized testing, Støle and her colleagues worry about the potential unintended consequence of digital education more generally on how much serious thinking we are encouraging students to do. They write:

> [T]here is a risk that the digital assessment in itself functions as a spear-head for "modern" digitally-based school activities which may or may not be well suited for promoting a broad range of reading skills, such as reflection and evaluation.[71]

We should all ponder this risk.

What else might be included in that "broad range of reading skills" besides reflection and evaluation? One essential addition is emotional engagement with texts, especially works of literature. I thank Anne Mangen and Maryanne Wolf for continuing to remind us of the centrality of literature to reading.

The importance of emotional engagement leads me to think about a newish book with the intriguing title *Literacy Beyond Text Comprehension*. The authors propose a different lens through which to view reading. Instead of emphasizing reading for comprehension, they argue that reading should be seen as a problem-solving activity that is goal directed and embedded in situational context.[72] The process of redefining what we mean by reading has been going on for centuries and continues to this day.[73] However, in the present climate, we should monitor potential unintended consequences of emphasizing information-seeking and problem-solving over contemplative reading and reading for the sheer joy of it.

Emily Dickinson wrote:

> There is no Frigate like a Book
> To take us Lands away

It would be a shame to reduce all those voyages to goal-directed exercises.

Key Takeaways About Reading Multiple Texts

Here are highlights of what we've learned about students reading multiple materials. As you think about these takeaways, it's important to keep several things in mind:

- *Not every study affirms the same conclusion.* And so, please take many of these highlights as "strongly probable", not definitive truth.
- *Discrepancies between study findings often reflect the sophistication of the questions asked.* Generally, more surface-level questions tend to yield comparable results with print and digital, while questions requiring more reflection or analysis frequently show better results with print. This conclusion parallels what we saw with reading single print versus digital texts.
- *Using multiple sources online is still a relatively new reading practice.* Our proficiencies might well alter in the coming years, as could our penchants for reading works of different genres and length.

Reading Multiple Documents Online
- Prior skills to build on:
  - Print reading
  - Prior background knowledge
  - Experience with online information-seeking
  - Working memory
- Skills to develop:
  - Search: much is new (though, remember, we also search multiple print texts)
  - Scrutiny: continues to need a lot of work
    - What's new with digital?
      - Less external vetting of online texts with print texts
  - Synthesis: continues to need work
    - What's new with digital:
      - Tendency to read digital more shallowly
      - Difficulty viewing multiple texts simultaneously

Single Versus Multiple Documents with the Same Information
- There is potential advantage of using multiple sources, perhaps aided by visual or tactile distinctiveness.

Multiple Documents in Print Versus Online
- For more cognitively complex tasks, performance with print is sometimes better.

Authenticity and Distinctiveness
- Authenticity of paper reading materials, including physical distinctiveness, seems to enhance reading performance.

Standardized Testing Trends
- Move from paper to digital for single texts
  - Results: Some findings show students do better on paper.
- Incorporation of online multi-site materials into reading tests
  - Still a work in progress
  - Key issue: Given pragmatic limitations on the number of test items, what should be the balance between online multi-document reading versus single informational and narrative texts?

Cautionary Notes
- Heavy use of social networking doesn't boost online performance with multiple informational documents.
- Limited student online experience may result in lower scores for reading multiple documents online.
- Online testing more generally may disadvantage students with reading challenges.
- The current emphasis on reading multiple informational texts online (in both teaching and testing) risks marginalizing literary reading and longer texts in the school curriculum.
- Online reading potentially encourages less complex and reflective thinking than reading in print, for both single and multiple document reading.

CHAPTER 6   Strategies for Effective Reading Onscreen

Finally, it's time for the rubber to hit the road and consider research-based strategies when reading for learning in a digital world. Yet recommendations come with a few caveats:

- *The research isn't complete or definitive.* While many studies we've been looking at offer clear directions for pedagogical decision-making, in other cases, findings are only suggestive or even conflicting. Welcome to the messy world of science!
- *Technology is a moving target, but reading persists.* The digital world changes incredibly quickly. Still, whatever technologies we have 5 or 10 years from now, we can safely assume people will continue to read. The questions will be using what devices, and with what benefits. We can anticipate expanding use of multimodal online documents, including text, graphics, and audio.
- *Students' beliefs about how they learn best are also a moving target.* We've seen a shift in whether students think they'll perform better on a print or digital exam. Nonetheless, they continue reporting they concentrate or learn better with print. Learning for a test isn't the same as learning for the long term. When talking about students' beliefs, we need to be clear what question we're asking.
- *Few guidelines exist for parents, teachers, administrators, or policy makers.* In most cases, there's a paucity of research-based decision-making. Handing each first-grader a tablet doesn't imply a sound basis for doing so, especially given common shortcomings in curricular design, wireless infrastructure, and teacher training.[1]

Despite such uncertainties, we still need to act.

Overarching Guidelines

In discussing strategies for supporting learning with print versus digital text, I'll roughly follow the organizational flow of Chapter 4 (young children, followed by single texts for school-age readers) and Chapter 5 (multiple texts). To help set the stage, here are six key issues to keep in mind.

WHAT IS THE GOAL?

What do we want children and young adults to derive from the reading we offer or require? The conundrum facing us is that almost all the research data come from studies using short amounts of reading, typically in formal testing situations.

However, as parents and educators, our aspirations for progeny and pupils are higher: to nurture a love of reading, a desire to enjoy long texts, an ability to analyze and ponder, and the vision to see learning as a long-term good, not a grade-driven end. And so, we sometimes may need to extrapolate from experiment-based conclusions to what reading looks like in more natural circumstances.

WHO IS THE READER?

In making recommendations, one size doesn't fit all readers. The first consideration is the role of *prior knowledge*. We've seen that prior knowledge can prove more important on a comprehension test than whether you read in print or digitally. Because levels of prior knowledge differ widely in classrooms, some children might flourish with screens, while others flounder.

A second issue is *individual preferences*. Adults often have their own platform preferences, and children do as well. Medium preference can make a difference in test results. As with prior knowledge, technology alone may not tell the full story.

Third, there's *motivation*. Some children are natural bookworms, while others need to be prodded to read. A U.K. project using eBooks to motivate children to read found a huge subsequent increase in enjoyment when reading on paper, from only 10 percent of the students at the start of the project to 40 percent at the end.[2] If eBooks (or, as we'll see in the next chapters, audiobooks) prove enticing, they might be options to explore.

It's tempting to assume that if we make digital devices available to students, motivation to read in their free time will magically rise. Margaret Merga and Saiyidi Roni tested a version of this hypothesis in Australia with 8- to 12-year-olds. Access to mobile phones was actually associated with lower levels of voluntary free-time book reading, while access to tablets and computers essentially had no effect.[3] If educators are looking to motivate reluctant readers with eBooks, scaffolding of the reading experience may be needed, as in the U.K. project.

Finally, we must pay attention to *needs of readers with challenges* of varying sorts. We've seen that children with lower reading scores seem to have more trouble with digital tests and that students with limited working memory capacity may struggle in handling multiple online documents. Other populations to keep in mind include second language learners or those with dyslexia. In some cases, digital technology can become part of the solution.

EXTENUATING FACTORS

Researchers (myself included) sometimes live in a bubble. The data may all line up indicating the best course of action, but pragmatism needs to factor in as well. We know, for instance, that preventive health care reduces ultimate costs, but not everyone has access. With reading, there are also realities to confront.

Cost is one of the biggest. In the late 2000s, an early push for using digital books in schools came from the state of California, which had been the edge of the wedge in the U.S. financial crisis. Then-governor Arnold Schwarzenegger proposed adopting free digital textbooks for students, beginning with high school classes:

> It's nonsensical—and expensive—to look to traditional hard-bound books when information today is so readily available in electronic form. Especially now, when our school districts are strapped for cash and our state budget deficit is forcing further cuts to classrooms.[4]

Today, school districts and colleges across the United States, not to mention in many struggling economies around the globe, have turned to digital books. Often the rationale isn't belief that eBooks are superior or even equivalent to print; it's that finances seemingly offer little option.

Another issue involves *decision-making*. Individual teachers may not be empowered to choose their class's reading platform. Sometimes departmental or central administrators rule that students will read digitally, regardless of teacher or student preference.

Next, no matter how much we argue that *standardized testing* may not be the best measure of students' reading accomplishments, those tests aren't going away any time soon, at least within middle school and high school. Our best tack is not to lose sight of the longer-range reading aspirations we have for students.

Lastly, there's *peer pressure*. Neither parents nor school systems want to risk their children being left behind in the digital revolution. Some educational systems (notably Waldorf schools) are committed to minimizing use of technology in the classroom.[5] But they're the minority. In a country known for wanting to keep up with the Joneses—and now worrying if your preschooler will get into Stanford—the advice parents give to parent-teacher associations and school boards can be fraught.

ACTIVE LEARNING

> *"Approaches that promote active learning focus more on developing students' skills than on transmitting information and require that students do something—read, discuss, write—that requires higher-order thinking."*
>
> Cynthia Brame[8]

The concept of "active learning", which started gaining prominence in the 1990s, argues that students should be involved in "doing things and thinking about what they are doing", rather than docile receptacles of information.[6] Initially influential in lower education, the idea has increasingly made its way into university classrooms. If you're not familiar with the approach, I recommend the excellent posting by Vanderbilt University's Center for Teaching.[7]

At the core of active learning is getting students to think about what they're learning and to work (individually or jointly with other students) to "construct meaning". While the phrase sounds a bit nebulous, it essentially indicates that learning and knowing are the products of personal engagement with subject matter.

There's a cornucopia of teaching techniques to help foster active learning. Examples range from pausing in the middle of a lecture so clusters of students can briefly discuss what you've been saying, to asking students to predict the result of a demonstration about to take place, to having the class construct a "concept map" (more on concept maps later in this chapter). As the chapter unfolds, we'll see multiple examples of how the notion of active learning specifically applies to reading.

CAPITALIZING ON PRINT READING STRENGTHS AND SKILLS

Whether we're reading on paper, working with a single digital text, or accessing multiple documents on a computer, we are still reading. Earlier we reviewed evidence that print reading skills often correlate with online reading competence, with both single and multiple documents. Continuing to build these print skills can benefit digital success.[9]

BOTH/AND, NOT EITHER/OR

Remember that food pyramid (MyPlate) analogy we suggested in Chapter 4? It's a handy way of thinking about what happened in the trade publishing industry half-a-dozen years ago, following its own "Great Debate" over whether books would essentially all go digital or print would persevere. A kind of truce was declared. Instead of talking about either/or, publishers began acknowledging that the world of books will continue to be both/and.

> "Schools should find a correct balance between comprehension instruction in print and on the Internet."
>
> Ladislao Salmerón et al.[10]

The same both/and logic applies in educational contexts. Instead of arguing for either/or, think in terms of proportions (back to MyPlate) for how much of each medium to use. A good example of such balance is Kristen Hawley Turner and Troy Hicks's *Connected Reading* (2015), a guide for teaching adolescents.[11]

And now to strategies.

Young Children

If I could put in huge neon lights one strategy for reading with young children, it would be this:

> *Don't let a headline in today's press make you flee print or swear off digital.*

Understandably, the news media highlight research that's attention-grabbing. The trouble is that readers generally aren't offered alternative perspectives or research details. Choosing a reading platform for young children based on a single news story can be like the case of the 10 blind men and the elephant: Depending upon which part you touch, you think you're dealing with a very different beast.

> "[R]eading digital books may be an activity that is very different from sharing paper stories with an adult."
>
> Adriana Bus et al.[13]

It's also important to remember that each year brings both new digital books for children and more research on how digital technologies can be used effectively for adult–child social interaction and for linguistic development.[12] One idea to keep in mind is that as digital books evolve from their early days as PDFs, EPUBs, and then gamified texts into new forms still being born, we may want to stop thinking of the electronic book for young children as a digital substitute for print and instead as a distinct form unto itself.

In the rest of this section on young children, I'll have suggestions regarding both print and digital reading. However, because readers likely know less about digital options and strategies, I'll put the emphasis there.

WHAT AGE?

The phrase "young children" stretches from birth to early primary school years. While there's still some debate over use of digital screens with kids under age two, reading experts working with children counsel sticking with print for infants.[14] As Natalia Kucirkova puts it,

> It is possible that over time, as more developers design digital books specifically for the youngest age group, the situation will change, but as things stand [now], the quality of digital books for babies can't match that of baby board books.[15]

WHICH GOAL?

Let your goal drive your choices. If your main purpose is *social interaction*:

- Print is the better choice with infants, and commonly with toddlers and preschoolers.
- As better-designed eBooks and apps become available, digital platforms potentially offer good opportunities for adult–child social interaction, without children being fixated on the technology. However, most digital books aren't there yet.
- Though not involving reading, a good potential use of digital platforms such as tablets and smartphones is to enable social interaction with people at a distance, such as parents and grandparents.

If your main goal is young children's *linguistic or cognitive development*:

- Recall that research results are mixed regarding the pros and cons of children's measurable development from using print or digital books. Also remember that results from formal testing may not reflect learning in more naturalistic settings.
- Regardless of the reading platform you choose, relating the text to children's own experience makes for a supportive learning environment.
- Think about how didactic you wish to be. While some parents—and cultures— see book reading as an opportunity for supporting vocabulary development, others focus on reading as a time for social interaction.

If your main goal is engaging young children's *attention*:

- Be honest with yourself when you're using a digital device to keep your child quiet and occupied. There's a difference between digital material being mesmerizing and encouraging active engagement.
- Recognize that for most of us, it's easier to share in a young child's active engagement with print (including through touch and manipulation) than with digital books. The difference reflects both our greater familiarity using print with young children and the fact that digital books are more inherently distracting. As our experience with digital books grows (and their educational quality improves), this ratio could become more balanced.

WHICH BOOKS?

How do you choose books for young children? Yes, there are the prize-winners and classic favorites. But when browsing print offerings in a bookstore or library, you can inspect the cover, leaf through the pages, and make a first-hand decision. With eBooks or apps, the selection process is more complicated. You might read a review online. There are recommendations from librarians, friends, or teachers. But you seldom have the chance to experience the book in full, the way your child might be doing at home. Given the paucity of well-designed, non–distraction-filled digital books, the task becomes yet more daunting.

What you can do is keep in mind the fruits of the research we talked about in Chapter 4, plus use common sense:

- *Be thoughtful when selecting digitally enhanced eBooks or apps.* If the aim is for children to focus on the storyline, then hotspots, games, and embedded videos are usually not productive.
- *Young children, much like older ones, sometimes need motivation* to spend time with books. Digital stories may kickstart interest in reading when print is proving less successful.
- *Think about the digital book's level of complexity.* Is it too simple or too intricate for your child to handle?

Natalia Kucirkova and Teresa Cremin offer a lot of additional sound advice.[16] I've gratefully incorporated some of it in these suggested strategies:

- Look for digital books (and ways of using them) that *encourage positive interaction between adult and child.* You'll find some research-based suggestions in the blog by Susan Rvachew and her colleagues at McGill University for their Digital Media Project for Children.[17]

- *Capitalize on multimedia features that can help teach new vocabulary* using a digital book. Research by Adriana Bus and her colleagues offers some helpful approaches, including using moving rather than static images, and having kids answer questions about the story rather than just read it (think active learning).[18]

- *Explore other interactive features,* such as letting readers select among possible story endings. Such choices offer opportunities for active engagement, both between the child and the book, and between adult and child. Talk about which ending to choose and why.

- *Touch is another way young children can interact with digital books* and, in the process, develop fine motor skills. Depending on the book's design and the digital platform, there may be options for tapping, swiping, or dragging.[19]

- *Try creating your own digital books with children.* Capitalize on opportunities for personalizing these books by including children's names, photographs, drawings, or own experiences as part of the storyline. Personalization can increase motivation, comprehension, and adult–children conversation.[20] Kucirkova's *How and Why to Read and Create Children's Digital Books* is an excellent guide, and it's available online as an open access book.[21] While some of the advice is for children of primary-school age, other suggestions are well suited to preschoolers.

- *Recognize the importance of keeping abreast* of new digital books or apps with sound educational design. Number of downloads or sales figures may not be good indicators.

DUO OR SOLO?

Often parents' prime motivation for handing children a digital book or app is to enlist an electronic babysitter. The role isn't new, as those of us will remember who parked children in front of the television while we did chores.

Now consider scenarios where you're not seeking time for yourself. Shared reading with a young child is always an appropriate option. But are there circumstances in which leaving children alone, specifically with a digital book, makes sense?

What it means to "read solo" varies with a child's age or stage of development. With books having no written text, reading solo translates into going through the digital pages, perhaps activating built-in sounds and music. For books with text, solo reading commonly means turning on voice narration corresponding to the written words. In Chapter 4 we mentioned research showing children recalled more information from a digital story when a parent read it aloud in person than with publisher-supplied audio narration.[22] Realistically, though, sometimes parents simply can't be available in the flesh, and some book experience is better than none.

Children reading digital books solo can be a sound option when:

- You are working to empower children to feel comfortable experiencing books by themselves.
- A parent or caregiver who can't be present has recorded the narration.

As we'll see in the next two chapters, simultaneous use of audio narration with written text can be a successful strategy for many students, ranging from beginning readers and those with learning challenges to adults who are prone to distraction.

School-Age Readers: Single Texts

When introducing digital reading strategies for young children, I wanted to put one message in neon lights. For school-age readers, I'll need three:

- *Slow down when you are reading digitally.*
- *Concentrate on the text* (quiet the urge to multitask).
- *Be honest with yourself* about how much you are understanding and absorbing.

Obviously, this advice is geared to focused reading, not skimming or hyper reading. Part of our role as parents and teachers is helping students recognize which kind of writing calls for which kind of reading. In the words of Lauren Singer Trakhman and her colleagues,

> Consider the conditions under which reading in print rather than digitally would seem advisable. By articulating those conditions, individuals can selectively move to print as the medium for reading when it seems warranted.[23]

That said, digital is increasingly part of the new normal. Even in contexts that seem better suited for reading in print, we and our students sometimes have no choice. Therefore, a vital job is strategizing how to level the playing field, where possible,

> "[G]iven the unavoid-
> able inclusion of digital
> devices in our contempo-
> rary educational systems,
> more work must be done
> to train pupils with per-
> forming reading tasks
> in digital media, as well
> as to understand how to
> develop effective digital
> learning environments."
>
> Pablo Delgado et al.[24]

between print and digital. It's also to acknowledge contexts where, even for concentrated reading, digital can be the smarter choice, especially for students with learning or reading challenges.

To frame our suggestions for single texts, let's start with goals.

GOALS

When we think about reading for learning, we usually have school settings in mind. And school conjures up reading assignments and tests. Since both of these can occur under time pressure, opportunities for quiet, reflective reading—whether with print or digital materials—may be all too infrequent.

We need to ask ourselves whether we want students to be reading for the short run (turn in the research report that's due tomorrow, cram for that test on Wednesday) or for the long haul. When I teach university students, I often ask, "What will you remember from this course five years from now?" Yes, I give reading assignments and tests. But what I really care about is whether the reading makes a difference in their thinking, not in their grade. In designing pedagogy, especially at the high school and university levels, we need to identify our own goals for students to help them in setting theirs.

TYPE OF TEXT

We'll begin by considering text length. Recall that when reading longer materials, students generally comprehend more with print. Also remember that in perception studies, most students say they prefer reading long texts in print. Accordingly, it's crucial to identify strategies to help students succeed when reading long texts digitally.

When the text is digital, here's general advice that sounds old hat by now but bears repeating:

- Slow down.
- Remove distractions.
- Set goals for what you want to derive from the reading.
- Actively engage with the text.

Later in this chapter when we talk about focusing the mind, I'll suggest ways of fostering active engagement.

Many of the shorter texts students encounter also merit careful reading, especially if they're detailed, complex, or nuanced. Good general advice includes:

- Don't assume that just because a text is short it will be an easy read.
- Especially if it's not an easy read, follow the above advice for long texts.

Turn now to genre. In Chapter 4 we saw potential differences between reading narrative writing (typically, though not exclusively, fiction) and material whose purpose is largely informational. When reading on a digital device, comprehension of narrative was generally on par with reading in print (with some exceptions), while comprehension of informational text was more likely to be higher with print.

Let's think about why. The "why" is inseparable from whether you're reading for pleasure, for a school assignment, or for a test. Formal research is overwhelmingly based on testing situations, most of which involve relatively short reading passages. But that's not the typical kind of text when people read of their own volition. After years of conversations with scores of people who use digital devices when reading for pleasure, I'm convinced it's every bit as possible to read "successfully" for enjoyment with digital. Success might mean speeding through a page-turner or pausing to savor the author's phrasing or plot complexity. I'll wager, though, that the number of readers who linger over the writing tends to be smaller for digital reading.

Are different reading goals reflected in how our brains process text? These days, we can utilize high-tech medical equipment to get a bird's-eye view as research partipants engage in various cognitive activities. Looking at fiction, literary specialist Natalie Phillips used an fMRI scanner to check for possible variation in brain activity when graduate students in literature read a chapter by Jane Austen with an academic mindset (what in Chapter 1 we called "close reading") versus the way they would read for pleasure. With close reading, the students had more blood flow in the parts of their brain responsible for executive functions (which include ability to plan, focus, and remember).[25] While I don't know of comparable fMRI studies when reading informational texts, I suspect we might find parallel results.

The takeaway? When we focus our minds—whatever the nature of the text—we read differently than when breezing through. Since digital reading, regardless of genre, tends to encourage breezing, here are some thoughts and advice, with a focus on formal learning contexts.

For Narrative Texts

- Assigned narrative reading is likely to be comparatively long (a short story or essay, a novel or play). When reading print, it's physically obvious how much of the text you've traversed (or haven't!). With digital, monitoring takes more effort.
- Think about your reading goal before you begin. What will happen after you do the reading? While there could be an in-class test, more likely you'll be asked to discuss the reading in class or write about it. As you read, pause at intervals to consider what you might say or put in an essay. (The same advice obviously goes for reading in print.)

For Informational Texts

- Assigned informational texts come in many lengths—book chapters, journal articles, news stories. Honor the length and complexity of what you're reading, giving the text the time and thoughtfulness it deserves.
- Remember that with digital texts, people tend to retain main ideas and concrete facts but fall short on details, abstractions, and inference-making. As you read, be aware of these common pitfalls.

Finally, here's some crucial genre *advice for teachers*:

Make time in your curriculum for reading long texts, especially fiction.

At the university level, there's a growing move away from the humanities (where longform reading has been the tradition) to subjects that are perceived as more practical—and happen to be less reading-intensive. The internet offers seemingly limitless access to information, which we tend to consume in quick bits and snippets. If the real goal of education is long-term learning, it's up to us to craft and then advocate for the importance of curricula that honor longform reading, including of narrative. If we help students develop habits of mind needed to read longer texts on digital devices, then digital could become a viable alternative to print.

Before leaving this discussion of text type, there's one more category to think about: complexity. Are the texts we're assigning students—whether short or long, narrative or informational—sufficiently challenging? In Chapter 3, we saw that some university faculty are now requiring less complex readings because they don't feel students were understanding earlier assignments.

One source of the problem could be K-12 education, which might not be providing an adequate foundation in grappling with complex reading materials. This is, in fact, the conclusion of a Common Core State Standards document in the United States:

> While reading demands in college, workforce training programs, and life in general have held steady or increased over the last half century, K–12 texts have actually declined in sophistication, and relatively little attention has been paid to students' ability to read complex texts independently.[26]

The report goes on to cite evidence of this decline from multiple research studies. Updates to the Common Core online documentation suggest new initiatives to assess reading complexity—and increase it—but long-term classroom results have yet to materialize.[27]

There's a worrisome paradox here. If texts being assigned aren't particularly complex, then reading digitally will likely be less problematic than if readings require more cognitive effort. However, by avoiding complex reading assignments, we are cheating our students of the education they need and deserve.

ROLE OF TECHNOLOGY

When it comes to reading digitally, the technology cuts two ways: some red flags but also opportunities for capitalizing on new possibilities, and not only for students with reading challenges.

First, potential downsides. The most obvious is the scrolling issue. While the evidence isn't conclusive, it's highly likely that scrolling as you read through a digital text (as opposed to paging) reduces comprehension. The reason is that with a page-worth of information, you not only process the words but establish a grounded sense of place for what you are reading.

What happens in real-world practice? Other variables are at play besides paging versus scrolling. The first is our goal: Are we trying to read the entire text (the research condition discussed in Chapter 4) or are we intentionally skimming or scanning? If skimming or scanning, then scrolling makes total sense. Other variables include how much text fits on a single screen. There's also the rate of scrolling—snail's pace? lickety-split? What's more, paging doesn't guarantee you actually pause to take in the page's real estate, and scrolling doesn't force you to keep the text moving, like credits rolling at the end of a movie.

With these issues in mind, here are some strategies for moving through digital text:

- Adjust the type font (where that's an option) to maximize the amount of text you're comfortable seeing at one time on a screen, whether you will be moving forward by paging or scrolling.
- Figure out for the device you're using if there's a way of doing "page down".
- If your goal is linear reading but you like to use scrolling, try removing your fingers while you're reading (at least to a hover), helping resist the temptation to read as if you're on a zip line.
- After you finish reading a page-worth, think about what you've read before moving on.

On this last point, I'm reminded of advice from the philosopher and educator Mortimer Adler, author of the classic *How to Read a Book*. It's an old book (first published in 1940), but its lessons still resonate. Adler advises readers to stop at the end of each page and process what they've just read. Here are the kinds of questions we might ask ourselves at each pause:

- What have I learned?
- Do I agree or disagree?
- What don't I understand?
- How does what I've read connect with what I already know or have encountered elsewhere?
- Why does what I've read matter?

> *"Reading entails the most intense mental activity. If you are not tired out, you probably have not been doing the work."*
>
> Mortimer Adler[28]

Technology also has its upside, including some clear benefits that digital reading can bring to students with learning challenges. In Chapter 4, we reviewed research suggesting that some children (particularly those with dyslexia or lower reading ability) benefit from increasing the amount of textual spacing—within words, between words, or between lines. Other work indicated that restricting the amount of text on the screen is helpful to students with dyslexia. Some researchers conclude that it's the use of short lines of text, not print versus digital technology, that contributes to these readers' success.[29] Of course, digital texts are easier to manipulate than works that are already printed.[30]

Mindful of this research, consider digital text manipulation techniques that might be useful for students in your classroom (particularly lower or middle school grades).

Most research has been conducted with children diagnosed with learning or specifically reading challenges. However, many of our students go undiagnosed, though we sense they could benefit from text adaptation. Consider experimenting with digital text adjustments that make reading more comfortable. As with adults who play with font size (not only because of diminishing eyesight), one size need not fit all. Some possibilities:

- Have students try adjusting font sizes and line spacing.
- Once students identify the amount of text on a screen they find most comfortable for reading, monitor if their reading benefits from such adjustments.
- Reducing screen brightness can prove beneficial for some students who suffer from eye strain.

Technology potentially enables many other kinds of tailoring that go beyond text or brightness manipulation. Natalia Kucirkova has helpful suggestions regarding digital books and apps appropriate for children with physical or cognitive challenges.[31]

FOCUSING THE MIND

"If you just put your mind to it!" The expression might apply to doing a yoga balancing pose, prying loose a boulder in the garden, memorizing a piano piece—or reading digitally. You're likely tired of hearing this refrain, but the advice to focus when reading onscreen remains central in this chapter. In Chapter 4, we saw that mindset accounts for a sizeable chunk of the differences in outcome between reading in print versus digitally.

Let's take as given the now-familiar advice about slowing down while reading digitally, resisting multitasking, setting reading goals, and being honest about how much we're understanding and retaining. Therefore, we can turn to different issues. While many suggestions we'll look at (Priming a Mindset, Practice Testing, Keywords and Summaries, and Solo Annotation) involve individual activity, others (Social Annotation and Concept Maps) are designed for or can be used in collaborative learning settings. For each of these six areas, we'll start with the recommendations and then follow with context.

Priming a Mindset
- Before you begin reading, prepare to focus your mind on the text.
- Preparation might include advance reading prompts (that is, issues to be thinking about as you read) or sizing up the length, along with the level of complexity or detail.

This advice isn't as obvious as it might seem. In Chapter 4, we saw ample evidence that readers are more likely to waltz through digital reading than the same material in print. But we also mentioned an experiment showing that if participants worked on an activity involving abstract reasoning before doing digital reading, they upped their scores on abstract questions about the text.[32]

Reading prompts are common in many secondary schools, though less so in college. While the technique has long been used with print reading, it could well have added value when students are reading onscreen, helping readers overcome their propensity to move so rapidly through digital text.[33]

Practice Testing

- Intersperse short practice tests within longer reading passages.
- Train students to quiz themselves more informally and to reflect on what they have read.

For most students, "test" is a dreaded four-letter word. However, as we explained in Chapter 3, frequent testing—not for a grade but while in the process of learning—can be a valuable study tool.[34] Such practice testing is useful regardless of the reading platform. But a particular advantage when reading digitally is that these pauses make you slow down. They also help you acknowledge you might not be understanding as much as you think you are.

Keywords and Summaries

- After you've finished reading, write down keywords to help you think about and remember what was important or otherwise thought-provoking.
- After doing the reading, summarize what you have read and learned.

Again in Chapter 4, we saw that listing keywords after reading digitally can support memory and comprehension.[35] These same strategies have long been advocated when reading print.

Keywords or summaries are steps in the right direction, given they're forms of active engagement with the text. But how active—and how useful? Remember the findings we talked about in Chapter 3: While practice testing was a highly useful tool for retention, such techniques as rereading, highlighting and underlining, and summarizing were less so.[36]

Solo Annotation

- Use digital annotation tools, but in a meaningful way.

- An alternative to digital annotation is making notes, either in a separate digital file or on paper.
- Don't assume students know how to annotate digitally or that they regularly engage in the practice. Since digital annotation can take more effort than annotating print, students need guidance on the value of the tool.
- Don't assume that when students do digital annotation, they necessarily are learning as much as when they annotate print. Outcomes tend to reflect energy expended.

The word "annotation" covers a wide swath of options. Highlighting and underlining are the most common. (You might also color-code your markings.) But highlighting and underlining are the most passive forms of annotation and seem to contribute the least to learning. The same goes whether you're using digital or print text.

Marginalia is a more active type of annotation. Notes coming from your own head inevitably require more mental effort than cruising along with a highlighter, pen, or cursor. Marginal notes may or may not boost your score on a comprehension test, but they are more likely to make your reading intellectually and personally meaningful.

Contemporary technology can help make digital marginalia feel more like traditional handwritten notes on paper. Tools such as the Apple Pencil, used with an iPad, enable users to annotate as they read digitally. A similar option is using the pen on the Microsoft Surface.

A different version of digital annotation that is gaining traction is visual notetaking, also called sketchnotes. The idea is to create illustrations (no art talent required), often accompanied by labels and arrows, that represent key events, issues, or relationships between them in the text. A clear benefit of sketchnoting is that students need to be actively involved in the reading process. While visual notetaking obviously makes sense using pen and paper, it can also work digitally, using a tablet.[37]

Digital annotation skills need to be taught and nurtured, much like hand annotation of print. While in K-12 education there's growing awareness of the importance of students learning how to annotate digitally, the extent of teaching—and student usage—is still all over the map. In the study my colleagues and I did with secondary students at the International School of Stavanger, 4 out of 10 said they had been taught to annotate digitally, compared with 7 out of 10 for annotating print. More than 85 percent reported instruction on taking separate notes.[38]

Research by Lauren Zucker and Kristen Turner, working with 11th- and 12th-graders in the United States, is yielding more detailed results. In the project, students were asked about their preferences for print versus digital annotation, both before and after being taught some digital annotation strategies. In the "after" condition, students still reported many reasons they preferred print annotation, including feeling more focused, feeling more relaxed, highlighting more, reading more quickly, and writing more notes with print. The virtues of digital annotation included easy access and not losing or misplacing a text.[39]

If Zucker and Turner's results turn out to generalize to larger student populations, then the mere act of teaching or doing digital annotation may not be a panacea. Smart pedagogies, coupled with smart design, will be needed to increase the probability that digital annotation is coupled with mental focus on and active engagement with what's written.

Social Annotation

- Use online tools to converse with others—fellow students or the instructor—about what you've been reading.
- Conversation might include marginal notes, questions, or answers to other readers' queries.

You likely noticed that the title of the previous section was "Solo Annotation". Though we didn't say so, all the discussion assumed individual students annotating their own copy of the reading. However, it's now increasingly common to find schools turning to shared annotation.

Think for a moment about Google Docs. There's a digital text (maybe written by someone you're working with, but perhaps a pre-existing document) that multiple people can annotate. In a school setting, the "document" could be an assigned reading that students are asked to annotate, working in small groups. Depending upon the sophistication of the social annotation platform, those annotations might be run-of-the-mill underlining or highlights, marginal notes, or questions for classmates to answer. Teachers who access the shared annotated document can see not only who is "doing the reading" but also what students' observations and questions are, along with responses to classmates. This vantage point offers a preview of what students are or aren't understanding, helping teachers better focus the next lesson.

A host of digital annotation tools are available, including Diigo, Evernote, Hypothes.is, Mendeley, and NowComment. The nonprofit organization Common Sense has excellent recommendations, under its Education section, for tools appropriate for K-12 settings. Some programs are specifically designed for either solo use or shared reading notes. Others can be used in both contexts.[40] In Chapters 7 and 8, we'll introduce several video annotation tools as well.

Innovative projects are under way to foster digital collaborative annotation. In Taiwan, a project with fifth-graders reported increased reading comprehension, both explicit and inferential, when using such a tool.[41] At the university level, there's a sophisticated system developed at Harvard called Perusall, designed by Eric Mazur and his colleagues.[42] A physicist, Mazur is also a leader in using technology that encourages active learning, helping students remember what they've learned long after the final exam.

Here's how Perusall is designed. As with most courses in the United States, students are asked to complete the assigned textbook reading before class. What's different is that the group is divided into small learning communities whose members share online which passages they find most important and post annotations, comments, questions—and answers. The prime audience is fellow students, not a professor they're trying to impress. By sharing their insights, along with confusions, students contribute to each other's understanding of the material. Another vital component of Perusall is the computer-generated Confusion Report that instructors receive just before the next class, identifying principal issues about which students have questions.

Evaluations suggest Perusall works. When it came to doing the assigned reading, 80 percent of the students completed at least 95 percent, a figure most teachers can only fantasize about. (Remember those statistics from Chapter 3.) As for test results at the end of the semester, students using Perusall did significantly better than those in comparison sections not using the system.

Here are some takeaways I've inferred from Mazur's social annotation platform:

- Seek ways of getting students to talk with each other about what they are reading.
- Strategize how to make such conversations meaningful (rather than devolving into one-person monologues or general chitchat).
- Find ways of recognizing student problem areas (or areas of disagreement, particularly in humanities or social science classes).
- While few of us have Mazur's sophisticated programming tools (and support staff), brainstorm either face-to-face or online systems enabling students to share with each other (and their instructors) the issues they most need to have addressed in class.

The welcome news is that Perusall has become a freely available tool that teachers anywhere can use with a host of digital materials. As of October 2020, the Perusall site listed almost 300,000 digital titles into which Perusall can be integrated. The only cost to students is acquiring the electronic book. You can also use open educational resources or your own uploaded materials. Perusall is compatible with a variety of learning management systems and has a rich supportive website.[43]

Try it out. There's even a built-in demo.

Concept Maps

- Visually map out relationships between issues, ideas, or people in the text you are reading.

Wait a minute, you might be saying: Didn't we already talk about sketchnotes (a visual form of notetaking) in the section on solo annotation? Yes, but there's a broader notion for us to think about, which draws upon a pedagogical theory designed to use graphics to map connections between ideas or information.

A bit of history: In the 1970s, Joseph Novak, a professor of education and biology at Cornell University, developed a technique known as concept mapping.[44] His aim was to help science students visually represent the ideas they were learning. The approach is predicated upon a learning theory espoused by psychologist David Ausubel, whereby students connect new information with prior knowledge. Use of concept mapping has spread far and wide, from science to the humanities, from college to primary school, from classrooms to boardrooms. An obvious virtue of these maps for learning purposes is that the creator needs to think through both what the central ideas are and then what the relationships are among them—a good context for active learning.

Today, educational practitioners talk about a wide array of visual constructions that collectively live under the umbrella "knowledge maps". There are "mind maps", "spatial maps", and "concept maps" (which themselves come in several varieties). What binds them together is that they are all graphic representations showing relationships between ideas or concepts.[45]

Initially, knowledge mapping was done by hand, but today there are digital tools that can be used individually or socially.[46] Because digital concept maps are commonly used when accessing multiple documents, we'll save the rest of our discussion for the later section on multiple texts.

BOTH/AND

- With reading platforms, "both/and" can mean combining print and digital for the same reading task.

When choosing a platform for reading single texts, you can obviously mix and match (this one in print, that one onscreen), depending on factors such as availability, length, subject matter, or personal preference. But there are also ways of using two media simultaneously, such as:

- Reading in print but taking notes digitally (or vice versa)
- Reading digitally but drawing a concept map by hand

In Chapter 8, we'll apply the same combination principle to reading a text (whether in print or digitally) and simultaneously listening to audio.

School-Age Readers: Multiple Texts

GOALS

Given the wealth of online resources available, it makes sense for teachers (especially in secondary school) to emphasize how to find, evaluate, and synthesize multiple digital documents. But pause for a second and think about the research we talked about in Chapter 5. Most of it focused on efficiency and on resolving conflicts between sources.

Don't get me wrong. These are critical skills for students to develop, and in a moment, we'll pinpoint strategies for fostering them. Before we do, though, let's acknowledge that not all education needs to be narrowly goal-driven:

- Build in opportunities for students to do online exploration that is less guided.

Think about the phrase "poke around". Think about serendipity in discovery and learning. Remember the times you've spent browsing bookstores or library shelves. Were you wasting time or going down rabbit holes? Sometimes. But creativity doesn't flourish on the clock. It needs breathing room.

Then there's the issue of controversy between sources:

- Resolving controversies isn't the only goal of reading multiple documents online. Don't shortchange the importance of information that is cumulative.

Not everything we read is fodder for debate. Yes, especially in today's charged political and fact-denying climate, it is vital that students understand how to evaluate alternative claims. But as the inscription on the temple of Apollo in Delphi cautioned back in the fourth century BC, "Nothing in excess".

Next, find ways of including in the curriculum a broad range of reading materials:

- Given the move in standardized testing to make navigating and appraising multiple online documents a large chunk of reading assessment, keep ample room for individual linear texts.

Again, nothing in excess.

Finally, think about our tendency in education to stress time constraints:

- Don't let accessing multiple online documents turn into speed dating. As with human relationships, one quick look is often a poor basis for decision-making that may have longer-term consequences.

SEARCH, SCRUTINY, AND SYNTHESIS

Having said my piece about the importance of balance in educational focus, let's dig into strategies for effective use of multiple online documents. There's a substantial research-based literature offering guidance. My goal here is to offer highlights and point you to additional resources.

All three components we're looking at (search, scrutiny, synthesis) have print counterparts, and many of the skills we strive to foster for print reading of multiple documents apply to digital as well. What's more, much of the advice we offered about reading individual digital documents is equally important for reading multiple documents (don't multitask, focus the mind, and so on). But we'll direct our attention here to strategies particularly relevant for reading multiple documents online.

Search

Here for starters is my "put this in neon lights" advice:

- *Don't assume Google knows best.* The first hits you come upon in a search may not be most relevant (not to mention most trustworthy).

Students, like many of the rest of us, tend to assume that hits in an online search are magically ranked by level of importance and maybe even trustworthiness. Not so. Page ranking—named after Larry Page, one of Google's founders[47]—is actually the result of complex algorithms. Google's algorithms are said to incorporate around

200 "ranking signals" for main searches, such as how the HTML code for the site is written (including what are known as title tags and meta-descriptions), page loading time, mobile usability, how often people have clicked on the site, how much the site has been referenced on social media platforms such as Twitter and Facebook, and how many other websites link to the page.

So much for content objectivity. Therefore:

- Help students recognize that the most useful (and accurate) information might not be the first hit or even on the first screenful in a search.

Obviously, you don't want students pursuing every possible site. (A February 2020 Google search on "impeachment" offered me about 388 million options.) But a bit of probing often bears valuable fruit. To reach a balance, it's important to define the parameters of what you're looking for and keep them in mind during the search process.

How long should readers spend on a site before deciding to move on?

- Don't dawdle, but do take enough time to fairly assess if the site seems worth reading.

A challenge with selecting online documents to read is that it's so easy to take a quick glance and move on, often without bothering to give sites a fair shake. Compare this with using multiple print documents, where there's a natural time delay built in—you need to pick up each source, maybe find the right page or heading. While I don't have comparative experimental data using a stopwatch, I strongly suspect readers move much faster—often too fast—with digital.

Once you're on a site that has hyperlinks, remember that:

- All that glitters is not gold.

Just because some words are underlined (or colored blue), indicating they are hyperlinked, don't assume these words are particularly important to the topic you're researching. Those of us who have written for online news outlets can vouch for getting not-so-gentle pressure from editors to load up our text with hyperlinks. You can't blame students for assuming text that visually stands out must be important and the hyperlinks worth following. Research confirms this tendency.[48] It's our job to teach students that's not always true.

Scrutiny

Begin with a tired but apt cliché:

- *Don't judge a book by its cover.*

In Chapter 5, when we talked about challenges students have in judging the veracity of an online site, we saw that aesthetics and professional look often counted more than content or authorship. Let's also not forget that conclusions we draw may be skewed by whether we're interested in the topic or the writer's opinion matches our own (confirmation basis).

What are sensible alternatives for judging the street creds of sites? These are some evaluation components researchers identify:

- Determine who created the site (what individual or organization).
- Identify (as best possible) when, where, and why the site was created.
- Learn about the author's credentials and professional affiliation. This research often entails going to other online sites.
- Characterize the author's point of view.
- On a scale from "very low" to "very high", rate the reliability of each source.
- Keep track of answers to these questions in a separate document (either print or digital).[49]

While these steps are commonly suggested for adjudicating when to give credence to websites taking opposing positions, the components are equally relevant for sizing up any online site.

There's evidence that teaching such vetting skills helps students make wiser decisions about which sources to trust. Researchers at the University of Oslo developed a training program for high school students, based on scripted lessons. Students using the lessons demonstrated greater sophistication in handling sources. They invested more time and effort in using the texts they selected, gave more justifications for their selections, and revisited sites more often than a control group without the training. What's more, the skills transferred when evaluating new multiple online documents.[50]

Synthesis

Weaving the parts into a coherent whole is a challenge with any research or writing endeavor. When the materials are digital (rather than physically at hand), it can be even harder keeping track of the pieces. We might think of the synthesis process as having three components: visualizing all the pieces of the puzzle (in the mind's eye or tangibly), comparing what different sources have to say, and creating an integrated ensemble.

For the visualization part,

- Use some tool—digital or by hand—to lay out the research questions.
- Concept maps (or some version thereof, hand-drawn or digital) can be useful, though simpler forms of visualization (even color-coding notes) sometimes suffice.

A variety of research supports the use of concept maps (by whatever name), both when reading single digital texts and when handling multiple documents online.[51]

While concept maps have attracted considerable attention both in schools and from educational psychologists, a review of prior studies reveals that a host of factors—including prior knowledge, reading skills, visuospatial memory capacity, metacognitive skills, and sustained attention ability—can influence the extent to which such mapping is useful. Some researchers have concluded that physical visualizations are most beneficial to students with lower abilities.[52] As with so much in education, one-size pedagogy doesn't fit all.

For the comparison part of synthesizing multiple online documents,

- Review the notes you made when scrutinizing individual documents.
- Compare where your different sources complement each other, agree, or disagree.

And finally, *for creating a coherent whole from reading multiple texts online,* some strategies that can prove beneficial include:

- Summarize your findings before trying to interpret them.
- Discuss potential conclusions with others, along with your reasons for reaching these conclusions.
- Use modeling of integration provided by your instructor or perhaps a video to help scaffold your own analysis.

As with the scrutiny discussion, there's much more to say about synthesis. For good research-based sources, see work by Sarit Barzilai and her colleagues.[53]

TACKLING FAKE NEWS

In Chapter 5, you got an earful about the problems students have in detecting fake information, especially when it comes to news. Our task now is identifying strategies to help address the challenges.

The first step is to distinguish what counts as fact from what doesn't. Recall the three questions that the Stanford History Education Group identified as central for developing civic online reasoning (Who is behind this information? What is the evidence? What do other sources say?). My neon-lights advice for helping students learn the importance of answering these questions is:

- *Look at the resources developed by the Stanford History Education Group.* Their website is a goldmine of freely available teaching materials, including their "Reading Like a Historian" curriculum (already downloaded more than 9 million times) and lessons on "Civic Online Reading".[54]

An additional valuable resource is:

- *Unpacking Fake News: An Educator's Guide to Navigating the Media with Students.* Chapters 6, 7, and 8 in the book offer concrete pedagogical recommendations for K-12 teachers.[55]

The Stanford group has one particular recommendation that bears highlighting for helping students separate fact from fabrication:

- Think like a professional fact-checker by reading laterally, not vertically.

Members of the group compared how professional fact-checkers versus historians (along with some Stanford undergraduates) went about evaluating the credibility of online content. While the historians and students focused within a site ("vertically") by looking at such features as logos and domain names, the fact-checkers made quick forays out to other locations ("laterally") to help verify the original source. It turned out that the professional fact-checkers "arrived at more warranted conclusions in a fraction of the time".[56]

What if you ascertain the facts but refuse to believe them? When we discussed fake news in Chapter 5, we reminded ourselves there's a psychosocial component that goes beyond evidence. Countering confirmation bias is at least as big a challenge as implementing a curriculum for recognizing fake news.

What's more, fake news tends to titillate. We know that online fake news is shared more often than factual reports.[57] Equally scary, research shows that when people repeatedly encounter misinformation, they increasingly feel it's OK (that is, not unethical) to share it—even when that information is clearly labeled as false and the senders don't believe the falsehood themselves.[58]

During World War II, an American propaganda poster read, "Loose lips sink ships", meaning, be careful about unguarded talk that might aid the enemy. When we spread fake news we don't even believe, the risk is erosion not only of truthfulness but also of our moral compass.

I wish I had magic solutions here. I don't. But part of the answer must lie in educating students (and, yes, adults) that when using social media, our responsibility as members of civic society is to think through potential consequences before we hit "send", "share", "like", or "retweet".

DECOMPOSITION, DISTINCTIVENESS, AND AUTHENTICITY

Towards the end of Chapter 5, we talked about several other issues relevant to reading multiple documents online: breaking texts into subcomponents, distinctiveness of the texts themselves, and authenticity of materials. Unfortunately, if you're asking students to find their own online information, it's not obvious how to capitalize on what we learned about the value of decomposing continuous lengthy passages into smaller sections. When it comes to distinctiveness, we already cautioned that flashy or professional-looking sites don't always translate into trustworthy sources, so you need smarter alternatives. And it's truly hard imagining how to think about online material as being authentic.

That said, here are a few ideas to consider:

- *Figure out what components there are to a text.* When readers come to sub-headers, it's time to pause to anticipate what might lie ahead. Unlike with print, the online option for scrolling tempts us to barrel ahead, not slowing down for what should be taken as stop—or at least yield—signs.
- *Look at different websites as being like identical twins* you're trying to tell apart. Imagine the worst-case online scenario, in which all the sites you look at have the same visual format, including identical type font and size. It's time to pause, probably jotting yourself some notes. What's specific to site 1 versus site 2? Your answers can feed directly into the strategies we talked about for scrutiny, such as working to identify the author, along with his or her credentials.

- *When it comes to authenticity, the best tools may be imagination* and, to invoke Aristotle, willing suspension of disbelief. Scholars might wish they could see for themselves the *Book of Kells* or Picasso's *Guernica*, but most need to make do with facsimiles, photographs, or, these days, digitally archived reproductions. Maybe you can't hold that book in your hand or contemplate that original painting from inches away, but virtual surely beats not at all.

Authentic print has many advantages, including aesthetic, physical, and cognitive. But realistically, you can't always access it. In working with students, a plausible strategy is to help them understand the relationship between authentic and virtual, and to recognize the importance of making space for both.

BOTH/AND

Wander into a school library or lounge, and you'll likely see many students engaged in some version of both/and with multiple documents. Maybe the "and" is taking notes by hand or drawing a graphic representation of ideas. Maybe it's reading a print textbook or reference book, while checking other information online. Handwritten notes can help anchor online text that often disappears all too quickly. Like the smile of the Cheshire Cat in *Alice's Adventures in Wonderland*, the tangible written word patiently remains.

Unintended Consequences: Digital Reading for Civic Good

In Chapter 5, we talked about unintended consequences—positive and negative—of the digital reading revolution. One promising constructive consequence we didn't explore was enabling students to harness their digital skills when confronting information and knowledge claims that go beyond the classroom.

A century ago, the philosopher and educator John Dewey wrote that "the chief advantage of education is the assurance it gives of not being duped".[59] In today's media-saturated world, education must entail not just background knowledge and analytical skills but also a keen awareness of the critical importance of trustworthiness of information, especially when it arrives unvetted. At stake is not only our individual sense of well-being but our success as citizens in a democratic polity.

In fall 2019, I met with Maik Philipps, a professor at the Zurich University of Teacher Education. Philipps has worked extensively on developing strategies to help students assess sources they find online. As our conversation unfolded, I probed a bit further, asking why he felt these skills were so important. His answer was simple but insightful: The skills we hope our students develop with online vetting are then applicable to assessing sources wherever they encounter them—including in print books or newspapers, on the radio, on television, in conversation, and yes, online.

With our digital devices, we can all become fact-checkers, regardless of where the reputed facts appeared. We'll also need ways to report fake news and correct it. The more we care about establishing veracity, the better equipped we become to vote knowledgably and to participate responsibly in civic discourse.

Sharing What We Know

Research findings are only valuable if they are shared with people who then act. In our case, this means when choosing and supporting reading platforms. Potential actors are everyone within the educational sphere: parents and teachers, librarians and administrators, students and the larger community of readers. A recent study urges us to take up this responsibility:

> The finding that children are . . . unaware of the detrimental effect of onscreen reading . . . further suggests that children are likely to make ineffective medium choices for their reading tasks. It might therefore be useful to share the current results with children and their teachers to help them make better choices to meet their reading goals.[60]

Please take this recommendation to heart.

PART III   READING WITH AUDIO

WHAT'S
AT STAKE?

Here are some issues to be thinking about as you read Part III:

- What are oral and written cultures, and why are they relevant?
- Is listening to audiobooks a form of cheating?
- Do we learn more from listening or from reading text?
- Is listening to an audiobook while following the text beneficial?
- Are podcasts productive learning tools?
- What are the pros and cons of video assignments?
- Are there practical ways to annotate audio or video?

CHAPTER 7 What Research Tells Us About Audio (and Video)

Even in literate societies, speech is the main way people communicate, as well as transmit culture and learning. The balance between spoken and written language has a complex history. That history helps us understand the prospects of audio complementing or even supplanting written text as an educational medium.

And so we begin with a brief look at the evolving roles of oral and written language.[1] From there we consider attempts to replace text with voice, extending from fictional imaginings to audiobooks and podcasts. The rest of the chapter examines research on audio—and some about video—as educational substitutes for the written word.

Speech and Writing: Cultural Shifts

In college, maybe you read some of Plato's dialogues or Shakespeare's plays. But wait: Doesn't "dialogue" mean a spoken conversation? And perhaps you learned (it's true) that Shakespeare intended his plays for live theatergoers, not to be read privately.[2] Not until 1623, with publication of the First Folio—the first printed collection of Shakespeare's dramatic works—were people urged to read rather than watch the plays. As for Plato's dialogues, they represent presumed accounts of conversations.

These two examples share a crucial trait: Although there were literate people in both late fifth century BC Athens and Elizabethan England, neither society yet had a written culture.

ORAL AND WRITTEN CULTURES

What do we mean by "oral" and "written" cultures? The terms describe how the bulk of society goes about its everyday business: How do people get their news? What is their entertainment? How are church services conducted? If these activities largely (sometimes exclusively) happen through spoken language, it's an oral culture. If the balance shifts sufficiently, we're dealing with a written culture.

It's deceptively simple to assume that when a technology exists, somehow, overnight, a fundamental mode of functioning changes. That assumption fails for the early personal computer revolution: How many people bought an Apple II when it appeared in 1977? It also fails for standardized English spelling: While many speak as if standardization magically happened in 1476 with the introduction of printing in England, it actually took almost 200 more years.[3]

Similarly, consider the place of writing in the history of English.[4] Up through most of the 17th century, England remained an oral culture. Yes, Chaucer wrote the

Canterbury Tales, but he also read his stories aloud to nobility. Yes, the Bible was written, but it wasn't until the Protestant Reformation that the populace was encouraged to read scripture for themselves. Common forms of entertainment were the likes of bear-baiting and theater, not private reading. Dissemination of news largely came via the town crier, along with gossip.

Two ingredients are essential for transforming a culture from oral to written: putting printed text within people's financial reach and increasing literacy. For the second, you need education.

FROM DISPUTATIONS TO WRITTEN EXAMS

One bellwether for distinguishing oral from written culture is how we assess formal learning. For lower education, memorization and recitation—an oral skill—have a long history. The same is true for higher education.

Imagine yourself at Cambridge University in the 14th century. You finished studying the "foundation course", meaning the trivium (grammar, logic, and rhetoric), followed by the quadrivium (arithmetic, music, geometry, and astronomy). Now it's exam time. The examinations, called disputations, are all oral. You're posed questions that you need to dispute or argue.

It took many centuries before written university exams began to appear. In 1702, Trinity College, Cambridge, was the first to start a shift, but initially only for mathematics. Written exams entered Oxford in 1800. In America, Harvard University's first written exams—again, in mathematics—didn't appear until 1833. The move from oral to written exams in public schools began in Boston in 1845.[5]

Today in the United States, we take written exams for granted. But I invite you to teach at a university in Italy, which I did for a semester. At the end of the term, I was supposed to give an oral examination to each student. Yes, modern Italy has a written culture, but oral vestiges remain.

Reading with Our Ears

Picture an article with the title "The End of Books". You likely assume the piece is about digital reading killing print. After all, since the rise of personal computers and then eBooks, riffs on the theme have been commonplace (to wit: Robert Coover's 1992 "The End of Books", Sam Leith's 2011 "Is This the End for Books?", or Rachel Nuwer's 2016 "Are Paper Books Really Disappearing?"). But the publication in question was dated 1894, long before Steve Jobs or Jeff Bezos was born.

And the replacement for print was not some new platform for the written word but sound.

TECHNOLOGICAL FEATS AND FICTIONAL IMAGININGS

The story begins in 1844 at the U.S. Capitol. It was there that a painter-turned-inventor named Samuel F. B. Morse tapped out the message "What hath God wrought!", which was sent on the first long-distance telegraph line, built between Washington and Baltimore. Written communication became possible without having to send a letter.

The next milestone came in 1876, when Alexander Graham Bell summoned his laboratory assistant with the words "Mr. Watson, come here. I want you", which was the first voice transmission on Bell's device known as the telephone. With telephones, you didn't need any writing to transmit messages at a distance.

Although Bell was the first to patent the telephone, his archrival in the pursuit, Thomas A. Edison, was nipping at Bell's heels. Just one year later, Edison introduced his new invention, the phonograph. Now you could record sound and replay it. Edison's initial idea was for businessmen to dictate letters, without requiring a stenographer. The voice message would be etched into a cylinder, then delivered to the intended recipient to replay. However, the phonograph ended up not as a system for sending personal messages but a device perfectly suited for playing recorded music.[6]

The phonograph could, of course, play back any recorded sounds, including the words in a book. In 1889, an acquaintance of Edison wrote:

> It is even possible to imagine that many books and stories may not see the light of print at all; they will go into the hands of their readers, or hearers, as phonograms.[7]

"Will letter writing be a proceeding of the past? Why not, if by simply talking into a mouthpiece our speech is recorded on paper. . . . Are we to have a new kind of books?"

Scientific American 1877[8]

And indeed, thinking ahead for a moment to the 21st century, some books now go directly into audio format without first being printed.[9]

In the late 19th century, authors began entertaining the prospect of audio replacing print. Writing in 1889, futurist Edward Bellamy envisioned writing being supplanted by recordings played on portable devices.[10] Five years later, Octave Uzanne, a French writer and publisher, concocted a related scenario in "The End of Books", complete with whimsical illustrations of possible hardware.[11]

AUDIO LISTENING 1.0

In the 20th century, we moved from fantasizing about replacing print with audio to enterprises making replacement possible. Matthew Rubery's *The Untold Story of the Talking Book* is an excellent history of what happened.[12] We'll focus on two major initiatives: audio recordings for the blind and recordings designed for the sighted. But first, there was radio. Taken together, I think of these platforms as Audio Listening 1.0.

Radio

By the early 1900s, Guglielmo Marconi's "radio telegraphy" was a technological reality. Initially used for communication between ships, radio came into its own by the 1920s as a general broadcast medium. The first U.S. commercial radio license was issued in 1920, while in England, the BBC launched in 1922.

Almost from the start, programming included so-called radio dramas, essentially dramatizations of stories, complete with actors' voices, music, and sound effects. A number of radio stations had their own acting troupes. During the 1930s, '40s, and '50s, radio dramas flourished. The spread of television in the 1960s undercut the radio audience somewhat, though the concept of radio dramas continues today through podcasting.[13]

Besides dramas, there was music—lots of it. Many radio stations maintained their own orchestras, initially to avoid paying royalty fees to the record business. Some radio orchestras still exist, such as the Swedish Radio Symphony.

Since its inception, radio has found a broad audience. A study by sociologist Paul Lazarsfeld showed that by the late 1940s, over 90 percent of people in the United States had a radio. What's more, 26 percent of those surveyed said that on an average weekday, they listened more than six hours a day.[14] Besides hearing the news, listeners were mostly interested in being entertained, not enlightened. As Lazarsfeld wrote, "It is well known that educational programs have low ratings".[15]

Initially, people listened at home. But given the growing love affair with driving, radios began appearing in American automobiles. The first car radios were installed in 1930 by the Galvin Manufacturing Corporation. Fun fact: The Galvin brothers decided to name their product "Motorola", a blend of "motor car" and "Victrola" (the popular "talking machine", aka phonograph). After car radio's robust success, the brothers renamed their company Motorola, now the multinational communications giant.

Radio brought music, news, drama, and other talk-based entertainment to vast audiences. But one thing radio didn't offer was books. For that, we needed war.

Books for the Blind

It all started with Napoleon Bonaparte. On the battlefield, exchanging written messages at night is a deadly risk. If you light a torch to read a missive, the enemy can spot your position. Napoleon demanded a system be devised enabling soldiers to decipher messages in the dark. A French captain named Charles Barbier de la Serre rose to the challenge, inventing "night writing", based on 12 raised dots on paper.

In 1821, when Barbier was lecturing at the Royal Institution for Blind Youths in Paris, sitting in the audience was 12-year-old Louis Braille, who was blind. Three years later, Braille had reworked Barbier's "night writing" to create the six-dot system we know today as Braille.

Jump forward nearly a century, to the years following World War I. England's Royal National Institute of Blind People began producing sound recordings of books for soldiers blinded in the war. By 1942, the American Foundation for the Blind and the Library of Congress launched a similar project.

Now there was an alternative to reading books in Braille. While debates would continue whether the blind community judged "talking books" to be preferable to Braille, two facts remained. First, not everyone who is blind can read Braille. And second, the average speed (for general listeners) when playing an audio recording is about 190 words per minute, compared with around 60 words per minute for reading Braille.[16]

On both sides of the Atlantic, large collections of "talking books" were created for the visually impaired. However, nothing prevents sighted people from listening to recordings. In the United States, a new industry blossomed, led by Caedmon Records. Their first release, in 1952, was poems of Dylan Thomas on one side and "A Child's Christmas in Wales" on the other, all read by the author. Caedmon went on to record many 20th-century literary greats, establishing there was a wider audience for recorded literature.

Caedmon's listenership was decidedly highbrow. It was assumed people would focus on the book, not simultaneously engage in other activities. Editors at Caedmon even encouraged listeners to follow along in the printed text.[17]

Such advice didn't survive the next technological development with audio and books.

Books on Tape

The year was 1973. Duvall Hecht, a one-time Olympic champion rower, was stuck in California traffic on his long daily commute. As Matthew Rubery retells the story, Hecht found the car radio's diet of Top 40 song hits, mixed with news and commercials, to be turning his brain "into cottage cheese".[18] Hecht's response was to found a company, two years later, called Books on Tape, which rented cassettes of full-length books. The intended audience was people seeking a better way to occupy their minds while doing something else—like driving.

Books on Tape was wildly successful, especially among commuters. With introduction of the Sony Walkman in the U.S. in 1980, those on foot (walking, at the gym, doing housework) or even sitting still could conveniently listen to books as well. Portable cassettes were later joined by compact discs. Over time, competitors entered the market, bookstores began selling rather than renting tapes, and the public became increasingly acclimated to reading with their ears.

While fiction (including serious literature) was available, the audio diet expanded to bestsellers and nonfiction. A 1992 survey of Books on Tape users showed most listeners were multitasking. About 80 percent listened while driving. Overall, three-quarters agreed that the ability to be "doing something else" while listening was the main advantage of Books on Tape.[19]

AUDIO LISTENING 2.0

By the first decade of the 21st century, the mobile digital revolution was upon us. Desktop and even laptop computers were yielding to eReaders, tablets, and mobile phones. Downloadable or streaming music became available on iPods, phones, and then smart speakers. New publications started appearing not just as print and eBooks but as audiobooks as well. Podcasts became increasingly popular, created by everyone from techies to journalists to university professors.

Enter Audio Listening 2.0. This second phase includes modern audiobooks and podcasts. But don't forget traditional radio, especially while driving.

Audiobooks

We'll start with audiobooks. The huge spurt in audiobook download revenues we reported in Chapter 2 suggests many people are listening. By early 2019, one out of five American adults had listened to at least one audiobook in the past year.[20] The largest audience is college-educated, comparatively affluent, and between ages 30 and 49. Audiobook listenership is heavily female, but the same is true for reading print or eBooks.

What are people listening to? The most popular categories are mysteries, thrillers, and suspense, followed by history, biography, memoirs, and humor.[21] Since much of this listening is done while multitasking, the genres make sense, as these materials don't tend to demand listeners' full attention. This list isn't far off from choices iden-tified in the earlier Books on Tape survey, which were bestselling fiction, the classics, mystery, adventure, war and history, and biography.[22]

Podcasts

Podcasts followed a different trajectory, given they aren't built on a print book model or commercial base. Rather, like so much on the internet, they have capitalized on mobile technologies and are often generated by the public.

By the early 2000s, as written blogging was burgeoning on the internet, netizens began experimenting with creating and sharing audio files. In 2004, journalist Ben Hammersley mused:

> With the benefit of hindsight, it all seems quite obvious. MP3 players, like
> Apple's iPod, in many pockets, audio production software cheap or free,
> and weblogging [the original name of blogging] an established part of the
> internet; all the ingredients are there for a new boom in amateur radio.[23]

You needed a name for these user-generated shared audio files. One of Hammersley's suggestions was "podcasting"—a cross between "iPod" and "broadcast". The name stuck.

Podcasts have been exploding. While exact statistics are hard to come by, one estimate for 2019 was over 800,000 different podcasts, containing over 30 million episodes.[24] And people are listening. Edison Research and Triton Digital reports that in 2019, nearly one out of three people in the United States age 12 or older had lis-tened to a podcast in the previous month. Men tend to listen more than women (the reverse of audiobook patterns).[25]

Much of the listening (49 percent) takes place at home, with 22 percent while driving, 11 percent at work, 4 percent while riding on public transportation, and an-other 4 percent when working out.[26] Among avid podcast listeners, the top genres are music, TV and movies, comedy, and technology.[27]

Radio

Just because radio is now an "old" medium, don't assume its audience is fading. A survey from late 2018 found that 92 percent of adults in the United States listened to the radio each week. Among adults, the most popular genre overall is country music, followed by news and talk shows. Pop chart music is second for teenagers up through adults in their mid 50s.

The bulk of listening is done in cars. Among those who had been in a car the previous month, 81 percent had listened to AM/FM radio. By contrast, 45 percent had listened to their own digital music, 43 percent to a CD player, and 26 percent to a podcast.[28]

DOES LISTENING COUNT AS READING?

Not everyone is convinced it's legitimate to call listening to a podcast or audiobook "reading". Despite the popularity of audio files, keeping separate nomenclature for what you do with your eyes has mattered to some authors and readers.

Take this question from Sven Birkerts:

> Is listening to books an extension of reading, or is it a simplification, yet another ingenious way of turning everything into entertainment?[29]

Birkerts's fundamental concern is with the level of engagement readers potentially have with an audiobook, compared with a printed work.

Part of the issue involves control, especially when the text is complex, subtle, or linguistically rich. With print, you easily linger whenever you choose. With audio, the narrator sets the pace. In fact, it was in this same essay that Birkerts coined the phrase "deep reading", which we talked about in Chapter 1. Birkerts writes:

> Reading, because we control it, is adaptable to our needs and rhythms. We are free to indulge our subjective associate impulse; the term I coin for this is *deep reading*: the slow and meditative possession of a book. We don't just read words, we dream our lives in their vicinity.

Birkerts continues: By contrast,

> Deep listening to words is rarely an option. Our ear, and with it our whole imaginative apparatus, marches in lockstep to the speaker's baton.[30]

Political commentator and essayist David Frum shares another of Birkerts's concerns about audiobooks, namely who is doing the imagining and interpreting: the reader or the narrator. Frum's worry with audio is that

> The [narrator's] interpretation asserts and inserts itself, stifling one's own understanding before that understanding can ever take form.[31]

Yet both Birkerts and Frum admit finding pleasure in audiobooks, especially when artfully narrated. And audio's availability is especially appreciated when consigned to boring tasks such as sitting in gridlocked traffic or waiting in an interminable line. What's more, Birkerts reminds us that the deep reading model he cherishes is frequently not practiced, thereby complicating the scorecard for print versus audio:

> Too often we read serious books at the same rate at which we read the morning paper, stripping the sentences for their sense and jamming phrases together like the pleats of a compressed accordion.[32]

In which case, audio has the advantage of at least putting every word before us.

Is listening to audiobooks a form of cheating, taking the easy way out? Psychologist and reading specialist Daniel Willingham reports frequently being asked this question. His response: Rather than talking about cheating by listening to your book club selection, don't think of audio and print as wholly interchangeable. For easy texts, equivalence is more likely. For harder texts, print has the advantage. But when you're driving or on the treadmill, audio can be a winner because it allows you to multitask.[33]

WHEN YOUR BRAIN LISTENS OR READS

Does your brain distinguish between listening and reading? The answer seems to be "no" and "yes", depending on the mental activity you're talking about.

First, the "no" part. Studies at the University of California, Berkeley, indicate that the brain's representation of words is nearly identical whether a person is reading a story or listening to it.[34] Of course, the brain does more than register word meaning. It also makes sense of longer units like sentences and paragraphs. What's more, it remembers what was read or heard, either in the short term or over time. For comprehension and memory questions, psychologists turn to different sorts of testing, which we'll talk about shortly.

We also need to think about genre. The Berkeley study used stories from a popular podcast, *The Moth Radio Hour*. What if they had used legal briefs? While the words themselves might get represented in the same brain locations regardless of input medium, it's unlikely that the level of mental effort would have been equivalent in the two media.

Now that we have laid the groundwork, it's time to focus on the place of audio in learning. We'll first consider audio by itself, moving next to audio plus text, and then on to audio with video.

Solo Audio

BUSINESS OR PLEASURE?

"Audio for learning". A natural or an oxymoron? The answer depends on what you're looking to learn and how serious you are about learning it.

Take the "what" question. If your goal is learning a foreign language, audio definitely can help with pronunciation and comprehension skills. An audio component makes obvious sense for music history or theory classes. What about novels or poetry? Maybe, especially if you have the right narrator. Fields that require memorization? Perhaps. Linear algebra? I'll wager not.

The issue of seriousness is relevant not just for students but for anyone curious about a topic. Here's where nonfiction audiobooks, along with podcasts, come in. In my spare time, I might eagerly—even intently—listen to a podcast on wildlife extinction. But what's my goal? I might share with my husband an interesting fact I learned. Will I remember it tomorrow? Next month? Possibly. I was listening for personal edification, not to be tested.

When it comes to audiobooks, remember that the most popular genres are mysteries, thrillers, and suspense. Plus, most audiobook users seem to be multitasking while listening. Highly popular podcasts are generally on the light side as well. What's more, since most podcasts are free, we don't generally perceive them as media demanding our focused attention. And yes, we're often multitasking. Partial attention is a theme we hear repeatedly in discussions of audio recordings. In her study of Books on Tape, Helen Aron found that survey participants looked

> to books on audiocassette for information and entertainment while they
> are engaged in activities that require little concentration.[35]

So much for attitudes and personal judgments. What does the research show?

THE PRIMACY OF PRINT: COMPARING LISTENING AND READING

For over half a century, psychologists have been comparing the way people listen and read. Most studies have concluded we remember more when we read. In the words of Adrian Furnham, there is a "primacy of print".[37] Some evidence:

> "[Audiobooks are] an emerging form of entertainment willing to sever its ties to the book altogether."
>
> Matthew Rubery[36]

- Adults who read news stories in print remembered more than people who listened to the same stories.
- Adults who read the transcript of a piece of fiction remembered more than those who either listened to the audio or watched the televised version (audio plus video).[38]

The question is why.

Focusing on physical differences between speech and writing, here are some reasons:[39]

- Durability of writing
  - Unlike audio, written text stays put, enabling several of the affordances below.
- Control over pace
  - Reading lets you set your own pace. With audio, you are at the mercy of the narrator.
- Ease of rereading
  - It's easy to reread sections when you wish. While there are ways of re-listening to audio, it's more cumbersome.
- Ability to skim or skip passages
  - With text, you can glide over material that seems uninteresting or irrelevant to your reading purpose. Audio has no easy option.
- Landmarks in the text
  - Written texts typically provide visual landmarks dividing the reading into chunks, using periods, new paragraphs, sub-headers, or page breaks. (In Chapter 5, we discussed the usefulness of decomposing longer texts.) Audio tends to be an unbroken stream.

Let's dig a little deeper. When comparing memory or comprehension of audio versus print, what happens when you take into account the length of the text or its complexity?[40] Research shows that with very short texts (say, a few words or sentences), recall can be better with audio. However, once the material gets longer, print has the advantage.

What about complexity? Eye-tracking studies reveal that when readers encounter text that's difficult, ambiguous, or important, they make more regressive saccades (going backward in the text with their eyes).[41] Written text enables readers to backtrack. So do audiobooks, though you can only conveniently rewind a short distance back. What's more, research suggests that in learning contexts, students are less likely to backtrack with audio than with text. When university students were given the opportunity to review or replay longer materials before being tested, they did so with the written version but not the audio.[42] These results aren't surprising, given the comparative ease of finding what you want to review in writing.

There's much more research comparing listening with reading.[43] But we'll focus here on a study done in Cyprus by Irene-Anna Diakidoy and her colleagues that looked at children ranging from lower to middle school and that included both narrative and expository texts. (While the authors use the term "expository", essentially think "informational".)[44]

Among reading scholars, there are two contrasting theories about the relationship between oral and written comprehension. One theory (the "dual process view") argues that although listening and reading share some elements, they are essentially two separate cognitive processes. The alternative theory (the "unitary process view") holds that the same comprehension mechanism underlies both listening and reading. As Diakidoy and her colleagues point out, if the unitary process view is correct, then once students have learned the decoding skills needed for reading, their comprehension scores on oral and written tasks should be equivalent.

But are they? More broadly, how does development of literacy skills affect proficiency in listening and reading comprehension? It stands to reason (and research confirms) that among younger readers, listening comprehension is stronger. But what happens then? And does genre matter?

To find out, the researchers in Cyprus had children either read two texts (one narrative and one expository) or listen to recordings of both. Afterwards, the children were asked questions about the material. The results:

- The relationship between listening and reading skills inverted as children got older. While second-graders had better comprehension with listening, eighth-graders had better reading comprehension.
- Overall, comprehension of narrative texts was higher than for expository texts, both aurally and when reading text.

So is there a primacy of print? The answer for beginning readers seems to be "no" (and understandably), but "yes" as students become more proficient with written text. Let's move, then, to what happens when older students encounter podcasts.

PODCASTS AND LEARNING

In school settings, podcasts are primarily used as a form of lecturing. In principle, though, podcasts can also substitute for written material. We'll look at both varieties.

A quick note on terminology is useful before we begin. When most people talk about podcasts, they have in mind audio programming used for news, entertainment, or other general public consumption. However, as the education world has increasingly embraced online learning, many teachers are producing audio recordings for their students with some or all of the content of a face-to-face lecture. (The same is true of teacher-generated videos.) In the research literature, these audio productions are typically called podcasts, though admittedly they are different in kind from what you find in the public realm.

As we'll see in a moment, sometimes educational audio podcasts are teamed with a PowerPoint slide set. However, I'm still classifying these as "solo audio" to distinguish them from pairing audio simultaneously with full written text, which we'll talk about a bit later.

Podcasts of Lectures

Over the years, as portable recording devices became available, individual students sometimes asked to record lectures. Some still do. However, for the last decade, institutionally hosted video recording ("lecture capture") has become common, providing both audio and video archiving.

Academic podcasts (aka audio recordings) come in three varieties:

- Distributed copies of classroom lectures (either audio or video)
- Flipped classroom mini-lectures
- Supplementary material

In the first case, the school gives students access to the classroom lecture, either for review purposes or in case students missed a class. In the second, the teacher records material (audio or video) for students to listen to (or view) before the class in which it will be discussed. The third variety provides additional course content.

Researchers have investigated university students' perceptions and usage of lecture podcasts. In a study of students in a medical radiology program, participants reported it was useful to listen to lectures a second time and to have the flexibility of listening when and where they choose.[45] In a second study, this time with university students from a range of social science courses, most participants reported that podcasts used for reviewing course material improved their overall understanding and helped them retain what they learned.[46]

But how do podcasts stack up against studying written materials? And what kind of written materials are we talking about?

Podcasts in Place of Written Text

In Chapter 4's discussion of reading in print versus digitally, we distinguished between student perceptions and experimental measures. We also talked about calibration—that is, comparing how well students think they'll do (or did) on a test against their actual score. Both issues are also at play with podcasts.

One straightforward comparison of audio versus text is pairing the audio recording with a written transcript of the same lecture. That's what researchers did with a group of dental students. Study participants were given the opportunity to use either format when preparing for an exam, when reviewing a lecture they had attended, and when listening to a lecture they'd missed. While course grades didn't reflect their choice of audio versus text, students were consistently more likely to use podcasts than transcripts.[47]

It's no coincidence that more than half the students listening to audio in the study played the podcasts at speeds one-and-a-half times or twice as fast as the original. Speeding up audio material for review is common among students in medical fields, based on conversations I've had with medical students. But it's also a practice among some general podcast users. The 2018 Edison Research and Triton Digital survey found that 19 percent of those who listened to podcasts said they sometimes sped up the podcasts "in order to listen to them faster".

What about comparisons of natively written educational materials (like textbooks or articles) versus audio recordings of the same words? I only managed to find a tiny handful of relevant studies—hardly the basis for definitive conclusions. However, they do hint at questions we need to be thinking about.

The first study, by David Daniel and William Woody, asked what many teachers want to know: If you give students the same words in a podcast or in a written assignment, from which medium do students think they learn more—and which is actually more academically beneficial?[48] Considering what students say about enjoying the benefits of podcasts, we might predict they'd assume more successful learning from audio. However, from what we learned about "the primacy of print", students might perform better with the written version.

University students in a developmental psychology class were asked either to read an article of about 3,000 words (roughly 10 typed pages) or listen to a podcast with the same text. Two days later, everyone completed a questionnaire. Among the items were questions about how much they thought they learned, how much they enjoyed the reading or podcast, and the extent to which they would prefer a podcast instead of reading when it came to learning "important material". Next, students were given a quiz, followed by a repeat of the question about which medium they would prefer for learning.

First, the quiz results: All the readers outscored those who listened to the podcast. What's more, those who read the text indicated they remembered more, understood more, had less difficulty, and learned more than reported by those in the audio condition. The "primacy of print" hypothesis prevailed.

> "Merely taking the test alerted them to the limits in their comprehension after listening."
>
> David Daniel and William Woody[49]

Now comes calibration. After listening to the podcast (but before taking the quiz), students said they preferred podcasts to reading. However, after taking the quiz—but before learning their results—students in the podcast group reduced their preference for podcasts.

After the quiz, the researchers conducted a focus group with the podcast group, looking to understand the challenges that podcasts might bring to learning. Among the students' near-unanimous observations:

- Podcasts lack "signalizing devices" such as bold or italics to emphasize what is particularly important.
- Podcasts lack visuals such as charts and graphs to reinforce learning.
- Students were far less likely to review portions of the audio than if they had been reading the same material.

The first comment reminds us that writing, unlike audio, has natural mechanisms for separating out or emphasizing portions of text that help readers organize the stream of language into meaning components. The second comment suggests that the usefulness of audio as a learning platform can be enhanced by visual complements. In the research with medical radiology students we just talked about, most students using podcasts to review lectures looked simultaneously at the lectures' PowerPoint slides.

It's the third comment, though, that gives me the most pause. Much like students in a study we mentioned earlier,[50] although Daniel and Woody's participants could have reviewed the audio material, they didn't. While some people re-listen to podcasts (and audiobooks) for pleasure, re-listening for learning seems far less frequent. If students are less inclined to review learning materials they encounter auditorily than ones in print, it likely follows they will be learning less from the podcast.

Further dredging the literature, I came upon an experiment that predated podcasts but compared undergraduates' comprehension of a printed magazine article versus an audio rendition (this time piped into the lab room). Besides looking at comprehension, the authors measured several other variables, including how much effort students said they invested in trying to understand what they read or heard. The results: better comprehension when reading, as well as more effort expended. In the authors' words,

> it is plausible that for these college students, one reason why listening comprehension lagged behind reading comprehension is precisely because they failed to invest mental effort in their listening.[51]

Another study I unearthed—this time with actual podcasts—was with German medical school students. To test the role of platform in learning about orthopedic diseases, one group was asked to read some textbook chapters while the other was given specially prepared podcasts on the same topics. However, the actual language in the written texts versus the podcasts wasn't identical. What's more, students using the podcasts were also given a PowerPoint presentation with which the voiceover narrative was synchronized. After reading or listening, both groups were tested. Students in the podcast (with PowerPoint) condition learned more and reported having more fun learning than students who read.[52]

The study is instructive in several ways. It reminds us that handing students textbooks and saying, "Go learn," may not be the most inspiring form of pedagogy. It also reinforces the theme that educational podcasts may be most successful when they're combined with relevant visual material.

AUDIOBOOKS AND LEARNING

As with podcasts, there's little research comparing learning from audiobooks versus written versions of the same text. An obvious challenge for researchers is how long it takes students to read an entire book, complicating the possibilities for comparative testing. Also, while audiobooks are a popular form of relaxation and entertainment, they're not part of the usual academic landscape.

A study by Beth Rogowsky and her colleagues comes closest to comparing audiobooks and written text for learning. The material used was about 3,000 words from Laura Hillenbrand's nonfiction novel *Unbroken: A World War II Story of Survival, Resilience, and Redemption*. The material was inherently engaging (unlike those textbook chapters on orthopedic diseases). The study design had three conditions: audio-only, text-only (digitally on a Kindle), and simultaneous audio and text (a situation we'll be exploring in just a bit).

After reading and/or listening, comprehension tests were given twice: immediately after reading/hearing the text and then again two weeks later. In neither case were there differences in comprehension across the three reading/hearing conditions.[53]

Do these findings contradict Daniel and Woody's conclusion that written text is better for learning than podcasts? Not necessarily. As Rogowsky and her colleagues point out, participants in their study weren't allowed to review the text (written or audio) before the test, while Daniel and Woody's students could if they chose. Even more relevant is the authors' comment about genre:

> We caution . . . that the non-fiction text material used in this study was more narrative in style, and may not be representative of the discourse style typically found in textbooks.[54]

Let's turn now from learning prospects for audiobooks with university students to use with younger readers. In Chapter 4, we talked about the potential for digital books to motivate school-aged children who don't like to read. If our first goal is getting children reading, and switching the medium can help, common sense dictates considering new options, including audio.

Take a U.S. study done with fourth- and fifth-graders who were struggling readers. The researchers asked if having these children participate in a library audio book club could jumpstart their interest in reading, along with their reading skills. The answer was "yes" on both counts. Students selected their own books. In each case, they were asked to read along with the written text as they listened to the audiobook. According to the researchers, after the year-long program, students went from identifying themselves as poor readers to declaring they were good readers. All participants said they were now reading more. And reading scores on standardized tests were reported to have improved significantly as well.[55]

On both sides of the Atlantic, researchers are increasingly interested in the role that audiobooks might play in both motivating and engaging children as readers.[56] A recent report from the United Kingdom's National Literacy Trust argues that audiobooks are not a shortcut to reading. Rather, they can build both vocabulary and emotional intelligence.[57] In the United States, the title of a master's thesis says it all: "Embracing Audiobooks as an Effective Educational Tool".[58]

The audio industry has taken notice of the potential of children using audiobooks for learning. The Audio Publishers Association[59] has an entire webpage called "Sound Learning". When you scroll down, you find an eye-popping infographic labeled "How Audio Promotes Literacy: Benefits of Audio to Learning How to Read" that is chock-full of impressive statistics, including:

- "Increases motivation by 67%"
- "Improves comprehension by 76%"

- "Test scores increased 21% when engaged in multimodal learning versus single-mode."
- "Combining print and audio increases recall 40% over print alone."

(We'll get to combining print with audio in a moment.) The infographic includes a bibliography that presumably contains all the data sources, though my moderate attempts didn't succeed in matching actual sources to most statistics. Accordingly, I view these numbers as possible trends, not definitive findings.

MINDSET AND MIND WANDERING

We've been talking about measuring the effectiveness of audio through traditional comprehension testing. There's another useful measure (likely correlated with comprehension), namely how much you perceive your mind to be wandering when you're reading.

Trish Varao Sousa and her colleagues compared the amount of mind wandering by university students in three conditions: reading aloud, reading silently, and listening. The test materials were excerpts from Bill Bryson's *A Short History of Nearly Everything*, a popular science book. To measure mind wandering, every 10 seconds students were asked to respond "yes" or "no" to the question "During the moments prior to the probe, were you mind-wandering?"

The most mind wandering came when listening to the audio. Next was silent reading, with the lowest level when reading aloud. This last finding make intuitive sense, since voicing the words yourself requires even more attention to the text than only having your eyes move across the lines. Not surprisingly, subsequent memory tests correlated inversely with mind wandering:

- Listening: most mind wandering, worst memory
- Reading silently: medium mind wandering, medium memory
- Reading aloud: least mind wandering, best memory[60]

Enough said.

We'll revisit mind wandering when we talk about video.

Audio + Text

We've looked at using audio by itself, plus several cases of adding in PowerPoint slides. What happens if you combine audio with full text?

In Chapter 4, we talked about young children using audio tracks in conjunction with digital books. In a moment, we'll turn to research on combining the two media with beginning and evolving readers, children with reading challenges, and second language learners. But first, an attempt to combine full text with not narration but sound effects.

THE SOUND OF THUNDER

If you ever listened to radio dramas, you remember the sound effects enlivening dialogue. A door slamming. A dog barking. The howling wind. Sound effects were sometimes added to "talking books" and now are included in a number of audiobooks.[61]

In 2011, two brothers from New Zealand launched a new pairing: digital books and movie-like soundtracks. The venture was called Booktrack. The company commissioned a study of adults reading a work on a Booktrack-enhanced text versus a conventional eBook. The researcher, Liel Leibovitz, reported that Booktrack resulted in better learning:

> Those reading with Booktrack's software have been shown to perform categorically better on information retention tests, and they attested to increased focus and greater clarity.[62]

Regrettably, the research report doesn't seem to be available online and (to my knowledge) was never published.

Another Booktrack study, this time by the University of Auckland working with middle school students, focused on those with low to mid level reading skills, including a small group specifically identified as having reading difficulties. Comprehension scores for this smaller group, when reading nonfiction, were 18 percent higher with Booktrack than with a normal eBook. Booktrack students also reported 35 percent greater satisfaction. For the larger group (more than 200 students), comprehension rates after reading a history text were 17 percent higher with Booktrack.[63]

Booktrack developed an academic initiative, Booktrack Classroom, but shuttered the project in August 2019, at the same time it stopped producing soundtracks for eBooks. The company now focuses on audiobook services such as providing narrators for new audiobooks and developing soundtracks for existing ones (booktrack.com).

When Booktrack first launched, there were many skeptics. Here's an example from a review in *Wired* magazine:

It's incredibly jarring. The beauty of a book is that the whole world is as real as you can imagine it to be. Adding tawdry effects doesn't enhance the experience—it just makes the whole thing seem fake.[64]

Apparently, the larger reading public agreed. Given the paucity of research in learning contexts, it's unclear if the initial studies reflected a novelty effect or perhaps the soundtrack helped hold students' focus on the text.

DOES REDUNDANCY HELP?

What if instead of coupling sound effects with written text you added the entire voiced narration? This is the model we talked about in Chapter 4 for young children, most of whom couldn't yet read by themselves. Might this technique be useful for those learning to read or who have reading challenges? Let's start with practice, and then get to theory.

These days, if we're talking about audio plus text for young children, the term is "read-along books" (or sometimes "listen and read books"). The commercial market is full of paired offerings, and not just for children. For older readers, including adults, Amazon markets "Kindle Books with Narration", combining its eBook platform with Audible, its audio arm. Using Audible's Whispersync software, you can toggle between an audio and eBook. You can also combine the two in what Amazon calls "immersive reading", which highlights the text in sync with the audio narration. For children, there are targeted products from Bookshare and Learning Ally, among others. We'll have more to say about Learning Ally in a moment.

Popular media have been praising the combination of audio and written text for young and old alike. But what do researchers think? To address that question, we need a bit of theory concerning multimedia and cognitive load.

There's a sizeable literature in psychology about the effects of receiving information in more than one channel—say, written plus oral, or text plus graph.[65] The issue is whether redundancy bolsters learning or reduces it by requiring the mind to do the same work twice—increasing the load on our cognitive faculties. Research suggests that while some kinds of redundancy seem beneficial (such as graphics plus audio narration), others apparently aren't (graphics plus audio plus text on screen). Such negative impact of dealing with two or more sources of the same information has been called "the redundancy effect".[66]

Does listening to an audio track while following along with a written text result in a redundancy effect, meaning poorer performance? Or does it lead to better learning?

Beginning and Evolving Readers

Enter many preschool or lower school classrooms, and you'll find audio headsets. Besides enabling children to listen independently to audiobooks, sometimes classrooms pair audio with text. Combining audio with text isn't just for beginning readers. There's evidence the multimodal approach can also be effective for evolving readers. A study of 9- and 10-year-olds found higher comprehension scores when simultaneously listening to and reading *The Little Prince* than when only reading.[67]

Many discussions of using audio with children don't specify whether audio is being used alone or paired with text. However, here are some of the potential benefits of pairing, gleaned from a blog post by Denise Johnson on the Reading Rockets site:

- Introduce students to books above their reading level
- Introduce new vocabulary
- Introduce students to new genres
- Model correct pronunciation of new or difficult words, including names[68]

Particularly the first three are equally applicable to just listening without text.

Children with Reading Challenges

Audio assistance for children with a variety of reading challenges traces back, yet again, to war and the blind. In this case, it was an initiative launched by Anne Macdonald in 1948 to provide recorded textbooks for American soldiers who had lost their sight in World War II but now wanted to attend college under the GI Bill of Rights. An organization named Recording for the Blind was formed. Over time, vinyl records morphed into tapes and computer discs. By 1995, the audience for audio textbooks expanded to include people with varied learning disabilities, including dyslexia, and the effort was renamed Recording for the Blind & Dyslexic. Again, as usership grew, so did the scope of offerings, now available to those of any age. And so in 2011, there was another renaming, this time to Learning Ally.[69]

Learning Ally has created over 80,000 audiobooks (textbooks and literature), all with human voice recording (not computer-generated text-to-voice synthesis). The organization has worked with 99,000 educators, who in turn have used Learning Ally audio materials with 472,000 students having reading challenges of all sorts, including limited vision, dyslexia, and a variety of learning disabilities. Wherever possible, the audiobooks are designed to be used synchronously with the written text. Hence, our reason for talking about Learning Ally under "audio + text" rather than "solo audio". And as we saw with beginning and evolving readers, a child doesn't need to have learning challenges to benefit from these tools.[70]

What does the research say about the effectiveness of combining audio and text for students who have reading challenges? Given the ubiquity of such students, you would think there would be a goodly amount of published formal research. Not so.

The research that has been reported comes in three varieties. First, there are informal recommendations and reports from teachers, parents, and industry journalists.[71] These articles, blog posts, and such report the positive experiences of students using audio + text for learning. The second group are school-specific studies, with research typically coordinated by academic reading specialists. Again, the conclusions are positive, though given the number of students participating and variations within the populations, formal statistics aren't always calculated. When they are, results don't always reach statistical significance. The third group are formal published studies available in the journal literature. We'll look at findings from the second and third groups.

A point of clarification here. Some of the reports simply use the term "audiobook" without explicitly saying the students followed along with the written text simultaneously. However, in many cases, it's possible to deduce from discussion sections in the articles (or other publications by the same authors) that the "audiobook" condition actually means "audio + text".

For school-specific studies, Learning Ally has taken the lead, working with university researchers and commissioning research. The Learning Ally website has summaries of individual success stories and case studies.[72] Learning Ally also commissioned a white paper reviewing the literature on use of audiobooks in K-12 education.[73] In some cases, research in this collective cluster exclusively looks at gains on various reading measures (including vocabulary development, reading comprehension, and/or motivation) by students using audio + text. Other studies have experimental and control groups, where the control group uses only the written text.

The findings from these studies, across multiple ages and types of reading challenges, are fairly consistent. Among them are that combining audiobooks with text resulted in these sorts of positive results:

- Increased word recognition and reading comprehension
- Faster reading rate
- More content acquisition
- Higher overall reading proficiency

The third cluster of research comprises studies for which I found more formal descriptions. Two dealt with reading disabilities more generally and one specifically with dyslexia. All looked at the effects of using audio + text. Here's what they found:

- Upper elementary students with learning disabilities read more words per minute correctly with audio + text than students reading with no audio.
- A meta-analysis looking at students with dyslexia, reading disabilities, or learning disabilities found a positive effect of audio + text on reading comprehension, though the authors caution that more research is needed before drawing definitive conclusions.
- Adolescents with developmental dyslexia showed improvement in reading accuracy after a five-month program of audio + text compared with a matched group only using text.[74]

The trends are clear. There are abundant indicators that dual input can be beneficial for many students with reading challenges. However, both practitioners and researchers are seeking more hard evidence, since we don't have enough formal studies, since gains weren't found on all reading measures assessed, and since what works for one student may not for another.

Second Language Learners

The bulk of research on audio with text has been with second language learners, especially those learning English. Sometimes the test conditions have been audio + text versus text-only, while other times an audio-only condition has been included.

Most studies suggest that audio + text can be advantageous for second language learners, generally measured by comprehension scores. For instance, two experiments with university students learning English showed better performance when simultaneously listening and reading.[75] Another study, this time with sixth-graders, found the audio + text combination was most beneficial for weaker students.[76]

Not all investigators agree. At least two studies of English language learners—one of 13-year-olds and the other of university students—reported that simultaneous audio and text proved detrimental to learning. Both studies argue that poorer performance resulted from increased cognitive load from having to process two language signals (the redundancy effect).[77]

Were these last two studies flukes? Was the issue the kind of comprehension measures used? The type of students tested? It's hard to know.

When you look at teacher forums and teacher-generated publications, you find strong praise for multimodal reading. Advocates argue that audio (either solo or with text) motivates reluctant readers or helps those with decoding challenges. We'll need more research to corroborate or discredit grassroots support for multimodality as part of academic reading. My sense is that teachers and parents know something that academic research will end up substantiating.

Video

While this chapter is about audio, we can't ignore the increasing role of video in education, especially of video materials available online. And so, we'll look at some video issues, including research comparing learning from video versus from text or just audio.

VIDEO RISING

Do you watch videos online? If so, you're hardly alone. Over a billion hours of YouTube videos are viewed daily. Zeroing in on videos geared towards learning (often posted on YouTube), think about TED Talks, with more than 3,500 to choose from. Add in TEDx Talks, which have been seen roughtly 5 billion times. And don't forget Khan Academy, which has 100 million users every year.[78]

We saw in Chapter 3 that video materials are making their way into classrooms in place of reading assignments, especially in the United States. In my study with Anne Mangen, almost 32 percent of American faculty participants said they were now assigning some video instead of text.[79]

Video is a powerful medium. To learn about melting of the polar icecap or tool use by chimpanzees, video can be invaluable. A video of a lively lecture (think TED Talks) can prove more engaging than reading the same words. After all, the "E" in "TED" stands for "entertainment".[80] But is video effective for academic learning? Specifically, how does it measure up against written text or just audio?

> *"Students come to expect more films and alternatives to reading and are disappointed when a class is more reading-heavy."*
>
> U.S. university faculty member in Baron and Mangen survey

VIDEO VERSUS TEXT

Begin with comparisons of learning with video versus written text. Each of the studies we'll look at has its own design twist, but collectively they present an instructive montage.

The first study was interested in how fourth- to sixth-graders in Spain integrated multi-source information presented either in videos or in written transcriptions of the audio track. Because the sources took opposite positions on a controversial topic (here, the pros and cons of bottled versus tap water), the goal of the research was to see if medium affected the kinds of arguments students made.[81]

In Chapter 5, we looked at how students engage in synthesis ("integration") of multiple sources, either print or digital. In this study, the media being compared were video versus digital text. Results showed no difference between media for remembering the source of their information when it came time to write an essay about whether bottled or tap water was better for health and the environment. However, there were differences in how students constructed their arguments:

- Students were more likely to defend the views presented in the videos than in the text.
- Students who read the texts made almost twice as many inferences as those who saw the videos.

The allure of video reminds us of students' tendency to believe what they read online without questioning its validity. The finding about inferences is reminiscent of what we saw in Chapter 4, where comprehension of basic ideas was generally similar for digital and print, but superior for print when it came to more detailed or inferential understanding.

The study's authors hypothesize that students may have been "reading" the videos more superficially than the written text because their familiarity with video is largely for leisure, not formal learning. I suggest we call it "video shallowing".

The next study, this time of high school students in Germany, also compared video and text, but added opportunities for users to interact with the materials. As we explained in Chapter 6, contemporary educators emphasize that active student engagement leads to better learning. In this study, participants either viewed a 16-minute film about the political and economic situation in Germany following World War II (composed of audiovisual documents and voiceover commentary) or read a print text containing a transcript of the film's audio, illustrated by several dozen screenshots from the video. The video offered opportunities for navigation and re-play, while the printed text provided a table of contents and index. (The actual study had a more complex design, with two versions of the video.) Both formats included chapter labels and key terms. The study's main conclusion was that if videos can be interactive—letting users regulate their pacing and the way they encounter information—their effectiveness can match or even exceed that of traditional print.[82]

A third research project worked with university students in the United States. Participants either read or viewed two information sources (one about penguins, the other about sea turtles) and then annotated both sources, with the purported goal of helping younger students understand the material better. For the text versions (transcriptions of the videos), students used the "track changes" function in Microsoft Word. For the videos, annotation was done using a tool called VideoANT, which we'll talk about in Chapter 8. Students were then asked to explain the strategies they used for processing the information.

One research report from the project focused on these strategies. Some were common to text and video conditions, including notetaking, identifying the main idea, and connecting content to prior knowledge. However, other approaches were specific to a particular medium. For instance, when reading text, students also did highlighting (not an option with video). More interestingly, with text, students reported trying harder to understand difficult vocabulary. They also took less time to process the material with text than with video.[83]

A second report from the project looked at the actual annotations. Students annotated the written text more often, perhaps because of the relative ease of using Word annotation tools. More important were differences in the kinds of annotations made. With the written text, students were more likely to ask deep-level questions whose answers required making inferences, rather than low-level questions that essentially required restating information directly provided in the sources.[84] This result reminds us of the Spanish fourth- to sixth-graders who made nearly twice as many inferences in their arguments if they had read texts rather than seen videos.

These aren't a lot of studies to go on, but some important patterns emerge, including:

- Basic comprehension shouldn't be the only measure of whether video or text makes for better learning. We also need to consider such measures as depth of understanding or attempts to understand words whose meaning you don't know.
- Interaction with video seems to increase its value as a learning tool.

VIDEO VERSUS AUDIO

Switching the pairing of platforms, is it more effective for learning to watch a video lecture (both seeing and hearing the instructor) or only hear the audio?

One study compared graduate students who watched a video lecture with those who only heard the audio. However, the experiment didn't just involve audio versus video, since in both cases, a set of slides with bulleted text was shown simultaneously. The topic was privacy issues relating to U.S. health care legislation. Students were given a comprehension test and also asked their opinions about format. Test scores for both groups were essentially the same. There was, though, an interesting asymmetry in opinions about the experience:

- Audio group: Most said they wished they also had the video.
- Video group: Less than half felt the video contributed to learning, and one-third found the video to be distracting.[85]

A second study had more theoretical underpinnings and a more complex design. The researchers wanted to test whether adding video to audio increases cognitive load, through the redundancy effect. Another question was whether presence of the instructor (in the video) affects learning. In addition, the investigators asked about participants' perceptions regarding their own learning.

Lecture material was presented in multiple formats, using different combinations of audio, full text, just text captions, and video. Participants ranged in age from 19 to 68. Four different studies were done, with variations on the test conditions and questions asked. Subject materials included university-level lectures on global problems of population growth and on early modern English history.

Here's what the study revealed, starting with user perceptions:

- Seeing the instructor on video was judged more enjoyable and interesting than just having audio or text.
- Learners believed that video facilitated their learning.
- Learners judged they expended the most attentional effort when reading the full text and the least when watching the video or using simultaneous audio plus text.

When it came to actual comprehension scores:

- Video resulted in the least learning.

That is, participants' expectations that video would make for better learning didn't calibrate well with actual test results. Given self-reports of not expending a lot of effort with the video, this looks like another case of video shallowing.[86]

What role might seeing the instructor have in reducing video learning outcomes? One hypothesis: An instructor can prove a distraction from concentrating on the lecture material. Thinking about real classroom situations, ask yourself how much of your students' attention is focused on the content of what you're saying and how much on your clothing, your hairstyle, or the way you pace around the room. If you doubt me, try reading open-ended comments on student course evaluations.

MIND WANDERING AND TESTING

When we compared listening to audio with reading text, our final topic was mindset and mind wandering. The same issues are important for understanding how students are prone to watch videos in school.

Benjamin Hollis and Christopher Was measured how much mind wandering undergraduates were doing when viewing videos. The researchers had students who were already enrolled in an online class watch two online lectures, using their own digital device and in a place of their choosing. Each lecture was about 13 minutes long. Four times during each lecture, the video was stopped and students were asked, "In the last 5 seconds, what were you just thinking about?" Choices included (1) the video, (2) how well I'm understanding the video, (3) a memory from the past, (4) something in the future, (5) a current state of being (such as hunger), (6) thinking about or using another technology (such as texting or Facebook), and (7) other.

Overall, students reported thinking about something unrelated to the video a whopping 43 percent of the time. Thinking about or using another technology accounted for the majority of off-task mental attention.[87] Linger for a moment on the "thinking about" part. Back in Chapter 2, we discussed the research of Adrian Ward and his colleagues showing that the mere presence of a mobile phone next to you, even if you weren't using it, drained cognitive resources.[88] We can all imagine how much less focus students are likely to have if they're watching video lectures in the comfort of their residence and simultaneously checking Twitter.

While we can't solve the problem entirely, other research on video lectures offers a strategy addressing both mind wandering and overestimating performance. The strategy entails using a form of active learning, namely intermittent testing. You'll recall our discussion in Chapter 3 about practice testing, which might mean intermittent quizzes. Using a video of slides plus voiceover, a study of university students showed that embedding quizzes throughout improved final test performance.[89] This same principle is behind adaptive learning digital textbooks that insert assessment measures throughout.

Focusing on actual video lectures, Karl Szpunar and his colleagues wanted to see how intermittent testing affected not just mind wandering and calibration, but also how often students (in this case, high schoolers) took notes on the lecture. Mind-wandering probes were inserted into the video lectures. After the lectures, students were asked to predict how well they thought they would do on a subsequent test. However, in addition, some (but not all) of the students were quizzed at several intervals during the lectures themselves.

Intermittent quizzes during the video lectures had multiple beneficial effects. Students who were quizzed:

- Showed less overconfidence in how well they would do on the final comprehension test
- Performed better on the final test
- Took more notes during the lecture

Mind wandering was also reduced, but only marginally.[90]

Key Takeaways About Audio (and Video)

Here are highlights of what we've learned about students listening with audio, along with a bit about video, in comparison with written text. For both audio and video, our focus is on using the technologies for learning.

Audio and Video Trends
- Both audio and video are deeply entrenched in contemporary culture as entertainment platforms.
- We have relatively little research on the educational effectiveness of audio and video, especially in one-to-one comparisons with written text.

Solo Audio
- For students who already have fundamental reading skills, comprehension is generally better with text than with audio.
- Students are less likely to review audio than written text.
- Multitasking with audio can be problematic.
- Calibration with audio can be problematic.
- Mind wandering with audio can be problematic.

- Adding a written component (such as PowerPoint slides) can improve audio performance.

Audio + Text
- Formal research findings on combining audio and text are mixed.
- Informal evidence is more supportive of the benefits of combining audio and text, especially for beginning and evolving readers, children with reading challenges, and second language learners.

Video
- As with solo audio, comprehension seems to be better with text than with video.
- As with solo audio, calibration with video can be problematic.
- As with solo audio, mind wandering with video can be problematic.
- Use of intermittent interactive activity (such as quizzing) can improve video performance.

Given what the research tells us about reading with audio (and video), what kind of strategies might we call upon to support learning from these non–text-based media? Our focus here will be on four themes that emerged in the last chapter: multitasking, calibration, mind wandering, and intermittent testing. We'll also talk about annotation as an active learning strategy.

To set the stage, we return for a moment to oral versus written cultures.

"Secondary Orality" or "Learning Lite"?

Before the advent of writing, communication was necessarily oral. As we saw in Chapter 7, even in societies where some of the population was literate, the broader culture might still be heavily based on the spoken word. Only with more widespread education and print distribution could we sensibly talk about a written culture.

With the coming of radio in the early 20th century, followed by television several decades later, the role of print was downgraded a notch, as spoken and visual media assumed many of print's functions. Walter Ong, one-time student of Marshall McLuhan, described these two sound-based technologies as ushering in what he called a "secondary orality".[1] Although radio and television still rely on writing for their production, they are projected through speech—much as speech had been the fundamental communication medium centuries back ("primary orality").

Today, audiobooks and podcasts are the new kids on the block. Like radio and TV, both are oral. Are modern audio technologies leading to "a new age of orality", as one author suggests?[2] No, and here is why.

In historically oral cultures, careful listening and speaking were valued skills. For listening, you had to focus your ears and your mind on what others were saying. Memory abilities were essential. Prepared speeches (along with poems and sermons) were commonly memorized, a skill rapidly fading in today's educational landscape. Likewise, as a speaker, you needed to craft arguments and deliver them, often extemporaneously—again, skills that today are not especially common, even among the highly educated.

If radio and television, and now audiobooks and podcasts, were actually spearheading a new age of orality, we would need to rethink education dramatically. Students would have to be trained to prize careful listening (an excellent idea, but proving hard to cultivate) and memory (which modern education has significantly dismissed as rote learning). The goals for speaking and listening skills as sources of learning would presumably closely mirror written culture aspirations for print.

Putting aside the question of desirability, is this a feasible enterprise?

Research we looked at in Chapter 7 suggests that students don't view audio (and video) the same way they do writing. Rather, audio and video are cast as "learning lite". As for their teachers, especially in higher education, most haven't thought through the pedagogical differences between media. University professors are hired for their subject expertise, not their knowledge of how best to utilize alternative teaching platforms. Most of us tend to assume—wrongly, it turns out—that students learn as much from listening or viewing as from reading a text. We haven't understood that additional effort (from the students) and guidance (from us) may be needed.

I'm not voting to revamp educational practice to put audio (and video) on the same footing as text. However, as with digital text, both audio and video will likely continue to assume expanding roles in education. Accordingly, what follows in this chapter are practical attempts to address some of the gaps in student performance between use of written versus audio/video learning platforms.

Overarching Guidelines

WHO IS THE READER AND WHAT IS THE GOAL?

In educational circles, the concept of "learning styles" has generated much discussion in recent decades. Are some children more likely to succeed through written, auditory, visual, or kinesthetic teaching methods? Contemporary research indicates that while students may voice a preference for one modality or another, test scores don't show better performance in their preferred medium.[3]

Yet beyond the question of whether "learning styles" predict learning, let's not forget that we have our own personalities, likes, and dislikes. If the goal is getting someone to do something, then an alternative path to the same end often makes sense. My husband has never liked eating carrots, ignoring all my reminders about that vital beta-carotene. But ultimately I found several recipes that alter the taste and have him asking for seconds.

Just so, if our goal is getting children to read but they treat print as my husband has done with carrots, it behooves us to find alternative strategies—including audio and maybe video. For younger readers, we're talking about getting them launched, and then hopefully transitioning to reading written text with equal comfort. For older students, teachers need to balance students' attraction to podcasts and videos against the probability that these media may not be the best platforms for focused learning.

We're back to mindset.

READER MINDSET

Our review of research on audio (particularly solo) and video revealed two important user issues that both platforms have in common:

- Calibration can be problematic.
- Mind wandering can be problematic.

With solo audio, we also have ample evidence of multitasking. I'll wager research will confirm multitasking as an issue with video as well. If we want to turn audio and video into serious learning tools, all three concerns need to be addressed head-on.

CAPITALIZING ON TEXT READING STRENGTHS AND SKILLS

In Chapter 6, we talked about ways of transferring traditional strategies for reading print to the way students read digital texts. A parallel approach makes sense for audio and video.

What text reading strategies can be useful with these new media platforms? Some obvious ones are notetaking, reviewing, and previewing with question prompts so students know what to be listening or looking for. Active learning (including inter-mittent testing, even informally) is always a good idea. The form of active learning we'll focus on here is annotation.

ANNOTATION

We talked in Chapter 4 about the value of annotating when you read, especially making your own written comments. The concept is clear for print and even digital text, but what happens when the "text" is spoken or visual? Both speech and video are ephemeral—here for a fleeting moment and then gone.

The challenge has precedence.

Imagine yourself in the 17th-century court of Louis XIV of France. You likely con-jure up the splendors of Versailles or "*L'état, c'est moi*". But you also should think about dance, for Louis was an accomplished dancer and insisted his courtiers develop skills as well.[4] Everyone needed to learn new dances, but how? Louis directed his dancing master, Pierre Beauchamps, to create a system for "making the art of dance compre-hensible on paper" so people could learn dances "without need of personal instruc-tion".[5] And so was born the idea of choreography, literally "dancing in unison" (Greek *khoreia*) plus "writing" (*-graphy*)—that is, a written notation for dance. People could now learn new dances by following written instructions representing when to move forward or back, when to turn or hop. While today's dance notation systems have changed, the transcribing principle endures.

Now let's think about signing systems such as American Sign Language (ASL). Words and sentences are expressed through hand configurations, placements, and movements, along with facial expressions and bodily stance. The most natural way to learn a sign language is face to face. But could you also write it down?

Following several 19th-century French proposals, the first modern notation was designed by William Stokoe, a professor at Gallaudet College (now University).[6] Paralleling linguists' use of phonology to analyze speech sounds, Stokoe created a system of "cherology". (The name derives from the Greek word for "hand".) The resulting cheremes, analogous to sound-based phonemes, were then represented by graphic symbols.[7] Again, new notation systems have evolved, but the idea of making ephemeral signs concrete remains.

You're likely wondering why I'm talking about written systems for dance and sign language. The answer is that as with dance and signing, it's easy to assume that audio and video aren't candidates for applying written tools. As we'll see later in this chapter, there are some promising options for school-age students. But first, a few comments about use of audio and video with young children.

Young Children

AUDIO

In Chapter 4, when we were talking about digital books for young children, we cautioned that many of the digital offerings on the market are better at distracting with bells and whistles than helping kids follow a storyline. With audiobooks, we're on safer ground, since in most cases a written version already exists, whose merits have been weighed by parents, teachers, or reviewers.

Where might you look for good age-appropriate audio options? Your local bookstore or library is always a good starting point. So, too, are recommendations from the Association of Library Services to Children (ALSC), a division of the American Library Association. If you're searching for the latest recordings for children up to age 14, check out the ALSC's list of "Notable Children's Recordings—2020".[8] Some of the titles are solo audio, while others come with both audio and text.

VIDEO

Video for young children is a whole new can of worms we didn't open in Chapter 7. We won't open it here either! The subject of young children and screen use (beginning with television, and then with the COVID-19 pandemic) is vast and beyond our scope.

School-Age Readers

When automobiles were introduced, you didn't need a license to drive one. Far more important was having a mechanic, preferably sitting alongside you, since those early cars kept breaking down. Henry Ford's Model T appeared in 1908. By 1918, U.S. states all required license plates for cars—but not licenses for drivers.[9] As late as 1930, merely 15 states had a mandatory driver's exam. Not until 1959 did the last state— South Dakota—join the ranks.[10]

Audio and video materials for learning are a bit like those early days of automotive history: You have a car (or are assigned a podcast or video or audiobook) and others assume you'll figure out how to operate it. While some teachers develop strategies for guiding students in making productive use of audio or video assignments, the practice isn't widespread, especially when it comes to older students. In my experience at the college level, we put audio and video materials on our syllabi and blithely presuppose students will use them effectively. Hardly sound pedagogy.

There are better approaches. We'll look at some, especially for solo audio and video.

SOLO AUDIO

I'll start with my "neon lights" messages about using solo audio for learning:

- *Don't assume you comprehend and remember as much with audio* as you do with comparable written text.
- *Focus on what you're listening to.* Your mind is more likely to wander with audio than with written text.
- *Think twice before multitasking while listening.* When multitasking, you reduce your chances of listening carefully.

I know, you were expecting this advice. But it's critical to repeat if audio is to be a meaningful learning platform.

Turn now to goals, type of text, and strategies for focusing the mind with solo audio.

Goals

Not all reading has the same objectives. With reluctant readers, audio may provide needed motivation. For fluent readers, informational audio can be an excellent source of new background knowledge, while narrative audio (even when multitasking) enlarges opportunities for encountering literature, albeit more casually.

For children with learning issues, audio may have the potential to remove roadblocks that solo text throws up. In Chapter 7, we saw from the Berkeley study that the brain handles spoken and written word meaning the same way. Fatma Deniz, the lead author on the study, is interested in possible implications for children with dyslexia or other reading issues. In an interview she hypothesized:

> If, in the future, we find that the dyslexic brain has rich semantic representation when listening to an audiobook or other recording, that could bring more audio materials into the classroom.[11]

Admittedly, it's a leap from word meaning to understanding connected prose, but audio is an avenue worth pursuing in both formal research and classroom experimentation.

Type of Text: Genre

Narrative prose finds a natural home in audio. The question (back to goals) is what we want readers to derive from hearing, say, a novel. In Chapter 6, we talked about Natalie Phillips's fMRI study comparing the way literature students approach a chapter by Jane Austen with either a "close reading" mindset or one of reading for pleasure. The brain worked differently with close reading. I can't say what the fMRI would look like if the story were read aloud to those same students, but it's a question we need to think about, especially given all we know about audio and "learning lite". If you're listening to that novel for enjoyment, no problem. But what about when the novel is assigned for a literature class?

When listening to informational podcasts for academic purposes, the challenges are much clearer. After all, these were the kinds of materials used in several of the studies we discussed in the last chapter. We saw that informational audio didn't measure up well against written text when it came to inference-generation and sometimes even comprehension. Hence, the importance of strategies for focusing the mind.

Focusing the Mind: Familiar Tools

As my "neon lights" messages stressed, focusing the mind is critical if you're trying to learn from audio. Some of the traditional strategies involve writing things down:

- Take notes as you listen.
- After listening, generate lists of keywords, summaries, or maybe a concept map.

Other strategies require someone else doing the writing in advance:

- Think about teacher-generated "reading" prompts before you listen.

- While listening, follow along with written aids such as PowerPoint presentations of lectures or relevant graphics.

Then there are some by-now-familiar review strategies:

- Re-listen to parts of the audio that warrant a second hearing.
- Quiz yourself about what you learned.

Since we know students are less likely to review audio than written text,

- Explain this propensity to students rather than just decreeing, "Review!"

On the quizzing issue, we'll have to devise creative ways of making quizzing—especially intermittently—a natural part of listening. Teachers need to take the lead here. One strategy (borrowed from some of the research designs we saw in the last chapter) is this:

- Break the audio into chunks, with activities to do after each section.

In Chapter 6, we talked about the advantages of decomposing texts (digital or print) into sections or even separate documents, given the learning advantage of working with distinct pieces of information. The same principle can apply to audio, though again, the burden is likely on the teacher to do the chunking and create the activities.

Focusing the Mind: Annotating Audio

We all know about doing annotations on printed text. Many of us are familiar with annotating digital texts, a skill we talked about in Chapter 6. But what about annotating audio? Are there tools—or could there be?

The answer at this point is "a technological work in progress", but one that already has some possible workarounds. Let's start with the basic concept.

We learned in Chapter 7 that the predecessors of today's audiobooks were recorded books for the blind or visually impaired. It's no surprise that as technology has evolved, so have the audio reading platforms available to those with vision challenges. These audiobooks are now digital, with much of the production coordinated under standards maintained by the international DAISY Consortium (Digital Accessible Information Systems).[12] Books can be heard using a DAISY player, but also on a computer or mobile device loaded with appropriate software.

Why talk about an audio system for the visually impaired? Because some of its features get us thinking about applications useful for the larger population listening to audio. With DAISY audiobooks you can search for a section or subsection, make a bookmark, and regulate the speed of play. And there's nothing stopping users from dictating or writing separate notes while listening.

Much as "talking books" for the blind were later joined by commercial ventures for the sighted, Amazon's Audible boasts some of the same features as the DAISY system. Without getting into product details (particularly because they change), Audible also lets you bookmark and save audio clips to which you may add notes.

A variety of methods exist for annotating audio "text", though as of when I'm writing this chapter, there's no slick turnkey system. An internet search yielded multiple approaches, including dictating notes into a mobile phone using a personal digital assistant such as Siri or typing separate notes on your phone as you listen. A third option I saw was bookmarking clips as you listen to an audiobook and, when you've finished the book, writing up annotations in one fell swoop for those bookmarked spots.

Given how clumsy such annotation currently is—especially compared with annotating print or even digital text—I hardly envision students or teachers now gravitating to audio annotation other than through externally written notes. However, I anticipate commercial tools will evolve, making audio annotation a smooth application. Judging from online discussion posts I've read, I suspect the impetus will come from professionals who want the convenience of using audiobooks but whose line of work necessitates eventually producing written annotations.

Education may not be the driver of such innovation but will be a beneficiary.

AUDIO + TEXT

We saw in Chapter 7 that not all researchers agree on the usefulness of combining audio with text, given the redundancy effect that potentially increases cognitive load on the reader. As I suggested in that discussion, there's real-world evidence that dual inputs can prove effective, especially for children with reading challenges. But I leave it to parents and practitioners to offer the best advice here.

What I can address is a study strategy first mentioned to me several years ago by a master's candidate in literature—let's call her Beth. While Beth loved to read, she often found herself getting distracted and unable to focus on the book. Her solution?

- Play the audiobook at the same time you read the written text to help you keep on track.

At the time I was skeptical, but now I've been thinking about those students we talked about in Chapter 3 who often won't do the assigned reading, along with those we mentioned in Chapter 1 who said reading printed books was boring. (We'll have more to say in Chapter 10 about students being bored by print.) Might combining audio with text help?

As I mulled over Beth's technique, I considered other situations where we enlist help in keeping up the pace. It might be a running partner or a diet buddy or "competing" on a stationary bike at the gym against a digital challenger. I even thought about the mechanical pace rabbits used in greyhound races.

In the case of reading, especially with a good audio narrator, you have support, but also control. The audio entices you to keep going while encouraging you to take in each word. And if you take the trouble, you can pause the audio to think about a phrase, reread a passage, or make written annotations. Audio + text isn't for every reader or every book, but it's an option for those helped by an assist to stay on track.

VIDEO

Once again, some familiar "neon lights" messages, this time tailored for learning from video:

- *Don't assume you comprehend and remember as much with video* as you do with comparable written text.
- *Focus on what you're watching.* Your mind is more likely to wander with video (including attending to the lecturer rather than the content) compared with written text.
- *Think twice before multitasking* while viewing a video. Doing something with your phone definitely counts as multitasking.

No surprises here. But students need to hear these cautions.

Goals

Those of us who teach need to ask ourselves honestly why we are assigning students videos, especially where in earlier years we assigned written text. Is it because video (or this one in particular) is an especially powerful educational medium or because students are more likely to watch a video than do the reading?

We know videos can be highly useful for "learning lite". They are often excellent sources of background information. However, when the goal is focused learning, we need to think about strategies for productive viewing.

Focusing the Mind: Familiar Strategies

This list will look familiar from the "solo audio" section:

- Take notes as you watch.
- After watching, generate lists of keywords, summaries, or maybe a concept map.
- Think about teacher-generated "viewing" prompts before you watch.
- Re-view parts of the video that warrant a second watching.
- Quiz yourself about what you learned.

As with solo audio, since we know students are less likely to review video than to review written text,

- Explain this propensity to students rather than just decreeing, "Review!"

Again as with audio,

- Chunking of video, with appropriate intermittent activities (including quizzing), can support learning.

Focusing the Mind: Annotating Video

Educational tools for annotating video are more developed than for audio. We might see YouTube as leading the way. YouTube launched in 2005. By 2008 it had added an annotation feature. Yes, YouTube annotations were formally discontinued as users moved from computers to mobile devices with less screen real estate (making it difficult to see the annotations), but the idea of marking up a video is now a familiar concept. These days, you might think about writing comments on a program being livestreamed or using the chat function on Skype or Zoom.

In the education world, several video annotation tools have been gaining footing. Here are two.

The first, Vialogues, was developed at Teachers College Columbia University's EdLab. The goal was to combine video and dialogue (hence the word Vialogues) to create a "community of learners using video to ignite discussion".[13] You may be reminded of Harvard's Perusall project, a form of digital social annotation, which we talked about in Chapter 6.

Like Perusall, Vialogues is a free tool. You begin by uploading a video or a link to a YouTube or Vimeo recording. Users then enter time-stamped comments, or perhaps surveys or multiple-choice questions. The idea is to increase engagement with the video content through interaction with a learning community.

A second video annotation tool is VideoANT, created at the University of Minnesota. This free platform is, like Vialogues, designed to promote creation and sharing of comments with peers (and maybe instructors). Again, you can download or link to videos created elsewhere or to your own video. VideoANT has a split screen between video and text boxes and lets you move comments to other points on the video timeline.[14]

Interestingly, the website's demo video explains that "Ants" (as annotated videos are called) can be marked for sharing or as private. While VideoANT was designed for social use, in principle it also enables individual students to annotate videos for their own learning purposes.

I'm not envisioning today's students downloading every video we assign (assuming they're downloadable) and annotating the way they might with written text. But as we increasingly include videos in our curricula with the goal of serious learning, we might keep some version of this scenario in mind.

Our journey over these eight chapters has covered extensive ground. In Part I, we "sized up reading", thinking about what is meant by "reader" and "reading", looking at how much reading people actually do, and questioning whether print reading is always the gold standard we envision. Part II delved into what we know about reading in print versus digitally, including research on reading single or multiple texts, along with suggested strategies for improving the effectiveness of digital reading. Part III turned to audio (and some video), examining the research and recommending strategies for enhancing audio and video learning.

In the last section of this book (Part IV), we will look to the future. We'll consider how print reading itself is being affected by the digital revolution. And we'll reflect on larger educational goals and the role that mindful reading can play in attaining them.

PART IV WHAT'S NEXT?

**WHAT'S
AT STAKE?**

Here are some issues to be thinking about as you read
Part IV:

- Are attitudes towards physical possessions helping
  propel digital reading?
- How much do we approach digital reading with an
  entertainment mindset?
- Are screen reading patterns changing the way we
  read print?
- Why do students say reading print is boring?
- Are shifting goals in higher education driving
  shallower and shorter reading?
- How are critical thinking and choice of reading
  platform related?
- Are we too reliant on the internet to do our knowing
  for us?

CHAPTER 9   Strategizing Reading in a Digital World

It's easy to romanticize the old ways. "Back when I was your age . . ."—fill in the blank. Someone else pumped your gas. Milk was delivered to the door. People used to read more.

In this book, we've spent a lot of time setting print against digital text, like boxers in a ring. In the process, it's understandable if you as reader have been tempted to interpret the discussion as suggesting a "back in the old days" nostalgia for print.

If so, please don't.

In Chapters 2 and 3, we tried to deromanticize the state of reading print, both in the "old days" (before the digital revolution) and now. For decades, students haven't been completing the reading (generally print) that we assign, and adults have been spending precious little of their spare time with books. But with the digital turn, something else has been happening when we do pick up printed works. Increasingly, we are approaching print as if it were digital.

In this chapter, I'll explain what I mean and what the consequences might be.

Phantom Rings: The Long Arm of Digital Technology

You hear your mobile phone ringing or feel it vibrating, but it's actually not. If you've fallen for this illusion, you're not alone. The Pew Research Center reported that 67 percent of the adults they surveyed fessed up to checking out a phantom ring.[1]

Is technology also affecting us mentally when it comes to reading? Many of us have sensed that we're having a harder time settling down to read something of substance than previously. Even serious writers and readers like Nicholas Carr (of "Is Google Making Us Stupid?" fame) and Maryanne Wolf (author of *Proust and the Squid* and *Reader, Come Home*) have worried they have shorter reading attention spans now, along with a greater tendency to become distracted. Here's how Carr summed up the problem:

> Immersing myself in a book or a lengthy article used to be easy. . . . That's rarely the case anymore. Now my concentration often starts to drift after two or three pages. . . . The deep reading that used to come naturally has become a struggle.[2]

> "I missed my old brain."
>
> Nicholas Carr[3]

Shift the focus from your brain to the print book itself. My mind keeps returning to a conversation I had with a college student, around age 20, who loved reading in print. But, as he explained, he now had difficulty concentrating. The problem wasn't a shortened attention span but the fact that he continually anticipated the book would beep at him when a new message or alert was arriving, just as it would on his smartphone. The next phase of phantom rings.

Our puzzle in this chapter is whether digital technologies are reshaping the attitudes and approaches we take with print. To tackle the question, we need to start with a much broader trend: the growing shift from what's tangible and lasting (that is, "durable") and what isn't ("ephemeral").

The Move from Durable to Ephemeral

Maybe you still have an old record collection, music on cassette tapes, or a carefully curated set of CDs. How often do you listen to any of them? With the coming of iTunes, Spotify, Pandora, Apple Music, or name your favorite, we are moving our music listening online.

Music is hardly the only part of our lives that has gone digital. Think of these:

- Interpersonal communication (email, IM, texting, Facebook, WhatsApp)
- Recordkeeping (email files, cloud storage)
- Currency (Bitcoin)
- Online banking

Then there are eSports, where fans pay good money to watch the newest type of athletes match off to play not live baseball or basketball but video games. And yes, your son or daughter really might win an eSports college scholarship.[4]

Now think about how you access news or entertainment. There is still radio, along with network or cable television, but count up how much is digital on demand. There are podcasts and webcasts, TED Talks and other YouTube videos, Netflix, and audiobooks or eBooks. Digital is increasingly replacing print newspapers and books, the TV show you could only see on Tuesdays at 9 p.m., or the need to stand in line at a movie theater. But something subtler is happening: an attraction to things that are short-lived—ephemeral—rather than those with physical shape, heft, and durability. The irony, as we'll see, is that while we increasingly opt for the ephemeral, we objectively value it less than the durable.

This growing turn towards the ephemeral is manifest in a variety of ways. One of the most trendy is the desire for "experiences" over possessions.

EXPERIENCES VERSUS POSSESSIONS

Say you're planning to visit Modena, the Italian medieval city and university town that is the home of balsamic vinegar and tenor Luciano Pavarotti. You need a place to stay, so you go online to Airbnb to find lodgings. While on the site, you scroll down and check out popular "experiences". How about cheese tasting on "The Secrets of Parmigiano Reggiano" tour? Or, for the health-conscious, there's "Easy Run Discovering Modena's Beauties"? Companies like Airbnb are going into the "experiences" business because an increasing number of people are preferring to spend money on a one-off adventure rather than on some durable possession.

Social scientists and survey companies have been tracking this trend. American research on adults across the age spectrum reported that "experience purchases" were a greater source of satisfaction because they enhanced people's social relationships, formed a larger part of their identity than physical possessions, and evoked fewer social comparisons.[5] A U.K. study of 18- to 34-year-olds calculated that 66 percent of those surveyed felt more fulfilled by a life experience than by purchasing an item of equal value.[6]

Why prize having an experience rather than owning something tangible? Scholars remind us of the role that geographic mobility plays in the attitudes people have towards consumption.[7] If you're frequently on the move—from one city or country to another—it's hard lugging physical possessions with you. I'm reminded of an undergraduate student of mine who was a prodigious reader, especially of print. However, she wasn't building up a personal physical library because she didn't know where she would be living after graduation and how much space she would have.

The technical term for talking about reducing your physical possessions because of mobility is "liquid consumption". When you do want to take things with you, they are increasingly digital.

CHOOSING DIGITAL OVER PHYSICAL

Why digital? Focus for a moment on textual material or photographs. Some of the reasons are abundantly obvious. Digital objects are weightless—not adding pounds to your suitcase. They are invisible—not taking up shelf space. They are convenient—they're always available. One study summed up the advantages of portability this way:

> [P]lacelessness provided [study participants] with a feeling that their collections of virtual possessions could travel with them across social and physical contexts.[8]

There are, however, some hitches. The first is that with many digital goods, you don't actually own them. In the words of computer scientist Abigail Sellen, "people think of using an e-book, not owning an e-book".[9] And as we know, you don't actually own that eBook (unless you get it free of digital rights management [DRM]). You're only leasing it. Even with digital objects that really belong to us, such as photographs, we don't always feel a sense of ownership. As one participant in a study put it, the digital photos on her phone

> are my possessions, but I don't know exactly what's in there anymore and that sense of not knowing . . . makes possessing them feel somewhat different.[10]

Another problem is the nagging feeling people sometimes have that digital goods aren't as valuable as their physical counterparts. In a novel experiment, two consumer researchers set up shop at Boston's Old North Church.[11] This is the church from whose steeple Paul Revere received his lantern signal on April 18, 1775, that the British would be arriving "by sea" (meaning rowing across the Charles River into Cambridge). Revere made haste towards Lexington and Concord to give warning, and the American Revolutionary War was soon on.

The experiment went like this. The researchers dressed up an assistant to look like Paul Revere and offered visitors the opportunity to have their picture taken with him. People were given a choice of receiving a physical photo there on the spot or having a digital copy emailed to them. The visitors were also invited to make a monetary contribution to the historical society that maintains the church. Those opting for the physical photo contributed three times as much.

The same researchers conducted another experiment, this time with undergraduate business majors. The question now was how much students would pay for a print copy or a digital copy of a particular course textbook. There was the added caveat that this was the last year of the book's current edition, meaning the print version wouldn't have strong resale value. Questions were asked both about purchasing the book (print or digital) or renting it for the semester (again, in print or as an eBook).

When it came to purchasing, print commanded a higher imagined price. (No money actually changed hands.) You owned that physical book, even though you probably couldn't resell it. But when it came to rental, there was no difference in how much students were willing to pay for print versus digital. Why not? Probably because that rented print copy wasn't your physical possession. Not only did you need to send it back at the end of the semester but you probably hesitated to annotate the pages, since you might be penalized monetarily for doing so.

EFFECTS OF GROWING DIGITAL USE

On the one hand, many people seem more interested in amassing experiences than possessions. Combined with this pattern is a growing trend to live our lives in digital space. Yet on the other hand, when confronted with a question about perceived monetary value, the durable, the physical, comes out on top.

What might these findings tell us about attitudes towards reading digitally? Reading onscreen is often highly convenient. But for all the convenience, are we also inclined to place less "value" on digital text, where "value" might translate into the amount of time and effort we are willing to put into reading it? If so, the challenge of doing serious reading on a digital platform isn't just the fact we can multitask (remember the shallowing hypothesis). Maybe part of the problem is that intrinsically, we feel that if texts are virtual, they literally aren't worth as much as those words in print.

The same issue may help explain results we reported in Chapter 7 about learning with audio versus text. The audio medium is ephemeral. In comparison with transient audio signals, even digital text has more durability. (A caveat about audio: Price may be less relevant with commercially purchased audiobooks, since some can be expensive, even more so than eBooks.)

A Digital Mindset When Reading Print

Return to the reality of how much our everyday lives are lived in the digital world. Think of all those hours spent on the internet, including on social media. What about educational settings? There are assignments to be completed or information to be accessed from school online learning management systems. There are online courses with online readings, coupled with publishers' mounting commitment to digital textbooks.

> "[W]e develop an unconscious set toward reading based on how we read during most of our digital-based hours. . . . [W]e begin to read that way even when we turn off the screen and pick up a book or newspaper."
>
> Maryanne Wolf[12]

Digital is becoming the default condition, leading to what I call a digital mindset when it comes to reading, regardless of medium. While the mindset potentially affects everyone, our main concern here is the impact on reading for learning.

What is this mindset, and what are its consequences when it comes to reading not just digitally but in print?

DEFINING A DIGITAL READING MINDSET

Here's my working definition:

> A digital mindset when reading is an approach to written materials that reflects the affordances of digital devices (that is, what digital devices are good for), especially when connected to the internet.

These are the main digital affordances at issue:

- Ease of skimming and scanning

- Focus on information, not concepts
- Opportunities for multitasking
- Reading speed
- Entertainment value

Let's unpack these components.

The skimming and scanning parts are obvious. Who doesn't love moving quickly through a text to decide if it's worth our while to read in detail? And who doesn't miss the Find function when we're trying to locate a particular name or phrase in a digital text that's been scanned (where Find doesn't work)? Similarly, since search engines work best with concrete search terms, it's no surprise that digital reading is a natural match for informational texts. As for multitasking possibilities, you can easily fill in the details yourself.

Less obvious are the last two items on the list: reading speed and entertainment. Take reading speed. Assuming high-quality resolution on a digital screen, it should, in principle, take the same amount of time to read a text onscreen as to read it in print. (For the sake of argument, assume the person is only reading the text, not engaging in multitasking or daydreaming.) Yet there are multiple examples of readers giving the digital text shorter shrift.

In Chapter 4, we saw evidence from one experiment that when university students were left to decide how much time to spend reading a digital and a print text, they went through the digital version more quickly and performed worse on a subsequent comprehension test.[13] In my own studies, several students revealed their assumption that digital reading should take less time than print. When asked what they liked least about reading in print, one undergraduate complained that it took too long— "I read more slowly"—while, as we've already mentioned, another admitted that his reason for disliking print reading was that "it takes me longer because I read more carefully".[14] Then there are the middle and high school students we also talked about in Chapter 4. When asked what they liked best about reading digitally, one wrote, "It looks shorter to read on".[15]

OK, you might say, people are more likely to zip through digital texts than comparable print reading. But there's a follow-up question we need to be asking: As students increasingly do their academic reading in digital form, will attitudes towards "appropriate" print reading speed shift to more closely resemble how at least some students are now approaching digital reading? Will the digital mindset come to encompass print? We don't have an answer yet. But as with the looming consequences of climate change, we don't want to find out the hard way.

THE ENTERTAINMENT FACTOR

What about the entertainment value of reading digitally? One student in the secondary school study came right to the point when asked what she liked most about reading onscreen:

> It can be a bit more entertaining.

Another praised digital reading as

> [N]ot that pla[i]n (boring)

Besides its opportunities for sought-after interruptions involving multitasking, digital reading offers technological enticements generally exceeding those available in print. Think about animation, sound, and possibilities for user interaction with the text or an online social community. Can print compete?

Let's reflect for a moment on the trajectory of print textbooks over the past 40 or 50 years. Given the high costs for running full-color photographs or illustrations, the books traditionally tended to be heavy on text. Over time, textbooks began to fill up with color graphics, along with other material (including cartoons) meant to attract students to do the reading. The price of textbooks soared in the process, though there wasn't comparable growth in how much reading students were doing.

Digital books offer multiple opportunities for entertaining readers. At the same time, there is the movement in many educational circles to incorporate "gamification" into learning, a process that dates back to early educational software such as Reader Rabbit and Math Blaster. The adult world has its own counterpart: infotainment. The underlying purpose is to teach something, but using an entertainment-based delivery system.

Our goal here isn't to evaluate the use of entertainment as a vehicle for learning, either for children or for adults. Rather, the point is that the digital revolution has been changing our expectations about what kinds of learning formats—in this case, when learning through reading—children are willing to engage with.

It's natural for expectations to evolve in many aspects of our lives. Often the catalyst is some form of technological development. The list of potential examples is vast, ranging from how long it takes to traverse a distance (weeks on a Conestoga wagon or hours on a plane), how fast an internet connection is (landline dial-up or 5G), or what the options are for reading a book (sitting in a library with a print volume or pulling up the same text on your phone while lounging at the beach).

The question in each case is whether the new set of expectations should cancel out the old. For speed of internet access, no one is looking to return to the not-so-good old days. But for traversing distance? For the sake of our health and our planet, people are increasingly realizing there are often alternatives to planes or cars (though I'm not advocating for covered wagons). What about for reading books?

No one's objecting to reading on your phone at the beach. The fundamental issue here is whether the mindset that has been developing for digital reading is now entering the "airspace" of print reading. If the answer is "yes", a number of troubling consequences potentially follow:

- Students will increasingly not want to read print, because it is boring in comparison with digital alternatives. (We'll return to the "boring" charge in the next chapter.)
- When students read print, they will approach it with a digital reading mindset, which can lead to the same shallow reading that too often now characterizes digital reading.
- Designers of print books will increasingly try to up the entertainment level, potentially undermining the effort we want students to devote to their reading.

Don't get me wrong. I'm not advocating a cod liver oil approach to learning, admonishing students that since reading is "good for you", you can't expect to enjoy it. Mindful reading of text—whether print or digital—can and should be both pleasurable and rewarding. Our responsibility as teachers and parents is to find ways of leading students to such realization.

No one said the task is easy. It wasn't easy before digital technologies came along. But I suspect it's now even harder. The growing encroachment of digital reading technologies over print, coupled with the less-than-contemplative tendencies so many people have when reading onscreen, should be warning signs. Simply instructing students to do at least some of their reading in print hardly guarantees the idealized reading experience we might envision.

Print is no panacea for learning. And digital is no inherent villain. Much of the issue is the mental attitude we bring to reading. Our task as educators is to help ensure that the typical digital mindset when it comes to reading doesn't become like Georgia kudzu and that it doesn't obliterate the more measured approaches to reading that print has represented, even though they are not always practiced.

Strategizing Print—and Digital—Reading in a Digital World

We all develop habits, some more laudable than others. Eating a healthy diet? Most of us know what we should do, but our follow-through is sometimes problematic. Exercise? Same story. An important key to success is conscious awareness of our goal and our reason for having it.

When it comes to reading habits, there are three major challenges. The first is that we often forget that different reading goals require different levels of mental focus ("You mean I shouldn't be watching a Netflix movie while writing an analysis of Hegel's dialectic?"). The second is that most people—that goes for teachers and students—are unaware that the default setting of a digital reading mindset tends to be shallower than a traditional print reading mindset. And third, the sheer volume of reading we're doing onscreen is poised to remake print reading mindsets in the digital image.

If teachers from kindergarten to college regularly say reading digitally is an appropriate substitute for reading in print, we can hardly fault students for believing them. And if digital reading is often cursory or distracted, what stops students from assuming the same approach to the "equivalent" experience with print?

In Chapter 4, we encountered a paradox in students' beliefs about reading in print versus digitally. When asked about broader learning issues (including concentration or remembering), the overwhelming majority of participants in the research we reviewed said they did better with print. Yet when asked to judge how well they scored (or would score) on a comprehension test after reading a print or digital passage, they particularly overestimated their success with digital. (As we saw in Chapter 7, the same mismatch went for audio and video.) We shouldn't be surprised at students' calibration problem, given all the emphasis that both lower and higher education is putting on digital reading.

We've had a lot to say in this book about potential challenges for sustained, in-depth learning when using digital materials. At the same time, we've been clear that overstated assumptions that print consistently leads to deep reading are more visions than reality. Yes, digital tends to engender different approaches to reading than print, but our question is: What can we do about it?

At the core of any answer must be conscious attempts to nurture reading habits that foster learning with both digital and print materials. That is, we first need to recognize there is a problem with the way so many readers approach the task—regardless of medium. That goes not just for text but for audio and video as well. Medium matters, but even more critical are awareness and mindset.

Maryanne Wolf has proposed a model of reading that she calls "biliteracy". Just as bilinguals can switch between languages as circumstances dictate, Wolf advocates educating children to become biliterates, able to switch between reading styles (and reading platforms) as the goal warrants. While the model emphasizes the contrast between reading in print versus digitally, it applies as well to alternative reading styles within each medium.

Here are some initial ideas for helping us brainstorm reading strategies. Many apply to any medium, while others focus on screens. I'm sure you can add to the list.

Identify your reason for reading.

- *What are you trying to derive from what you're about to read?* Depending on your goal, decide if the text merits skimming, scanning, or a linear read.

- *Keep in mind there are different kinds of linear reads*: once through and done (fine for a murder mystery or news story) or pausing to think as you go (some version of deep reading). Maryanne Wolf's ideas on biliteracy offer us a useful model.

> *"The ultimate goal . . . is the development of a truly biliterate brain with the capacity to allocate time and attention to deep-reading skills regardless of medium."*
>
> Maryanne Wolf[16]

Put in the effort needed to make your reading medium work.

- *Actively engage with what you read.* Too often we slide into making reading a passive spectator sport. Use engagement tools such as notetaking or other annotation, self-quizzing, or discussing with others what you are reading.

- *Read at the pace the text warrants*, which may include referring back to earlier passages or rereading larger sections. Most times, speed is not your friend. School settings notwithstanding, life is not a timed test.

- *With audio, capitalize on the fact it plays every word.* If you find yourself rushing ahead too much when reading text (print or digital), audio may help coach you to slow down with the written word.

Be realistic about your ability to read carefully.

- *Don't let your digitally saturated environment lull you into believing* you can skim and whiz your way through text that calls for more of your attention. This lesson is especially important when reading digitally but increasingly applies to print as well.

- *Reading is not a competitive sport.* How long it takes you to read a passage with understanding (and, one hopes, insight) may not correspond to the pace for others.

Take stock of your reading environment.

- *Reduce onscreen distractions.* Possibilities include minimizing tabs or windows (other than the document you're actually reading) or muting notifications.
- *Know when it's best to block online connectivity temporarily.* You can still choose to read on a digital device, but limit access to the outside world.
- *Consider some version of "digital detox".* The mere presence of a mobile phone nearby can drain some of your cognitive focus. If people can do a "digital detox" for several days or weeks at a time, try a mini version while you're reading material that merits your full attention.

Learn to accommodate when you can't choose the reading medium.

- *Sometimes it's not up to you which medium* you—or your students—will be using for reading. If your school has adopted a digital-only policy for textbooks, build on what you have learned about our propensities when reading digitally to guide students how to be mindful readers with digital texts.
- *Seek ways of encouraging opportunities for using multiple reading platforms.* Print still abounds—in libraries, in bookstores, in homes. If we aspire to fulfill the goal of biliteracy, we need to keep experiencing both the physical and digital reading worlds.

CHAPTER 10   The Road Ahead

Predictions that "this will replace that" are common in the history of technology. One poignant prophecy appeared in Victor Hugo's novel *The Hunchback of Notre Dame*. There is a scene when the archdeacon

> first points to the great cathedral and then stretches out his right hand toward a fifteenth-century printed book and announces, "*Ceci tuera cela;*" "*This* (the printed book) will kill *that* (the cathedral, which had served for centuries as an encyclopedia in stone)."[1]

However, hindsight often reveals that "both/and" is more likely than "either/or". Despite the devastating fire that made her the worse for wear, Notre Dame, with its stained-glass windows visually depicting religious history, still stands. Television didn't drive out radio. Audio hasn't obliterated print, and neither have digital screens.

Rather than tilting at windmills, it's time to declare a truce. Print—and reading— aren't dying. At the same time, digital texts (along with audio and video) are now an intrinsic part of our classrooms, at least for the foreseeable future. And that's a blessing, given their potential for enriching education. The trick, as we've argued, is to work out which medium makes sense for what kind of learning.

How We Read Now has covered a lot of territory about reading with print, screen, and audio. We've laid out the issues, reviewed contemporary research findings, and suggested ways of using these results when choosing reading materials, designing curricula, and crafting teaching strategies. In this last chapter, we'll begin by highlighting paradoxes we need to confront about both print and the educational enterprise, and then offer parting suggestions for moving ahead as parents, teachers, librarians, and policy makers.

Print Paradoxes

Two paradoxes about print keep puzzling me. The first concerns market forces and the second, reader attitudes, particularly among students.

WHAT'S SELLING?

If you want to know what's trending in users' approaches to print, digital text, and audio, follow the money. What are people buying?

Here's the conundrum. As we saw in Table 2.2 in Chapter 2, the pattern for book sales in the United States has been fairly consistent of late: Print books are largely steady-state, eBooks are continuing to decline, and audiobooks are soaring. To recap the numbers for the last two years for which I have data:

	Print	eBooks	Audio Download
2019	−1.3%	−4.2%	+22.1%
2018	+1.3%	−3.6%	+37.1%

But pause for a moment to focus specifically on higher education. According to the Association of American Publishers, overall sales for higher education course materials declined 7.2 percent in 2018 and another 10.7 percent in 2019.[2] To repeat a few other numbers from Chapter 2: College students are spending less and less on course materials. Instead of the roughly $1,200 or more that the College Board suggests students should budget annually, the average spent is now closer to $200 to $500, depending on which survey you look at. Again, depending on the survey, the drop between 2014 and 2019 has been between 29 and 35 percent.[3]

Good news for students? Yes and no. Faculty are concerned about the high cost of textbooks and naturally welcome opportunities for students to save money. But part of that decline reflects renting books rather than buying them, which means that at the end of the semester, the books are gone. While we don't have definitive data, some of the decline in expenditures could reflect more students simply not acquiring course materials. One significant factor we can identify is the move we talked about in Chapter 2 for major textbook publishers to push digital bundling over print—think "inclusive access", whereby students pay a comparatively low fee to access digital books issued by that publisher.

The hitch, of course, is that the majority of students report they learn or remember or concentrate better when using print, especially for longer reading. And so the paradox, particularly in the United States: While print sales for the overall readership remain solid, educators are increasingly accepting the publishers' gambit to replace print textbooks with digital.

In higher education, the transition is already well under way. In lower education, preparations are proceeding afoot. At the November 2019 conference of the National Council of Teachers of English, I stopped by the exhibit booth of Pearson, curious to see what the publisher's plans were for K-12. (Pearson, remember, has adopted a "digital first" policy for higher education texts.) The enthusiastic sales representative waxed eloquent about the current availability of all their materials in both digital and print but also about the company's plans for K-12 print to soon fall by the wayside.

If the educational establishment increasingly adopts digital materials, replacing print, what reading platform decisions do we anticipate students will make once they leave school? My concern is that we are socializing the next generations to assume digital is always an adequate substitute for print. Technology won't be responsible for the dwindling of print. Publishers and educators will be.

Are kids ready to say goodbye to print? Data from the publisher Scholastic suggest otherwise. For a number of years, Scholastic has asked children for its U.S. *Kids & Family Reading Report* whether they agreed with this statement: "I'll always want to read books printed on paper even though there are eBooks available." In 2012 (nearing the crest of meteoric growth in U.S. eBook sales), 58 percent of 9- to

17-year-olds surveyed and 64 percent of those age 6 to 8 said they agreed.[4] By 2018, the number of 6- to 17-year-olds overall who agreed had *risen* to 69 percent.[5]

If children have their way, print is not yet an endangered species.

WHAT'S BORING?

We've looked at tons of data in this book. A lot of it confirms many of our intuitions about the pros and cons of different reading media. But one finding I hadn't expected: students saying that reading print is boring.

Some of their complaints showed up when answering an open-ended survey question on what they liked least about reading in print. In my cross-national university study, a couple responses of "boring" surfaced. The proportion rose among secondary school students at the International School of Stavanger.[6]

> "[Print] can tire you out really fast and get boring no matter how interesting the book is."
>
> Student, International School of Stavanger

Then I came upon a report from the United Kingdom's National Literacy Trust on the impact of eBooks on children's reading motivation and skills.[7] At the end of the project, the researchers conducted student focus groups in which participants were queried what they liked and disliked about reading with paper or on a screen. Here's some of what they said:

"When you read on paper, it's a bit boring, unless it's something you're really into. . . . On a tablet, it feels more interesting, it reminds me of when I'm texting someone."

"I get bored when I'm reading paper books, I don't know why it just seems to drag."

Other replies may hint at answers to the "why" question. One student observed that

"On paper, there's just too many words on the page and it's too long, you get confused."

Sounds familiar. In our earlier research review, we found students perceiving the same amount of text looking longer in print than on a screen. Another student in the U.K. study favored eBooks because of their similarity to the internet:

"People our age we love using the internet so most of us don't like reading books because it's not on the internet, we prefer ebooks, that's more like the internet."[8]

Reading print is a drag. Too long. Too many words. Not enough like texting or using the internet. What are students trying to tell us? While I don't know for sure, I have several hypotheses.

The first is that in comparison with the bright shiny possibilities when reading onscreen, print looks staid. There's no animation, no sound, and often no color. Even stand-alone digital texts have more glitz. Worse still, print has no online connection. Unless you turn to your mobile phone for distraction while reading print, you have few opportunities to multitask.

When I think about assertions from secondary school and university students that print is boring, I harken back to an experiment with young children that we talked about in Chapter 4, comparing reading with digital versus print books. When designing their study, the researchers had to abandon their plan for half of the children to first get the digital book and then the print. The problem? In a pilot study, "children who were assigned to read [electronic books] first [then] resisted reading traditional books afterward".[9] Apparently—and troublingly—such resistance persists among older readers.

The second hypothesis is that today's students subliminally feel that when reading print, they're supposed to go more slowly and expend more effort. That is, there's a mindset at work. Given the choice of print versus digital for the same text, can you blame students for resenting the extra burden they presume that print imposes, even though many of these same readers likely acknowledge they concentrate or learn better with print?

Third, there's validation from authority figures. When teachers across the grade spectrum tell students that print and digital are educationally equivalent (at least for many types of reading), students believe them. How can we fault students for making the choice between "equals" that's not just less expensive and often more convenient but also perceived as reducing the time and mental energy they need to expend?

We don't just have a student learning problem on our hands. There's also a public relations challenge. Maryanne Wolf's advice to train our students to be biliterate is a step in the right direction. But knowing is not the same as doing. We need to explain to students (and to remind ourselves) why digital technologies can be so tempting and also why they're not always the best choice.

A major reason why digital can fall short lies in our broader educational goals.

The Aims of Education

I borrowed this section title from a 1929 essay by the mathematician and philosopher Alfred North Whitehead. The question of what we teach and why must be posed anew for different times, different cultures, different priorities. Our answers won't be the same as Whitehead's, but the importance of thinking through educational rationales remains constant.

Because my own experience is largely in higher education, I'll begin the discussion there. However, the rest of the section expands to students spanning the age range.

WHY GO TO COLLEGE?

What do entering college students say they want from their education? Perceptions shift with time, often in tune with the economy. Researchers at the University of California, Los Angeles, have long been surveying freshmen across the country on a spate of issues.[10] When asked their reasons for attending college, first-year student responses from 1971 and 2015 stacked up this way:

	1971	2015
Get a better job	70.0%	85.2%
Make more money	44.5%	69.9%
Gain a general education and appreciation of ideas	62.7%	71.5%

It's good news that a broad educational foundation continues to be valued. But then consider these responses from entering students regarding objectives they considered "essential" or "very important":

	1971	2015
Being well-off financially	37.1%	81.9%
Developing a meaningful philosophy of life	72.7%	46.5%

A few years earlier (in 1967), the votes on a meaningful philosophy of life were even higher—85.5 percent. Now, financial success is in the driver's seat.

These trends are further reflected in sobering statistics on whether Americans feel going to college is important. A 2019 Gallup poll of adults (age 18 to 65+) found only 51 percent thought getting a college education was "very important"—compared with 70 percent in 2013. The numbers are even more chilling for those age 18 to 29: In 2019, only 41 percent felt college was "very important", down from 74 percent in 2013.[11]

The shifting value proposition for higher education is reflected in what students who do attend college choose to study. Looking at all bachelor's degrees conferred in the United States, the largest number continues to be in business.[12] Considering some of the most prestigious undergraduate institutions in the United States, the most popular major as of 2016 at Brown, Columbia, Dartmouth, Harvard, Princeton, and Yale was economics, with finance being number one at the University of Pennsylvania.[13] Computer science and, where available, engineering weren't far behind. What you don't find high on the list are literature and history—disciplines that traditionally have been grounded in longform reading.

So much for what disciplines students are choosing to study. But what are we aiming to teach them?

THE CRITICAL THINKING PARADOX

Listen to college presidents or deans extolling the virtues of their institution, and the teaching of critical thinking inevitably emerges as one of the school's promised strengths. My own university obviously got the memo. A quick trip online revealed teaching of critical thinking as an explicit goal for departmental programs ranging from business to government, public communication, international studies, writing studies, and women's, gender, and sexuality studies. Even art history and studio art made the list. The library and the career center offer to help out as well. In fact, the university's Faculty Manual counsels that

> Excellent teaching enables students to acquire knowledge, develop critical thinking skills, and become active participants in the learning process. (American University Faculty Manual)

Higher education is not alone. Interest in teaching critical thinking can be found throughout the K-12 spectrum.[14]

What exactly is this educational elixir? It depends upon whom you ask. A typical definition highlights abilities to evaluate evidence and solve complex problems.

Figuring out what you need to know is another common component, as are being able to formulate a coherent argument and spot flaws in someone else's. We'll get to a couple of sample definitions in a moment.

Epistemologists (philosophers who study what it means to know) sometimes define knowledge as "justified true belief". It is this notion of justification that lies at the heart of much of the critical thinking movement.

While people have been thinking for millennia about what it means to think, John Dewey is generally credited as the modern founder of talk about critical thinking. In his 1910 book *How We Think*, Dewey used the term "reflective thought" to refer to

> *Active, persistent, and careful consideration of any belief or supposed form of knowledge in the light of the grounds that support it, and the further conclusions to which it tends.*[15]

Over the ensuing decades, the term "reflective thought" came to be replaced by "critical thinking" or "clear thinking". Initially, the concept was most closely related to teaching logic and the scientific method.[16] A link was also being made between critical thinking and good citizenship. As psychologist Edward Glaser wrote at the time,

> Competent citizenship in a democracy calls for a good deal more than the ability to read and write. Among other things, it requires the ability to think critically.[17]

By the 1950s, a high school science teacher named Robert Ennis decided to incorporate critical thinking into his pedagogy. Ennis went on to become a major spokesperson for critical thinking, later writing a two-part history and analysis of the movement. After something of a hiatus in public interest in the 1960s and 1970s, the idea of critical thinking began receiving new attention in the 1980s.[18]

Given more than a century of talk about the importance of critical thinking (by whatever name), a cascade of definitions have been offered for the concept. Here are a few:

- "Reasonable reflective thinking focused on deciding what to believe or do"[19]
- "The art of analyzing and evaluating thinking with a view to improving it"[20]
- "A habit of mind characterized by the comprehensive exploration of issues, ideas, artifacts, and events before accepting or formulating an opinion or conclusion"[21]

You get the drift.

These days, there's a sizeable industry for training students to think critically, as well as for assessing outcomes. Some examples:

- The Critical Thinking Company helps "students of all abilities achieve better academic results with highly effective lessons that sharpen the mind as they teach standards-based reading, writing, mathematics, science, and history".[22]
- The Foundation for Critical Thinking runs an annual conference and offers books for teachers and students at all levels.[23]
- The critical thinking course on Lynda.com (an online tutoring source) has been accessed more than 1.6 million times.[24] For something more formal, Coursera has several offerings.[25]
- A host of textbooks on critical thinking are available, including one by Brooke Moore and Richard Parker, now in its 12th edition.[26]
- The online learning management system Blackboard has an assessment tool called a "critical-thinking coefficient" that "classifies words according to the degree of critical thinking represented".[27]

Is all this teaching and assessing of critical thinking skills working? Maybe not. A cascade of essays with titles such as "Can Colleges Truly Teach Critical-Thinking Skills?"[28] and "The Holy Grail of Critical Thinking"[29] lay out some of the challenges.

For even more objective evidence, a couple of recent studies should give us pause. We've already talked in Chapters 5 and 6 about the findings of the Stanford History Education Group when it came to measuring students' ability to apply civic online reasoning (certainly a skill under the critical thinking umbrella) to materials they read on the internet. The results, as we saw, were bleak.

A different study by the same Stanford group reveals that trouble lies not just in student capabilities but also in the measures we use to assess them. Here's the story.[30]

The National Assessment of Educational Progress (NAEP) has been measuring student progress in U.S. K-12 for several decades. Its 12th-grade U.S. history test purports to evaluate critical thinking, not just recall of names and dates. NAEP claims it can use multiple-choice questions to assess such skills as explaining points of view and developing (and defending) perspectives.

Are they right? When history education scholars at Stanford compared what skills NAEP said it was measuring against interview answers from students who had taken the assessment—as well as scored 3 or better on the U.S. History Advanced Placement exam—the discrepancies were stark. The reasoning students said they actually used in selecting answers didn't include *any* of the thinking strategies NAEP maintains it is measuring.

What do students say about their critical thinking skills? Given the climate of grade inflation that envelops education in the United States, we shouldn't be surprised that American students are largely confident about their abilities. Others aren't so sure.

A 2017 survey by the National Association of Colleges and Employers found that 80 percent of college students judged themselves proficient in critical thinking/ problem-solving skills, but only 56 percent of employers shared this view of recent college graduates.[31] An earlier study commissioned by the American Association of Colleges and Universities yielded a similar mismatch. Among students, 66 percent rated themselves prepared in critical/analytical thinking, while only 26 percent of employers agreed.[32] In Europe, where the reform of higher education known as the Bologna Process included critical thinking as an important pedagogical goal, research suggests that like their American counterparts, European students give themselves high marks in critical thinking, while more objective measures do not.[33]

How do you teach people to think critically? If the results of the Stanford study are any indication, we have yet to figure that one out. What we can be sure of is that in a literate society, reading that is careful and reflective will be part of the answer. To the extent that a particular reading platform leads us to minimize this kind of reading, then medium matters.

Here is the paradox. Educators tout the importance of nurturing critical thinking skills in students. Yet at the same time, they advocate for a reading medium—namely digital—that is often at odds with the task. Digital technology is well suited to locating information and to fact-checking online but doesn't typically encourage contemplation and thorough evaluation.

> *"It seems likely that digital devices are useful for concrete, short term learning goals, whereas complex cognitive skills like reading comprehension are best developed through traditional print reading. Reading ability is long term learning, developed throughout life."*
>
> Hildegunn Støle et al.[34]

Part of the issue is speed. When thinking through a problem, weighing the evidence, challenging your own argument, speed is rarely of the essence. Deliberation and depth are. But then readers often believe they can successfully read more quickly with digital text.

A second part of the problem is durability. With print, the words, the ideas, the arguments pro and con continue to stare back at us as readers, ready to help nudge our thinking forward. By contrast, while digital text can be re-summoned, its default state is ephemeral, and rereading is less likely than with print. With audio, the chances of words being revisited are even smaller.

A third component is length. Yes, people might apply critical thinking skills to texts of any length. However, to get to the heart of some issues, it's often necessary to grapple with genuinely lengthy longform reading. Not 500 words but maybe 5,000 or more. And even students tell us that for longer reading, print is preferred.

Finally, there's mindset. If digital reading is prone to encourage a shallower read than when using print, we need to ask how much mental energy is likely needed for the cognitive task at hand when asked to think critically. Not all problems call for the same extent—or depth—of analysis. But it's important to remember those calibration studies in Chapter 4 showing we tend to overestimate our performance more when reading onscreen than with print.

KNOW IT OR LOOK IT UP?

When talking about critical thinking, teachers don't typically imagine digital technology to be a relevant factor. There is, though, an aspect of today's education that fundamentally involves such technology: what we hope students commit to memory and what makes sense for them to look up, which these days nearly always means online.

In this age of ubiquitous internet access, there's considerable talk about what the role of a teacher is. Historically, responsibilities included disseminating information and nurturing the development of knowledge. Now that information is everywhere online, what's left for those proverbially on the other side of the desk? In principle, a lot, including guiding students in locating information, evaluating what they find, and making sense of it. Equally vital is helping students develop the mental tools (and moral fiber) necessary to tackle problems whose resolution you can't simply look up, such as how to deal with climate change or to reduce ethnic and racial strife.

In light of all these educational aims, we need to figure out whether it matters if students "know" things, independent of what they might access online. I ask my university students: What do you know when the internet is down? I ask faculty colleagues who are strong advocates of both digital technology and crit-

My challenge to students: What do you know when the internet is down?

ical thinking skills: If students don't have ample knowledge in their heads, what do they have to think critically about?

In earlier chapters, we saw correlations between reading scores (both with print and digital materials) and prior knowledge. While there are many ways of gaining prior knowledge—including life experience, listening to others, and watching educational videos—the most consistent pathway in literate societies has been through longform reading.

There's also a cognitive values issue. If you go online to locate information, which in principle could help build prior knowledge as you go forward, does it matter if you remember what you found? Or is it OK if the memory trace washes out like the tide? Research is increasingly showing that we commonly go online not to learn over the long term (building an accumulation of prior knowledge) but rather to pluck out facts for momentary use and then abandon them. Here's some of the evidence.

Psychologist Betsy Sparrow and her colleagues reported that after doing a Google search, people are more likely to remember their search path than the results of what they sought.[35] If we remember the path, we can always look again, not needing to remember what we found. And that seems to be exactly what many of us tend to do.

Studies by Kaspersky Lab have probed ways in which we are lured to stop making the effort to remember things for ourselves, now that, in the words of psychologist Paul Marsden, digital devices have become "the new flash drives of the mind". Kaspersky Lab used the term "digital amnesia" to describe "the experience of forgetting information that you trust a digital device to store and remember for you".[36]

In Kaspersky surveys of Europeans and Americans, 61 percent of both groups felt it wasn't necessary to remember facts unearthed online but only to recall where you located them. When asked if they forgot an online fact as soon as they found it, more than a quarter said "yes". Even scarier, many people surveyed didn't feel motivated to bother trying to remember something they once knew before resorting to their virtual Jeeves. Among Europeans, 57 percent said they first tried to remember, while 36 percent reported going directly online. Americans were quicker to throw in the towel: Only 39 percent reported first attempting to remember, while 50 percent made a beeline for the internet.[37]

The problem isn't just a fact here and there. Psychologist Maria Wimber warns that

> the trend to look up information before even trying to recall it prevents
> the build-up of long-term memories, and thus makes us process infor-
> mation merely on a shallow, moment-to-moment basis.[38]

In the cautionary words of Susan Greenfield, a neuroscientist:

Imagine in the future people become so used to external access for any form of reference that they have not internalized any facts at all, let alone put them into a context to appreciate their significance and understand them.[39]

It's all too easy to turn the internet—and what we read and listen to (or watch) on it—into our memory keeper. Or into our sole research resource. Or into our data analyzer. Or into our standard for what's worth knowing. Since the appearance of Wikipedia, teachers have struggled to train students to have healthy skepticism about its accuracy as well as to seek out additional sources and to develop their own point of view. But the challenge I'm talking about is even greater. It's believing that like gravity, the internet will always be there for you. Why do your own mental heavy lifting?

In short, the challenge teachers are faced with is not just figuring out which reading platform is likely to best foster what kind of learning. It's also dealing with the very real possibility of students failing to grasp that what they know is not the same thing as what they can look up, and that their fund of knowledge might be paltry indeed when the internet is down.

Pathways Forward

What is to be done? Digital amnesia is just one of the challenges for which there are no easy solutions. And as with so much in education, what works in one classroom or with a particular student doesn't always generalize. That said, here are some parting ideas for helping achieve a meaningful balance with print, screen, and audio reading.

READING MATTERS—FAST AND SLOW, SHALLOW AND DEEP

Begin with the obvious: Reading matters. If you picked up this book, I'm preaching to the choir. But my message here is about advocacy, not personal belief.

We need to speak up for the kind of reading we want children and young adults to do. Yes, there are state or national curricular requirements. Yes, so many components of education—from textbooks to testing—are going digital. Yes, students commonly don't complete the reading we assign, in whatever medium. And yes, some students are complaining that print is boring.

But these realities make it even more incumbent upon us to help students see reading as filling many purposes, among which are quick access to information, absorbed light reading, and contemplative reading, which is slower paced. We need to find ways of incorporating fuller-length reading into the academic agenda, helping cultivate an understanding among our students and our own children that such reading matters.

DON'T JUST BLAME THE MESSENGER

As we think about student reading patterns over the years, it's clear that digital technologies aren't the only driver of how much students read. More accurately, the move onscreen and online has reinforced trends already in motion.

Here's an analogy to think about, drawing on earlier research I've done on whether online communication affects how we write and speak. In the early 2000s, there was much public angst over the linguistic patterns showing up in email, instant messaging, and texting. All those misspellings! Those abbreviations and acronyms! Sloppy grammar! Helter-skelter punctuation! As one newspaper put it,

> [T]he changes we see taking place today in the language will be a prelude
> to the dying use of good English.[40]

It turns out that news of these presumed atrocities was much exaggerated. When you look carefully at actual data, the picture changes. There aren't as many misspellings as you might think (some are intentional), and punctuation tends to follow logical patterns (including generally using question marks when they're required and omitting final periods because you're hitting "Send" anyway).[41]

Equally importantly, the origins of many such linguistic "deviations" in online communication predate the digital revolution. Looking at the history of English composition pedagogy in the United States, along with print-based publishing, you find several relevant trends at work. First, you see a growing educational focus, especially from the 1960s, on students' ideas rather than their spelling, grammar, or punctuation. Second, you find a surprising number of errors (in spelling, grammar, or punctuation) in books published by highly respected publishers or in magazine advertisements that must have cost a pretty penny.[42]

But third, particularly in the United States, there has been a palpable move towards informality: in the way we dress, how we speak, and in our writing patterns. Text of all sorts (even in some professional journals) increasingly looks more like casual spoken language. Concerns about proofreading continue to decline. These trends predate spellcheck and predictive texting.[43]

In *What We Talk About When We Talk About Books*, Leah Price reminds us that throughout their history, books have evolved, as have the ways we read them. She argues that differences over time as to what books, reading, and readers have looked like seem to "outstrip differences between print and digital". What's more, she says,

> The long dominance of books designed to be searched, skimmed, and discarded needs to be airbrushed out of our memories because it challenges the digital-age fantasy that print inculcates patience, strengthens work ethics, and stretches attention spans.[44]

That is, we've searched and skimmed for centuries when reading print, not just now in the digital world.

And yet, we shouldn't deny the multiplier effect. In the case of online communication and written language conventions, I've argued that the writing we do on computers, tablets, and mobile phones is contributing to (though not the source of) our increasingly casual approach to what used to be called sentence mechanics. A parallel conclusion holds for the influence of digital technologies on reading patterns. Online reading isn't the source of shallow or hurried reading, but it has been magnifying practices and attitudes that already existed.

YOU CAN FIGHT CITY HALL

Over the years, I've been following the expanding presence of digital pedagogy, especially in higher education. Faculty are offering more online courses, and use of digital textbooks continues to grow, though in some people's eyes, not fast enough. To wit: Consider this comment from a director at a nonprofit organization dedicated to integrating digital learning into higher education:

> Instructors who model effective use of digital texts in learning can help students overcome their preference for print and take advantage of the convenience and lower cost offered by digital texts.[45]

I understand the author's mission, but asking students to "overcome their preference for print" ignores the reasons behind that preference, even in light of cost and convenience.

Is digital reading a moving train that can't be stopped? Can we successfully fight City Hall? The answer is up to us. Not every technology eradicates its predecessor. Hardcopy book purchases put the lie to predictions of the end of print. When it comes to education, those of us in decision-making positions have more clout than we might think. Hopefully, the research in this book provides arguments for supporting your case for giving students a balanced reading palette.

When it comes to choosing a reading platform, current educational trends aren't immutable. Your course of action needs to fit your own circumstances, but here are a few ideas to think about:

- *Share research findings* with those who make textbook and curricular decisions, as well as with parents and students. Put the chapters in this book to productive use!
- *Brainstorm options.* When a school policy argues for moving to digital strictly for cost reasons, remember such alternatives as print on demand for open educational resources or print books that are less expensive than bestselling texts.[46]
- *Encourage a "both/and"* rather than "either/or" approach to platform choice.
- *Find ways to go around.* If the school system or department chair selects a reading platform that doesn't match your own choice, explore ways of providing alternatives or supplements. There are medical schools that have moved entirely to digital books, but in response to student protest, now have print copies of a core collection, including textbooks, available in the library. High school or college students who prefer print but whose schools (or courses) have gone all digital may find ways to purchase, rent, or borrow hardcopy texts.
- *Compromise is not defeat.* Mindful of student budgets, many faculty are willing to use digital materials "even if the lower cost options are of lesser quality".[47] But textbooks are only one course component. In fields such as history and mathematics, some faculty don't assign specific textbooks but suggest a few reference options. After all, the professor is teaching the course, not the publisher.
- *Don't underestimate your own influence* as a parent or teacher. The behavior you model—including how you read with or in the presence of your progeny or students—can have an impact on children's perceptions of which reading platform might be most beneficial when.

I also have some advice for publishers. Over the past several decades, I witnessed commercial warfare in which companies vied with one another to see who could have the most color photographs, the funniest cartoons, or the glossiest paper. I also saw the price of the introductory linguistics textbook I was using nearly triple and new editions appear at an unnecessarily feverish pace. No wonder my students complained! And no wonder publishers are now abandoning print. Here's my plea to textbook publishers:

- Consider what is driving up production costs. Are there ways of publishing print textbooks that are educationally inviting without trying to make them decorative candidates for coffee tables?[48]

LIFE IS NOT A TIMED TEST

We've spent considerable time in this book talking about standardized testing, particularly in secondary schools. Love the tests or hate them, they persist. The irony is that a growing number of U.S. colleges have stopped requiring scores on the ACT or SAT as part of the admissions process. One of the arguments is that a timed test doesn't necessarily reflect students' skills, prior knowledge, ability to analyze and evaluate, or willingness to work hard.

How much credence is put in results from tests such as the NAEP (in the United States) or the PISA (internationally) is a moving target. In Europe, for instance, national PISA scores for 15-year-olds are taken very seriously, while in the United States, they receive far less attention (perhaps, in candor, because Americans don't do especially well on them). In countries such as Japan, where the college entrance exam remains all-important in determining so much of a student's future prospects, it's hard to know how to lessen the pressure. But in many other countries, particularly in the U.S., we should find ways of learning from the declining importance of the ACT and SAT.

In Closing: MyReadingPlate

How We Read Now has been my attempt to size up what we know about nurturing productive reading practices in children and young adults, especially when it comes to using print, screen, or audio materials. Raising the next generation of adults, including as readers, is one of the hardest jobs in the world. It's also potentially one of the most important and rewarding.

Journalist and food crusader Michael Pollan began a piece in the *New York Times Magazine* with these memorable words:

Eat food. Not too much. Mostly plants.[49]

His succinct counsel is unambiguously clear. After thinking about an equally concise way of offering closing advice about reading platforms and learning, here's what I came up with:

Read more. Focus when you do. Medium matters.

These words are intended for all of us.

We each need to work out our personal reading plate. But we also must acknowledge that we don't always get to use the platform we prefer or believe is best suited for the reading we are undertaking. That same reality exists in our classrooms. Being aware of the strengths and weaknesses of each medium—and of our reading mindsets—can go far to help compensate.

May this book assist you in the venture.

Acknowledgments

This book has two godmothers. I had known their research for years, but only met both in January 2018.

The setting was the Stanford Center for Advanced Study in the Behavioral Sciences, nestled in the foothills above the university. It was a bit of a homecoming for me, having done my doctoral work at Stanford long ago and later having been a visiting scholar at CASBS (as the center is familiarly known). That January, Maryanne Wolf (Godmother One) brought together about two dozen researchers for a Global Literacy and Neuroscience Workshop, areas about which she is passionate. One of those researchers (Godmother Two) was Anne Mangen, with whom I also promptly bonded, especially given our shared interests in comparing print and screen reading.

The goal of the workshop wasn't just scholarly talk. At the final session, Maryanne powerfully charged us to turn ideas into action, to take what we knew in our respective fields of expertise and make a difference in the lives of readers.

As I listened, I fathomed my own task: to gather current research findings on the pros and cons of reading in different media, and then share what we know with those educating the next generations of readers. From work on my earlier book *Words Onscreen: The Fate of Reading in a Digital World*, I already had a grasp of the literature up through early 2014. And from my cross-national study of university student reading habits, I had some first-hand data. But I needed to find out what scholars were discovering now, as well as do more data collection myself.

In the months that followed, I launched a project I called "Medium Matters". Its goal was to connect with researchers who could help me map the questions that should be asked, and share with me their own work. While I looked to the group for tackling issues of print versus digital reading, I realized that given the explosive growth of audiobooks and podcasts, I also needed to think about audio as a third medium for reading.

Maryanne and I brainstormed a short list of people to invite to the project. Then Anne's help was invaluable as she introduced me (virtually) to several dozen members of the research community she had formed with Adriaan van der Weel known as E-READ (Evolution of Reading in the Age of Digitisation). This COST Action, funded by the European Union, was an immense—and immensely fruitful—four-year undertaking that brought together almost 200 scholars working on reading, publishing, and literacy in the context of the digital revolution.

A profound thank-you to Medium Matters colleagues from throughout Europe, from Israel, and from the United States who answered my call. I learned so much from you. And I'm equally grateful for the friendships forged.

Maryanne, Anne, and our Medium Matters partners: There would be no book without you.

Over the next year, as I started amassing questions to confront, articles to read, and new manuscripts my colleagues graciously shared, I began strategizing how the project should transition from theory to practice. Should I focus on education conferences? Approach school principals or central policy makers? While these would be necessary steps, I realized that first I needed to write down what I was finding—and recommending.

And so this book was born.

Like many authors, I owe a debt to those who shared with me their information and expertise. To begin:

- For educating me about use of audio plus text for those with learning challenges: George Kerscher (from the DAISY Consortium) and Edward Bray (from Learning Ally)
- For information about open educational resources: the Creative Commons USA team at the Washington College of Law (Meredith Jacobs, Michael Carroll, Jeselyne Andrade, and Bilan Jama)
- For reading statistics in Europe, plus lively conversations about the role of print: Adriaan van der Weel (Leiden University) and Miha Kovač (University of Ljubljana)
- For information about the 2021 PIRLS test: Ina Mullis (TIMSS & PIRLS International Study Center)

- For discussion of audio and video annotation: Ian O'Byrne (College of Charleston)
- For conversation about using multiple documents online: Maik Philipp (Zurich University for Teacher Education)

My sincere apologies to anyone I inadvertently omitted.

I'm also grateful to colleagues for facilitating opportunities to present some of my thinking to a variety of audiences:

- Leopoldina Fortunati and Marina Bondi: lecturing in Italy to groups at the University of Udine and the University of Modena and Reggio Emilia
- Pamela Hurst-Della Pietra: speaking at the inaugural conference of her Children and Screens institute
- Tove Rye Andersen: speaking at the Modes of Reading Seminar at the University of Aarhus (Denmark)
- Patricia Alexander: sharing my work with her Disciplined Reading and Learning Research Laboratory at the University of Maryland
- Ann Friedman: speaking with the board of directors of Ann's fabulous new museum, Planet Word
- David Fortin: speaking at researchED in Philadelphia
- Satomi Sugiyama: lecturing to classes at the Franklin University of Switzerland in Lugano
- The Digital Society Initiative and the URPP Language and Space Colloquium: lecturing at the University of Zurich
- Kristen Turner: organizer of our Medium Matters Roundtable at the National Council of Teachers of English Conference in Baltimore

A very big thanks to those who hosted me for short-term visiting appointments, where I had the opportunity to continue my research and writing, and equally importantly, to talk with new colleagues:

- At the Norwegian Reading Centre, located at the University of Stavanger: Anne Mangen
- At the University of Zurich: Elisabeth Stark, Simone Uberwasser, and the Digital Society Initiative

I also won't forget the warm hospitality during my stays at the Ydalir Hotel in Stavanger and Hotel Hottingen in Zurich.

Next, those who taught and guided me, as well as supportively critiqued what I had written. Here's an accounting:

- For helping me think about the importance of audio as a form of reading: Iben Have and Birgitte Stougaard Pedersen (both at the University of Aarhus) and Anisha Singh (University of Maryland)
- For broadening my understanding of children and digital books: Natalia Kucirkova (University of Stavanger), Lisa Guernsey (New America), and Michael Levine (Nickelodeon)
- For their conversations, research support, manuscript-sharing, and encouragement: Rakefet Ackerman (Technion), Mirit Barzillai (University of Haifa), Frank Hakemulder (Utrecht University), William Harder (Goucher College), Tami Katzir (University of Haifa), Karin Kukkonen (University of Oslo), Diane Mizrachi (UCLA), Alicia Salaz (Carnegie Mellon), and Ladislao Salmerón (University of Valencia)
- For incredibly helpful comments on a draft of the book: Rakefet Ackerman, Mary Findley, Natalia Kucirkova, Anne Mangen, and Anisha Singh
- For working with me, over the years, to hone my writing for the larger public: Rebecca Basu (American University)
- For her critical eye, boundless patience, and friendship: my literary agent, Felicia Eth
- For her fine editorial hand: my editor at Oxford University Press, Meredith Keffer
- For helping guide the publication process: Macey Fairchild, at Oxford, and the folks at Newgen KnowledgeWorks

And finally, to the friends and family who encouraged, tolerated, and good-naturedly listened when I needed a sympathetic ear: Please know I treasure you.

It genuinely takes a village. I am most grateful to you all.

Notes

INTRODUCTION

1. See Goldstein 2020 for an overview of current positions. Seidenberg 2017 presents an extended rationale for phonics.
2. Have and Pedersen 2016.
3. Rubery 2016.
4. Examples include Guernsey and Levine 2015; Kucirkova 2018.
5. For insights on pleasure reading, I highly recommend Natalia Kucirkova and Teresa Cremin's 2020 *Children Reading for Pleasure in the Digital Age*.

CHAPTER 1

1. Price 2019; Stallybrass 2002.
2. For audio versus text, see Chapter 7; for print versus digital text, see Baron 2015a and Tyo-Dickerson et al. 2019.
3. Brower 1962, p. 4.
4. See, for instance, John Miedema's 2009 manifesto *Slow Reading*.
5. Guillory 2010.
6. Birkerts 1994, p. 146.
7. Wolf and Barzillai 2009, p. 33.
8. Stavanger Declaration Concerning the Future of Reading 2019.
9. See, for example, Garfinkle 2020.
10. Sosnoski 1999, p. 167.
11. Hayles 2012, p. 12.
12. Gibson 1979; Norman 1988.
13. Cazden et al. 1996, p. 60.
14. For an introduction to new literacies, see Lankshear and Knobel 2011. For an update on the movement, see Serafini and Gee 2017.
15. For discussion of how new literacies and technology intersect, see Coiro 2020; Coiro et al. 2008; and Leu et al. 2004.
16. Spence 2020, p. 6.
17. Mangen 2016, p. 465.
18. Mangen 2008; Merchant 2015.
19. Brasel and Gips 2014.

20. Baron et al. 2017.
21. Kuzmičová et al. 2018. For more discussion of embodiment and reading, see Burke and Bon 2018.
22. For a user-friendly overview of the psychology of reading, including eye movement, see Rayner et al. 2012. Other useful references are the seminal 1986 article of Carpenter and Just, and Conklin et al.'s 2018 book on eye-tracking.
23. Ashby et al. 2005.
24. Kretzschmar et al. 2013; Siegenthaler et al. 2011; Zambarbieri and Carniglia 2012.
25. Mol and Bus 2011.
26. Krashen 2004; Wu and Samuels 2004.
27. Biancarosa and Snow 2004.
28. For a short overview of the issues, see Willingham 2017.
29. A classic study is Daneman and Carpenter 1980.
30. For insightful discussions, see Furedi 2016 and Jackson 1932.
31. Cited in Rowold 2010, p. 35.
32. In the United States: Rideout and Robb 2019; Scholastic 2017. In the United Kingdom: Clark and Douglas 2011; Egmont 2019. Cross-nationally: OECD 2011.
33. Bureau of Labor Statistics n.d.; National Endowment for the Arts 2012; Perrin 2015.
34. Nation's Report Card 2017.
35. National Center for Education Statistics n.d.
36. TIMMS & PIRLS International Study Center n.d.-1.
37. OECD 2019b.
38. Scholastic 2019a.
39. See Penny Kittle's "Why Students Don't Read What Is Assigned in Class" (https://www.youtube.com/watch?v=gokm9RUr4ME).
40. Baron et al. 2017.
41. Tyo-Dickerson et al. 2019.
42. Perrin 2018.
43. Rea 2020.
44. Scholastic 2017, p. 15.
45. Scholastic 2019a, p. 30.

CHAPTER 2

1. For useful insights, see Biancarosa and Snow 2004, as well as Zabrucky and Ratner 1992.
2. For an overview of the literature, plus discussion of how these distinctions play out in on-line communication, see Baron and Campbell 2012.
3. Fottrell 2015.
4. See Perrin 2015 for U.S. statistics and Eurostat 2016 for European data.
5. Jerrim and Moss 2019.
6. Duncan et al. 2016, p. 233.
7. Pfost et al. 2013.
8. Torppa et al. 2019.
9. Torppa et al. 2019, p. 888.
10. For data sources, see Baron 2015a, p. 7.

11. Sources: https://www.npd.com/wps/portal/npd/us/news/press-releases/; https://www.publishersweekly.com/pw/by-topic/industry-news/financial-reporting/article/82152-print-unit-sales-fell-1-3-in-2019.html; https://newsroom.publishers.org/aap-statshot-trade-book-publisher-revenue-increased-by-46-in-2018/; https://publishers.org/news/aap-december-2019-statshot-report-publishing-industry-up-1-8-for-cy2019/
12. Popken 2015.
13. https://newsroom.publishers.org/new-data-shows-continued-decline-in-student-spending--on-college-course-materials/
14. Seaman and Seaman 2020.
15. I'm grateful to members of the Creative Commons USA staff at American University's Washington College of Law for discussing OER initiatives with me, especially at the K-12 level.
16. CampusBooks.com 2019.
17. Hazelrigg 2019.
18. Quoted in Dimeo 2017.
19. Quoted in Cavanagh 2016.
20. https://www.pearson.com/news-and-research/announcements/2019/02/pearson-2018-results.html
21. Pearson 2019.
22. Gardner 2002.
23. Baron et al. 2017, p. 599.
24. See Jackson 2001 for a thorough discussion.
25. See Mueller and Oppenheimer 2014.
26. Misra et al. 2016.
27. Ward et al. 2017.
28. Ward et al. 2017, p. 140.

CHAPTER 3

1. Price 2009, p. 487.
2. Kuzmičová 2016.
3. Norway: http://www.bokhandlerforeningen.no/leserundersokelsen-2018; United States: Perrin 2019b; Italy: https://www.istat.it/en/archivio/178341
4. For example, National Endowment for the Arts 2007.
5. From Scholastic 2019b, p. 5, Figure 2a.
6. Rideout and Robb 2019, p. 9.
7. For past and present report highlights, see Ingraham 2018, 2019.
8. https://www.bls.gov/news.release/atus.nr0.htm
9. https://www.leesmonitor.nu/nl/wie-lezen-er
10. See, for instance, Ingraham 2016, 2018; Weissmann 2014.
11. Mokhtari et al. 2009.
12. Huang et al. 2014.
13. *Japan Times* 2018.
14. For a perceptive review and analysis, see Johnson 2019.
15. Burchfield and Sappington 2000.

16. 28 percent: Connor-Green et al. 2000; 27 percent: Clump et al. 2004; 25 percent: Baier et al. 2011.
17. Ribera and Wang 2015.
18. 10.9 hours: Mokhtari et al. 2009; 7.7 hours: Huang et al. 2014.
19. National Survey of Student Engagement 2019.
20. St Clair-Thompson et al. 2018.
21. See U.S. Department of Education 2008 for an explanation of the policy.
22. Ribera and Wang 2015.
23. More details are in Baron and Mangen 2021.
24. One analysis, based on cognitive approaches offered by accomplished readers, is Pressley and Afflerback 1995. Another discussion appears in the RAND Reading Study Group 2002.
25. Baker 2000, p. 8.
26. OECD 2015, p. 94.
27. See, for instance, Protopapas et al. 2012.
28. Wolf et al. 2019.
29. For a less technical version, see Dunlosky 2013.
30. Dunlosky 2013, p. 12.
31. Dunlosky 2013, p. 14.

CHAPTER 4

1. Australia: Nicholas and Paatsch 2018; Canada: Strouse and Ganea 2017a; United Kingdom: Kucirkova and Littleton 2016; United States: Zickuhr 2013.
2. Kucirkova 2019, p. 209.
3. Kucirkova and Zuckerman 2017.
4. For an overview encompassing all these aspects, though differently configured, see Barzillai et al. 2017.
5. Bruner 1981.
6. D. G. Smith 2017.
7. Tønnessen and Hoel 2019; Troseth et al. 2020.
8. Etta 2019.
9. Parish-Morris et al. 2013; Munzer et al. 2019.
10. Parish-Morris et al. 2013, p. 208.
11. Strouse and Ganea 2017a.
12. Munzer et al. 2019, Conclusions.
13. Chiong et al. 2012.
14. Courage 2019, pp. 31–32. See Takacs et al. 2015 for a meta-analysis of eBooks with features of both types.
15. Guernsey et al. 2014.
16. Bus et al. 2019a; Korat and Falk 2019.
17. Bus et al. 2019b.
18. Takacs et al. 2014.
19. Sarı et al. 2019.
20. Dore et al. 2018.
21. Parish-Morris et al. 2013, p. 203.

22. Strouse and Ganea 2017b.
23. For an excellent review of researchers' current understanding of the pros and cons of using digital books with young children, see Courage 2019.
24. See Mizrachi and Salaz 2020 for analysis of students' open-ended comments in the second university study.
25. For example, Delgado et al. 2018. See Annisette and Lafreniere 2017 for more discussion of the shallowing hypothesis.
26. Such studies include Duncan et al. 2016 and Pfost et al. 2013.
27. Clinton 2019; Delgado et al. 2018.
28. For a quick summary, see the Introduction to Baron et al. 2017.
29. Kaufman and Flanagan 2016.
30. Singer and Alexander 2017a; Singer Trakhman et al. 2019.
31. Singer and Alexander 2017a, p. 167.
32. Parish-Morris 2013, p. 206.
33. Clinton 2019.
34. Ackerman and Goldsmith 2011.
35. Ackerman and Lauterman 2012.
36. Singer Trakhman et al. 2019.
37. Lenhard et al. 2017.
38. Singer Trakhman et al. 2019, pp. 112–13.
39. Wickelgren 1977.
40. Lenhard et al. 2017, p. 440.
41. Ackerman and Lauterman 2012; Sidi et al. 2017.
42. Singer and Alexander 2017b.
43. For example, Margolin et al. 2013.
44. Clinton 2019; Delgado et al. 2018.
45. Mangen et al. 2019.
46. Parish-Morris et al. 2013, p. 206.
47. Baron et al. 2017; Tyo-Dickerson et al. 2019.
48. Baron 2015a, p. 87.
49. Mizrachi and Salaz 2020, p. 817.
50. Mizrachi and Salaz 2020, p. 818.
51. Wästlund et al. 2005; Wästlund 2007.
52. Delgado et al. 2018; Higgins et al. 2005; Pommerich 2004.
53. Sanchez and Wiley 2009.
54. Dutch study: Hakvoort et al. 2017; Israeli study: Dotan and Katir 2018; American study: Joo et al. 2018.
55. Schneps, Thompson, Sonnert, et al. 2013.
56. Salomon 1984.
57. Rieh et al. 2012.
58. Fifth- and sixth-graders: Golan et al. 2018; college: Ackerman and Goldsmith 2011; Ackerman and Lauterman 2012; Singer and Alexander 2017a; Singer Trakhman et al. 2019.
59. For example, Clinton 2019 and Sidi et al. 2017.
60. University: Baron et al. 2017; secondary school: Tyo-Dickerson et al. 2019.
61. Ackerman and Lauterman 2012.
62. Lauterman and Ackerman 2014.

63. Golan et al. 2018.
64. Daniel and Woody 2010.
65. For example, Fletcher and Nicholas 2016; Maynard 2010; Miranda et al. 2011; Picton and Clark 2015; Tveit and Mangen 2014.

CHAPTER 5

1. Goldberg 2009.
2. Blaustein 2001.
3. Tenner 1996.
4. Fitzpatrick 2017.
5. Uston 1983, p. 178.
6. "Online Learning Graduation Requirements" 2018.
7. Vaikutytė-Paškauskė et al. 2018, p. 6.
8. Also see Baron 2015, pp. 75ff; Baron 2019; McKenzie 2018; and Whalen 2019 for more details.
9. Eisenstein 1979, p. 72.
10. Eisenstein 1979, p. 74.
11. Wakefield 1998.
12. Guimarães and Carriço 2010.
13. Salmerón et al. 2018c.
14. For more detailed discussion, see Afflerbach and Cho 2009, pp. 209–12; OECD 2015, Chapter 4.
15. Coiro and Dobler 2007.
16. Afflerbach and Cho 2009.
17. For example, Afflerbach and Cho 2009; Coiro 2011.
18. For a useful overview, see Salmerón et al. 2018c.
19. Rouet et al. 2011.
20. Salmerón et al. 2018a.
21. Kornmann et al. 2016.
22. Naumann and Salmerón 2016.
23. OECD 2015, p. 121.
24. Salmerón et al. 2017.
25. Salmerón and Llorens 2019.
26. Fallows 2005, p. iv.
27. Hargittai et al. 2010.
28. See McGrew et al. 2019 for an overview and McGrew et al. 2018 for details of the study.
29. Halverson et al. 2010.
30. Robins and Holms 2008.
31. McGrew et al. 2018, p. 185.
32. Garrett 2019.
33. Segall et al. 2019, p. 88.
34. Garrett 2019, p. 27.
35. Middaugh 2019.
36. Beker et al. 2016; DeStefano and LeFevre 2007.

37. DeStefano and LeFevre 2007.
38. Braasch et al. 2018.
39. Wineburg 1991, p. 84.
40. Wiley and James Voss 1996.
41. Bråten and Strømsø 2006; Stadtler et al. 2013.
42. Stadtler et al. 2013, pp. 143–44.
43. Macedo-Rouet et al. 2003.
44. http://www.corestandards.org
45. Peterson and Alexander 2020.
46. Latini et al. 2019.
47. Bråten et al. 2011.
48. Coiro 2011.
49. Naumann and Salmerón 2016; Salmerón et al. 2018a.
50. Salmerón et al. 2018a, p. 39.
51. Naumann 2015; Salmerón et al. 2018a.
52. Macedo-Rouet et al. 2020.
53. Salmerón et al. 2018b.
54. Wang et al. 2008.
55. Mangen et al. 2013.
56. Norway: Støle et al. 2020; New Zealand: Eyre 2017; United States: Backes and Cowan 2019.
57. Backes and Cowan 2019, p. 90.
58. Walgermo et al. 2013.
59. Schulz-Heidorf and Støle 2018.
60. Støle et al. 2020.
61. OECD 2019a, p. 23.
62. The NAEP in the United States is also transitioning to digital. See National Center for Education Statistics 2019.
63. TIMMS & PIRLS International Study Center n.d.-1.
64. TIMMS & PIRLS International Study Center n.d.-1.
65. TIMMS & PIRLS International Study Center n.d.-2.
66. OECD 2015, p. 96.
67. OECD 2019a, p. 29.
68. My understanding of these issues is enriched by the perceptive analysis of digital testing by Støle et al. 2018.
69. Baron 2015, Chapter 3.
70. Pfost et al. 2013; Duncan et al. 2016, p. 233; Jerrim and Moss 2019; Torppa 2019.
71. Støle et al. 2018, p. 218.
72. Britt et al. 2017, p. 7.
73. Baron 2015, Chapter 2; Rubery and Price 2020.

CHAPTER 6

1. For lessons from the misadventures of the Los Angeles Unified School District, see Lapowsky 2015.
2. Picton and Clark 2015.

3. Merga and Roni 2017.
4. Schwarzenegger 2009.
5. Baron 2015, p. 13.
6. Bonwell and Eison 1991, p. iii.
7. Brame 2016.
8. Brame 2016.
9. Salmerón et al. 2018a, p. 39.
10. Salmerón et al. 2018a, p. 39.
11. Turner and Hicks 2015. For discussion of adolescent digital reading practices, drawing on the same database, see Turner et al. 2020.
12. For a new crop of research, see Bus et al. 2020.
13. Bus et al. 2020, p. 5.
14. AAP Council on Communications and Media 2016.
15. Kucirkova 2018, p. 71.
16. Kucirkova 2018; Kucirkova and Cremin 2020.
17. https://digitalmediaprojectforchildren.wordpress.com/people/
18. Verhallen and Bus 2010; Smeets and Bus 2012.
19. Roskos et al. 2012.
20. Kucirkova et al. 2014a, 2014b.
21. https://www.uclpress.co.uk/products/109473
22. Dore et al. 2018.
23. Singer Trakhman et al. 2019, p. 13.
24. Delgado et al. 2018, p. 34.
25. Goldman 2012.
26. Common Core n.d.
27. Common Core 2019.
28. Adler 1940, p. 110.
29. Schneps et al. 2013a.
30. For an excellent review of current research on the potential of digital technology for supporting students with learning differences, see Ben-Yehudah et al. 2018.
31. Kucirkova 2018, pp. 74–82.
32. Kaufman and Flanagan 2016.
33. Singer Trakhman et al. 2019.
34. Dunlosky et al. 2013.
35. Lauterman and Ackerman 2014.
36. Dunlosky 2013; Dunlosky et al. 2013.
37. For an introduction to sketchnoting, see Zucker 2019.
38. Tyo-Dickerson et al. 2019.
39. Turner and Zucker 2020; Zucker and Turner 2019.
40. https://www.commonsense.org/education/top-picks/top-tech-for-digital-annotation
41. Chen and Chen 2014.
42. For an extended discussion of Perusall, see Miller et al. 2018.
43. https://perusall.com
44. Novak 1991.
45. For an overview of knowledge maps, see Hanewald and Ifenthaler 2014.
46. For details, see Ifenthaler and Hanewald 2014.

47. https://web.archive.org/web/20010715123343/https://www.google.com/press/funfacts.html
48. Fitzsimmons et al. 2019.
49. For more details and suggestions on building scrutiny skills, see Brante and Strømsø 2018; Bråten et al. 2018.
50. Bråten et al. 2019.
51. Single texts: for example, Li et al. 2013; multiple documents: for example, Payne and Reader 2006; Philipp 2019.
52. Amadieu and Salmerón 2014.
53. Barzilai and Ka'adan 2017; Barzilai et al. 2018.
54. https://sheg.stanford.edu
55. Journell 2019.
56. Wineburg and McGrew 2017, p. 1.
57. Langin 2018.
58. Effron and Raj 2020.
59. Dewey 1922, p. 329.
60. Halamish and Elbaz 2020.

CHAPTER 7

1. See Baron 2000 for a fuller discussion.
2. Prouty 1954.
3. Baron 2000, pp. 96–99.
4. For more detail, see Baron 2000, especially Chapters 2 and 3.
5. See Hanson 1993, pp. 191–96, for a brief history.
6. For details on development of the phonograph, see Gitelman 1999.
7. Hubert 1889, p. 259.
8. "A Wonderful Invention", *Scientific American* 1877.
9. Alter 2014.
10. Bellamy 1889.
11. Uzanne and Robida 1894.
12. Rubery's 2016 book was an important source for the discussion that follows.
13. Brooks 2016.
14. Lazarsfeld 1948, pp. 115, 122.
15. Lazarsfeld 1948, p. 35.
16. Rubery 2016, p. 72.
17. Rubery 2016, p. 201.
18. Rubery 2016, p. 217.
19. Aron 1992, pp. 209, 212.
20. Perrin 2019a.
21. Audio Publishers Association 2019.
22. Aron 1992, p. 211.
23. Hammersley 2004.
24. Podcast Insights 2019.
25. Edison Research and Triton Digital 2019.

26. Edison Research and Triton Digital 2018.
27. Nielsen Company 2018.
28. All these data are from Nielsen Company 2019.
29. Birkerts 1994, p. 143.
30. Birkerts 1994, p. 146.
31. Frum 2009, p. 95.
32. Birkerts 1994, p. 149.
33. Willingham 2018.
34. Deniz et al. 2019.
35. Aron 1992, p. 212.
36. Rubery 2016, p. 24.
37. Furnham and Gunter 1989.
38. News stories: Furnham and Gunter 1989; fiction: Furnham 2001.
39. This list incorporates some elements from Schüler et al. 2013 and Furnham 2001.
40. For research references on both issues, see Schüler et al. 2013.
41. Just and Carpenter 1987.
42. Schüler et al. 2013.
43. Some useful sources: Hildyard and Olson 1982; Horowitz and Samuels 1985, 1987; Kintsch and Kozminsky 1977; Townsend et al. 1987.
44. Diakidoy et al. 2005.
45. Scutter et al. 2010.
46. Vajoczki et al. 2010.
47. Allen and Katz 2011.
48. Daniel and Woody 2010.
49. Daniel and Woody 2010, p. 202.
50. Schüler et al. 2013.
51. Rubin et al. 2000, p. 131.
52. Back et al. 2017.
53. Rogowsky et al. 2016.
54. Rogowsky et al. 2016, p. 8.
55. McAllister et al. 2014; Whittingham et al. 2013.
56. See Moore and Cahill 2016 for an often-cited discussion of adolescents and audiobooks.
57. Best 2020, p. 12.
58. Waite 2018.
59. Audio Publishers Association n.d.
60. Varao Sousa et al. 2013.
61. Rubery 2016, pp. 91–92, 267.
62. Quoted in Jones 2011.
63. "Evaluation Report" 2014.
64. Sorrel 2011.
65. The classic work is Mayer 2014.
66. Kalyuga and Sweller 2014.
67. Grimshaw et al. 2007.
68. Johnson n.d.
69. https://learningally.org/About-Us/Who-We-Are
70. I am grateful to George Kerscher, a trailblazer in developing audio technologies for the blind, and to Edward Bray at Learning Ally, for introducing me to Learning Ally's

history and resources, as well as to the importance of human narrators for books to be engaging.

71. For example, McReynolds 2016; WeAreTeachers 2013.
72. https://learningally.org/Solutions-for-School/Success-Stories
73. Elsayed et al. 2019.
74. Esteves and Whitten 2011; Wood et al. 2018; Milani et al. 2010.
75. Chang and Millett 2013; Woodall 2010.
76. Maryniak 2014.
77. 13-year-olds: Luchini 2015; university students: Diao and Sweller 2007.
78. https://www.youtube.com/about/press/; https://www.ted.com/talks; https://www.youtube.com/user/TEDxTalks/about; https://skoll.org/organization/khan-academy/
79. Baron and Mangen 2021.
80. https://www.ted.com/about/our-organization/history-of-ted
81. Salmerón et al. 2020.
82. Merkt et al. 2011.
83. List 2018.
84. Lee and List 2019.
85. Berner and Adams 2004.
86. Wilson et al. 2018.
87. Hollis and Was 2016.
88. Ward et al. 2017.
89. Rice et al. 2019.
90. Szpunar et al. 2014.

CHAPTER 8

1. Ong 1982.
2. Bednar 2010, p. 74.
3. See Khazan 2018 for an overview of the issues and Willingham et al. 2015 for a more formal analysis.
4. Hilton 1997.
5. Quoted in Harris-Warrick and Marsh 1994, p. 84.
6. Rée 1999.
7. Stokoe 1960.
8. http://www.ala.org/alsc/awardsgrants/notalists/ncr
9. https://americanhistory.si.edu/america-on-the-move/licensing-cars-drivers
10. Nix 2018.
11. *ScienceDaily* 2019.
12. https://daisy.org
13. https://www.vialogues.com
14. https://ant.umn.edu

CHAPTER 9

1. Mohn 2012.
2. Carr 2008.

3. Carr 2011, p. 16.

4. Heilweil 2019.

5. Gilovich et al. 2015.

6. EventBrite 2014.

7. Bardhi and Eckhardt 2017; Bardhi et al. 2012.

8. Odom et al. 2011.

9. Cited in Jabr 2013.

10. Odom et al. 2012.

11. Atasoy and Morewedge 2018.

12. Wolf 2018, p. 80.

13. Ackerman and Goldsmith 2011.

14. Baron et al. 2017.

15. Tyo-Dickerson et al. 2019.

16. Wolf 2018, p. 177.

CHAPTER 10

1. Eisenstein 1997, p. 1055.

2. https://newsroom.publishers.org/aap-statshot-trade-book-publisher-revenue-increased-by-46-in-2018/; https://publishers.org/news/aap-december-2019-statshot-report-publishing-industry-up-1-8-for-cy2019/

3. https://newsroom.publishers.org/new-data-shows-continued-decline-in-student-spending--on-college-course-materials/

4. Scholastic 2013, p. 20.

5. Scholastic 2019a, p. 30.

6. Baron et al. 2017; Tyo-Dickerson et al 2019.

7. Picton and Clark 2015.

8. Picton and Clark 2015, pp. 14, 15, and 16.

9. Parish-Morris et al. 2013, p. 203.

10. Eagan et al. 2016.

11. Marken 2019.

12. https://nces.ed.gov/programs/coe/indicator_cta.asp

13. https://www.businessinsider.com/most-popular-ivy-league-major-2017-4#columbia-university-2

14. See, for example, Gormley 2017.

15. Dewey 1910, p. 6. Italics in original.

16. Black 1946.

17. Glaser 1941, p. 173.

18. Ennis 2011a, 2011b.

19. Ennis 1991, p. 6.

20. Paul and Elder 2008, p. 4.

21. McConnell and Rhodes 2017.

22. https://www.criticalthinking.com

23. https://www.criticalthinking.org

24. https://www.lynda.com/Business-Skills-tutorials/Critical-Thinking/424116-2.html

25. https://www.coursera.org/courses?query=critical%20thinking
26. Moore and Parker 2016.
27. McKenzie 2017.
28. Schlueter 2016.
29. Warner 2017.
30. M. D. Smith 2017.
31. NACE 2017.
32. Hart Research Associates 2015.
33. Gojkov et al. 2015.
34. Støle et al. 2020.
35. Sparrow et al. 2011.
36. Kaspersky Lab 2016, pp. 5, 1.
37. Kaspersky Lab 2015a, 2015b.
38. In Kaspersky 2015b, p. 11.
39. Greenfield 2015, p. 206.
40. *Sun*, April 24, 2001, quoted in Thurlow 2006.
41. See Baron 2008, especially Chapters 4, 7, and 8 for details.
42. Baron 2000, Chapter 5; Baron 2008, pp. 164ff.
43. Baron 2008, pp. 164–72.
44. Price 2019, pp. 12, 65.
45. Barajas-Murphy 2017.
46. McKenzie 2019.
47. Jaschik and Lederman 2019.
48. See Baron 2015b for some ideas.
49. Pollan 2007.

References

"A Wonderful Invention—Speech Capable of Infinite Repetition from Automatic Records" (1877), *Scientific American* 37(20): 304.

AAP Council on Communications and Media (2016), "Media and Young Minds," *Pediatrics* 138(5): e20162591. Available at http://pediatrics.aappublications.org/content/138/5/e20162591.full

Ackerman, R., and Goldsmith, M. (2011), "Metacognitive Regulation of Text Learning: On Screen versus on Paper," *Journal of Experimental Psychology: Applied* 17(1): 18–32.

Ackerman, R., and Lauterman, T. (2012), "Taking Reading Comprehension Exams on Screen or on Paper? A Metacognitive Analysis of Learning Texts under Time Pressure," *Computers in Human Behavior* 28: 1816–28.

Adler, M. (1940). *How to Read a Book*. New York, NY: Simon and Schuster.

Afflerbach, P., and Cho, B.-Y. (2009), "Determining and Describing Reading Strategies: Internet and Traditional Forms of Reading," in H. S. Waters and W. Schneider, eds., *Metacognition, Strategy Use, and Instruction*. New York, NY: The Guilford Press, pp. 201–25.

Allen, K. L., and Katz, R. V. (2011), "Comparative Use of Podcasts vs. Lecture Transcripts as Learning Aids for Dental Students," *Journal of Dental Education* 75(6): 817–22.

Alter, A. (November 30, 2014), "An Art Form Rises: Audio without the Book," *New York Times*. Available at https://www.nytimes.com/2014/12/01/business/media/new-art-form-rises-audio-without-the-book-.html

Amadieu, F., and Salmerón, L. (2014), "Concept Maps for Comprehension and Navigation in Hypertexts," in D. Ifenthaler and R. Hanewald, eds., *Digital Knowledge Maps in Education*. New York, NY: Springer, pp. 41–59.

Annisette, L. E., and Lafreniere, K. D. (2017), "Social Media, Texting, and Personality: A Test of the Shallowing Hypothesis," *Personality and Individual Differences* 115: 154–8.

Aron, H. (1992), "Bookworms Become Tapeworms: A Profile of Listeners to Books on Audiocassette," *Journal of Reading* 36(3): 208–12.

Ashby, J., Rayner, K., and Clifton, C. (2005), "Eye Movements of Highly Skilled and Average Readers: Differential Effects of Frequency and Predictability," *Quarterly Journal of Experimental Psychology* 58(6): 1065–86.

Atasoy, O., and Morewedge, C. K. (2018), "Digital Goods are Valued Less Than Physical Goods," *Journal of Consumer Research* 44: 1343–57.

Audio Publishers Association (April 24, 2019), "New Survey Shows 50% of American Have Listened to an Audiobook." Available at https://www.audiopub.org/uploads/pdf/Consumer-Survey-Press-Release-2019-FINAL.pdf

Audio Publishers Association (n.d.), "Sound Learning: How Audiobooks Promote Literacy." Available at https://www.audiopub.org/sound-learning

Babcock, P. S., and Marks, M. (2010), "The Falling Time Cost of College: Evidence from Half a Century of Time Use Data." Working Paper 15954. Cambridge, MA: National Bureau of Economic Research. Available at http://www.nber.org/papers/w15954

Back, D. A., von Malotky, J., Sostmann, K., Hube, R., Peters, H., and Hoff, E. (2017), "Superior Gain in Knowledge by Podcasts versus Text-Based Learning in Teaching Orthopedics: A Randomized Controlled Trial," *Journal of Surgical Education* 74(1): 154–60.

Backes, B., and Cowan, J. (2019), "Is the Pen Mightier Than the Keyboard? The Effect of Online Testing on Measured Student Achievement," *Economics of Education Review* 68: 89–103.

Baier, K., Hendricks, C., Warren Gorden, K., Hendricks, J. E., and Cochran, L. (2011), "College Students' Textbook Reading, or Not!," *American Reading Forum Annual Yearbook* 31. Available at https://www.americanreadingforum.org/yearbook

Baker, N. (2000), "Narrow Ruled," *American Scholar* 69(Autumn): 5–8.

Barajas-Murphy, N. (September 25, 2017), "Instructors Can Help Students Prefer Digital Texts," *Educause Review*. Available at https://er.educause.edu/articles/2017/9/instructors-can-help-students-prefer-digital-texts

Bardhi, F., and Eckhardt, G. M. (2017), "Liquid Consumption," *Journal of Consumer Research* 44(3): 582–97.

Bardhi, F., Eckhardt, G. M., and Arnould, E. J. (2012), "Liquid Relationship to Possessions," *Journal of Consumer Research* 39(3): 510–29.

Baron, N. S. (2000). *Alphabet to Email: How Written English Evolved and Where It's Heading.* London, UK: Routledge.

Baron, N. S. (2008). *Always On: Language in an Online and Mobile World.* New York, NY: Oxford University Press.

Baron, N. S. (2015a). *Words Onscreen: The Fate of Reading in a Digital World.* New York, NY: Oxford University Press.

Baron, N. S. (2015b), "We Need a Smarter Approach to College Textbooks," *Inside HigherEd*. Available at https://www.insidehighered.com/views/2015/08/18/essay-calls-new-approach-college-textbooks

Baron, N. S. (September 19, 2019), "Textbook Merger Could Create More Problems Than Just Higher Prices," *The Conversation*. Available at https://theconversation.com/textbook-merger-could-create-more-problems-than-just-higher-prices-123120

Baron, N. S., Calixte, R. M., and Havewala, M. (2017), "The Persistence of Print Among University Students: An Exploratory Study," *Telematics and Informatics* 34: 590–604.

Baron, N. S., and Campbell, E. (2012), "Gender and Mobile Phones in Cross-National Context," *Language Sciences* 34(1): 13–27.

Baron, N. S., and Mangen, A. (2021), "Doing the Reading: The Decline of Long Longform in Higher Education," *Poetics Today* 42(2).

Barzilai, S., and Ka'adan, I. (2017), "Learning to Integrate Divergent Information Sources: The Interplay of Epistemic Cognition and Epistemic Metacognition," *Metacognition and Learning* 12(2): 193–232.

Barzilai, S., Zohar, A. R., and Mor-Hagani, S. (2018), "Promoting Integration of Multiple Texts: A Review of Instructional Approaches and Practices," *Educational Psychology Review* 30(3): 973–99.

Barzillai, M., Thomson, J., and Mangen, A. (2017), "The Influence of e-Books on Language and Literacy Development," in K. Sheehy and A. Holliman, eds., *Education and New Technologies: Perils and Promises for Learners*. New York, NY: Routledge, pp. 33–47.

Bednar, L. (2010), "Audiobooks and the Reassertion of Orality: Walter J. Ong and Others Revisited," *CEA Critic* 73(1): 74–85.

Beker, K., Jolles, D., Lorch, R. F., and van den Broek, P. (2016), "Learning from Texts: Activation of Information from Previous Texts During Reading," *Reading and Writing* 29: 1161–78.

Bellamy, E. (1889), "With the Eyes Shut," *Harper's New Monthly Magazine* 79(October): 736–45.

Ben-Yehudah, G., Hautala, J., Padeliadu, S., Antoniou, F., Petrová, Z., Leppänen, P. H. T., and Barzillai, M. (2018), "Affordances and Challenges of Digital Reading for Individuals with Different Learning Profiles," in M. Barzillai, J. Thomson, S. Schroeder, and P. van den Broek, eds., *Learning to Read in a Digital World*. Amsterdam, The Netherlands: John Benjamins, pp. 121–40.

Berner, E. S., and Adams, B. (2004), "Added Value of Video Compared to Audio Lectures for Distance Learning," *International Journal of Medical Informatics* 73: 189–93.

Best, E. (2020), "Audiobooks and Literacy." National Literacy Trust. Available at https://literacytrust.org.uk/news/we-release-research-review-benefits-audiobooks-literacy/

Biancarosa, G., and Snow, C. (2004). *Reading Next: A Vision for Action and Research in Middle and High School Literacy*. Report to the Carnegie Corporation of New York. Alliance for Excellent Education. Available at https://www.carnegie.org/media/filer_public/b7/5f/b75fba81-16cb-422d-ab59-373a6a07eb74/ccny_report_2004_reading.pdf

Birkerts, S. (1994). *The Gutenberg Elegies: The Fate of Reading in an Electronic Age*. Boston, MA: Faber and Faber.

Black, M. (1946). *Critical Thinking: An Introduction to Logic and Scientific Method*. New York, NY: Prentice-Hall.

Blaustein, R. J. (2001), "Kudzu's Invasion into Southern United States Life and Culture," in J. A. McNeeley, ed., *The Great Reshuffling: Human Dimensions of Invasive Species*. The World Conservation Union, pp. 55–62. Available at https://www.srs.fs.usda.gov/pubs/ja/ja_blaustein001.pdf

Bonwell, C. C., and Elison, J. A. (1991). *Active Learning: Creating Excitement in the Classroom*. ASHE-ERIC Higher Education Report No. 1. Washington, DC: The George Washington University, School of Education and Human Development. Available at https://files.eric.ed.gov/fulltext/ED336049.pdf

Braasch, J. L. G., Bråten, I., and McCrudden, M. T., eds. (2018). *Handbook of Multiple Source Use*. New York, NY: Routledge.

Brame, C. (2016), "Active Learning." Vanderbilt University Center for Teaching. Available at https://cft.vanderbilt.edu/guides-sub-pages/active-learning/

Brante, E. W., and Strømsø, H. I. (2018), "Sourcing in Text Comprehension: A Review of Interventions Targeting Sourcing Skills," *Educational Psychology Review* 30(3): 773–99.

Brasel, S. A., and Gips, J. (2014), "Tablets, Touchscreens, and Touchpads: How Varying Touch Interfaces Trigger Psychological Ownership and Endowment," *Journal of Consumer Psychology* 24(2): 226–33.

Bråten, I., Brante, E. W., and Strømsø, H. I. (2019), "Teaching Sourcing in Upper Secondary School: A Comprehensive Sourcing Intervention with Follow-Up Data," *Reading Research Quarterly* 54(4): 481–505.

Bråten, I., Britt, M. A., Strømsø, H. I., and Rouet, J.-F. (2011), "The Role of Epistemic Beliefs in the Comprehension of Multiple Expository Texts: Toward an Integrated Model," *Educational Psychologist* 46(1): 48–70.

Bråten, I., Stadtler, M., and Salmerón, L. (2018), "The Role of Sourcing in Discourse Comprehension," in M. F. Schober, D. N. Rapp, and M. A. Britt, eds., *The Routledge Handbook of Discourse Processes*, 2nd edition. New York, NY: Routledge, pp. 141–66.

Bråten, I., and Strømsø, H. I. (2006), "Effects of Personal Epistemology on the Understanding of Multiple Texts," *Reading Psychology* 27: 457–84.

Britt, M. A., Rouet, J.-F., and Durik, A. M. (2017). *Literacy Beyond Text Comprehension*. New York, NY: Routledge.

Brooks, R. (October 31, 2016), "A World in Your Ears—Radio's Dramatic Rebirth in the Digital Age," *The Conversation*. Available at https://theconversation.com/a-world-in-your-ears-radios-dramatic-rebirth-in-the-digital-age-67881

Brower, R. A. (1962), "Reading in Slow Motion," in R. A. Brower and R. Poirier, eds., *In Defense of Reading*. New York, NY: E. P. Dutton, pp. 3–21.

Bruner, J. (1981), "The Social Context of Language Acquisition," *Language & Communication* 1(2/3): 155–78.

Burchfield, C. M., and Sappington, J. (2000), "Compliance with Required Reading Assignments," *Teaching of Psychology* 27: 58–60.

Bureau of Labor Statistics (n.d.). American Time Use Survey, 2017 and 2018. Table A-1. Time spent in detailed primary activities and percent of the civilian population engaging in each activity, averages per day by sex, annual averages. US Department of Labor. Available at https://www.bls.gov/tus/#tables

Burke, M., and Bon, E. V. (2018), "The Locations and Means of Literary Reading," in S. Csábi, ed., *Expressive Minds and Artistic Creations: Studies in Cognitive Poetics*. Oxford, UK: Oxford University Press, pp. 205–31.

Bus, A. G., Hoel, T., Aliagas, C., Jernes, M., Korat, O., Mifsud, C. L., and van Coillie, J. (2019a), "Availability and Quality of Storybook Apps Across Five Less Widely Used Languages," in O. Erstad, R. Flewitt, B. Kümmerling-Meibauer, and I. S. Pies Pereira, eds., *The Routledge Handbook of Digital Literacies in Early Childhood*. New York, NY: Routledge, pp. 308–21.

Bus, A. G., Neuman, S. B., and Roskos, K. (2020), "Screens, Apps, and Digital Books for Young Children: The Promise of Multimedia," Introduction to "special topic" collection in AERA Open. Available at https://journals.sagepub.com/topic/collections-ero/ero-1-screens_apps_and_digital_books_for_young_children_the_promise_of_multimedia/ero

Bus, A. G., Sarı, B., and Takacs, Z. K. (2019b), "The Promise of Multimedia Enhancements in Children's Digital Storybooks," in J. E. Kim and B. Hassinger-Das, eds., *Reading in the Digital Age: Young Children's Experiences with E-books*. Cham, Switzerland: Springer Nature, pp. 45–57.

Bush, V. (1945), "As We May Think," *The Atlantic* (July). Available at https://www.theatlantic.com/magazine/archive/1945/07/as-we-may-think/303881/

CampusBooks.com (July 24, 2019), "New Data Reveals College Textbook Prices Decrease 26%." Available at https://www.prnewswire.com/news-releases/new-data-reveals-college-textbook-prices-decrease-26---college-students-are-getting-a-break-on-textbook-costs-for-the-first-time-in-more-than-a-decade-300890084.html

Carpenter, P. A., and Just, M. A. (1986), "Cognitive Processes in Reading," in J. Orasanu, ed., *Reading Comprehension: From Research to Practice*. Hillsdale, NJ: Lawrence Erlbaum Associates, pp. 11–29.

Carr, N. (2008), "Is Google Making Us Stupid?" *The Atlantic* (August). Available at https://www.theatlantic.com/magazine/archive/2008/07/is-google-making-us-stupid/306868/

Carr, N. (2011). *The Shallows: What the Internet is Doing to Our Brains*. New York, NY: W.W. Norton.

Cavanagh, S. (May 16, 2016), "Pearson CEO Fallon Talks Common Core, Rise of 'Open' Resources," EdWeek Market Brief. Available at https://marketbrief.edweek.org/marketplace-k-12/pearson-ceo-fallon-talks-common-core-rise-open-resources/

Cazden, C., Cope, B., Fairclough, N., Gee, J., Kalantzis, M., Kress, G., Luke, A., Luke, C., Michaels, S., and Nakata, M. (1996), "A Pedagogy of Multiliteracies: Designing Social Futures," *Harvard Educational Review* 66: 60–92.

Chall, J. (1967). *Learning to Read: The Great Debate*. New York, NY: McGraw-Hill.

Chang, A. C.-S., and Millett, S. (2013), "The Extent of Extensive Listening on Developing L2 Listening Fluency: Some Hard Evidence," *ELT Journal* 68(1): 31–40.

Chen, C.-M., and Chen, Y.-Y. (2014), "Enhancing Digital Reading Performance with a Collaborative Reading Annotation System," *Computers & Education* 44: 67–81.

Chiong, C., Ree, J., Takeuci, L., and Erickson, I. (2012), "Print Books vs. E-Books: Comparing Parent-Child Co-Reading on Print, Basic, and Enhanced E-Book Platforms," The Joan Ganz Cooney Center. Available at http://www.joanganzcooneycenter.org/wp-content/uploads/2012/07/jgcc_ebooks_quickreport.pdf

Clark, C., and Douglas, J. (2011), "Young People's Reading and Writing: An In-Depth Study Focusing on Enjoyment, Behaviour, Attitudes and Attainment." National Literacy Trust. Available at https://files.eric.ed.gov/fulltext/ED521656.pdf

Clinton, V. (2019), "Reading from Paper Compared to Screens: A Systematic Review and Meta-Analysis," *Journal of Research in Reading* 42(2): 288–325.

Clump, M. A., Bauer, H., and Bradley, C. (2004), "The Extent to Which Psychology Students Read Textbooks: A Multiple Class Analysis of Reading Across the Psychology Curriculum," *Journal of Instructional Psychology* 31(3): 227–32.

Coiro, J. (2011), "Predicting Reading Comprehension on the Internet: Contributions of Offline Reading Skills, Online Reading Skills, and Prior Knowledge," *Journal of Literacy Research* 43(4): 352–92.

Coiro, J. (2020), "Toward a Multifaceted Heuristic of Digital Reading to Inform Assessment, Research, Practice, and Policy," *Reading Research Quarterly* Early View Online. Available at https://ila.onlinelibrary.wiley.com/doi/abs/10.1002/rrq.302

Coiro, J., and Dobler, E. (2007), "Exploring the Online Reading Comprehension Strategies Used by Sixth-Grade Skilled Readers to Search for and Locate Information on the Internet," *Reading Research Quarterly* 42(2): 214–57.

Coiro, J., Knobel, M., Lankshear, C., and Leu, D. J. (2008), "Central Issues in New Literacies and New Literacies Research," in J. Coiro, M. Knobel, C. Lankshear, and D. J. Leu, eds., *Handbook of Research on New Literacies*. Mahwah, NJ: Lawrence Erlbaum Associates, pp. 1–22.

Common Core (2019). *English Language Arts Standards. Supplemental Information for Appendix A of the Common Core State Standards for English Language Arts and Literacy: New Research on Text Complexity*. Available at http://www.corestandards.org/wp-content/uploads/Appendix-A-New-Research-on-Text-Complexity.pdf

Common Core (n.d.). *Common Core State Standards for English Language Arts & Literacy in History/Social Studies, Science, and Technical Subjects*. Appendix A: Research Supporting Key Elements of the Standards. Available at http://www.corestandards.org/assets/Appendix_A.pdf

Conklin, K., Pellicer-Sanchez, A., and Carrol, G. (2018). *Eye-Tracking: A Guide for Applied Linguistics Research*. New York, NY: Cambridge University Press.

Connor-Greene, P. A. (2000), "Assessing and Promoting Student Learning: Blurring the Line Between Teaching and Testing," *Teaching of Psychology* 27(2): 84–8.

Coover, R. (June 21, 1992), "The End of Books," *New York Times*. Available at https://archive.nytimes.com/www.nytimes.com/books/98/09/27/specials/coover-end.html

Courage, M. (2019), "From Print to Digital: The Medium is Only Part of the Message," in J. E. Kim and B. Hassinger-Das, eds., *Reading in the Digital Age: Young Children's Experiences with E-books*. Cham, Switzerland: Springer Nature, pp. 23–43.

Daneman, M., and Carpenter, P. A. (1980), "Individual Differences in Working Memory and Reading," *Journal of Verbal Learning and Verbal Behavior* 19: 450–66.

Daniel, D. B., and Woody, W. D. (2010), "They Hear, But Do Not Listen: Retention for Podcasted Material in a Classroom Context," *Teaching of Psychology* 37: 199–203.

Delgado, P., Vargas, C., Ackerman, R., and Salmerón, L. (2018), "Don't Throw Away Your Printed Books: A Meta-Analysis on the Effects of Reading Media on Comprehension," *Educational Research Review* 25: 23–38.

Deniz, F., Nunez-Elizalde, A. O., Huth, A. G., and Gallant, J. L. (2019), "The Representation of Semantic Information Across Human Cerebral Cortex During Listing Versus Reading is Invariant to Stimulus Modality," *Journal of Neuroscience* 39: 7722–36.

DeStefano, D., and LeFevre, J.-A. (2007), "Cognitive Load in Hypertext Reading: A Review," *Computers in Human Behavior* 23(3): 1616–41.

Dewey, J. (1910). *How We Think*. Boston, MA: D. C. Heath and Co.

Dewey, J. (1922), "Education as Politics," in *The Middle Works of John Dewey, 1899–1924, Volume 13: 1921–1922. Essays on Philosophy, Education, and the Orient*. Carbondale, IL: Southern Illinois University Press, pp. 329–36.

Diakidoy, I.-A. N., Stylianou, P., Karefillidou, C., and Papageorgiou, P. (2005), "The Relationship Between Listening and Reading Comprehension of Different Types of Text at Increasing Grade Levels," *Reading Psychology* 26(1): 55–80.

Diao, Y., and Sweller, J. (2007), "Redundancy in Foreign Language Reading Comprehension Instruction: Concurrent Written and Spoken Presentations," *Learning and Instruction* 17(1): 78–88.

Dimeo, J. (April 19, 2017), "Turning Point for OER Use?" *Inside HigherEd*. Available at https://www.insidehighered.com/digital-learning/article/2017/04/19/new-yorks-decision-spend-8-million-oer-turning-point

Dore, R. A., Hassinger-Das, B., Brezack, N., Valladares, T. L., Paller, A., Vu, L., Golinkoff, R. M., and Hirsh-Pasek, K. (2018), "The Parent Advantage in Fostering Children's e-Book Comprehension," *Early Childhood Research Quarterly* 44: 24–33.

Dotan, S., and Katzir, T. (2018), "Mind the Gap: Increased Inter-Letter Spacing as a Means of Improving Reading Performance," *Journal of Experimental Child Psychology* 174: 13–28.

Duncan, L. G., McGeown, S. P., Griffiths, Y. M., Stothard, S. E., and Dobai, A. (2016), "Adolescent Reading Skill and Engagement with Digital and Traditional Literacies as Predictors of Reading Comprehension," *British Journal of Psychology* 107: 209–38.

Dunlosky, J. (2013), "Strengthening the Student Toolbox," *American Educator* (Fall): 12–21.

Dunlosky, J., Rawson, K. A., Marsh, E. J., Nathan, M. J., and Willingham, D. T. (2013), "Improving Students' Effective Learning Techniques: Promising Directions from Cognitive and Educational Psychology," *Psychological Science in the Public Interest* 14(1): 4–58.

Eagan, K., Stolzenberg, E. B., Ramirez, J. J., Aragon, M. C., Suchard, M. R., and Rios-Aguilar, C. (2016). *The American Freshman: Fifty-Year Trends, 1966–2015*. Los Angeles, CA: Higher Education Research Institute, UCLA, pp. 68–70, 83–5.

Edison Research and Triton Digital (2018), "The Infinite Dial 2018." Available at http://www.edisonresearch.com/wp-content/uploads/2018/03/Infinite-Dial-2018.pdf

Edison Research and Triton Digital (2019), "The Infinite Dial 2019." Available at https://www.edisonresearch.com/wp-content/uploads/2019/03/Infinite-Dial-2019-PDF-1.pdf

Effron, D. A., and Raj, M. (2020), "Misinformation and Morality: Encountering Fake-News Headlines Makes Them Seem Less Unethical to Publish and Share," *Psychological Science* 31(1): 75–87.

Egmont (2019), "Children's Reading for Pleasure: Trends and Challenges," Report on Egmont/Nielsen survey "Understanding the Children's Book Consumer, 2018." Available at https://www.egmont.co.uk/wp-content/uploads/2019/03/Reading-for-Pleasure-Paper-final.pdf

Eisenstein, E. L. (1979). *The Printing Press as an Agent of Change*. Cambridge, UK: Cambridge University Press.

Eisenstein, E. L. (1997), "From the Printed Word to the Moving Image," *Social Research* 64: 1049–66.

Elsayed, R., Ringstaff, C., and Flynn, K. (2019), "White Paper on Audiobooks and Reading Achievement." San Francisco, CA: WestEd.

Ennis, R. (1991), "Critical Thinking: A Streamlined Conception," *Teaching Philosophy* 14(1): 5–24.

Ennis, R. (2011a), "Critical Thinking: Reflection and Perspective, Part I," *Inquiry: Critical Thinking Across the Disciplines* 26(1): 4–8.

Ennis, R. (2011b), "Critical Thinking: Reflection and Perspective, Part II," *Inquiry: Critical Thinking Across the Disciplines* 26(2): 5–19.

Esteves, K. J., and Whitten, E. (2011), "Assisted Reading with Digital Audiobooks for Students with Reading Disabilities," *Reading Horizons* 51(2): 21–40.

Etta, R. A. (2019), "Parent Preferences: e-Books Versus Print Books," in J. E. Kim and B. Hassinger-Das, eds., *Reading in the Digital Age: Young Children's Experiences with E-books*. Cham, Switzerland: Springer Nature, pp. 89–101.

Eurostat (2016), *Culture Statistics. 2016 Edition*. Available at: http://ec.europa.eu/eurostat/documents/3217494/7551543/KS-04-15-737-EN-N.pdf/648072f3-63c4-47d8-905a-6fdc742b8605

"Evaluation Report: Booktrack Enables School Text" (March 2014). Auckland, New Zealand: The University of Auckland Faculty of Medical and Health Sciences. [No longer available online]

Eventbrite(December8,2014),"UKStudyRevealsMillennialsWantExperiences,NotPossessions," Press Report, Eventbrite. Available at http://www.pressat.co.uk/releases/uk-study-reveals-millennials-want-experiences-not-possessions-1f90ece0f2f8747abe7bf057dbcc443d/

Eyre, J. (2017), "On or Off Screen: Reading in a Digital World," *Assessment News* set 1: 53–8.

Fallows, D. (2005), "Search Engine Users: Internet Searchers are Confident, Satisfied and Trusting—But They are Also Unaware and Naïve," Pew Internet & American Life Project. Available at https://www.pewinternet.org/wp-content/uploads/sites/9/media/Files/Reports/2005/PIP_Searchengine_users.pdf.pdf

Fitzpatrick, R. (February 9, 2017), "A Brief History of the Internet," *ScienceNode*. Available at https://sciencenode.org/feature/a-brief-history-of-the-internet-.php

Fitzsimmons, G., Weal, M. J., and Drieghe, D. (2019), "The Impact of Hyperlinks on Reading Text," *PLoS ONE* 14(2). Available at https://journals.plos.org/plosone/article?id=10.1371/journal.pone.0210900

Fletcher, J., and Nicholas, K. (2016), "Reading for 11–13-Year-Old Students in the Digital Age: New Zealand Case Studies," *Education* 3-13: 1–12.

Fottrell, Q. (January 29, 2015), "The Huge Difference Between What Men and Women Read," Marketwatch.com. Available at https://www.marketwatch.com/story/fiction-readers-an-endangered-species-2013-10-11

Freire, P. (1970). *Pedagogy of the Oppressed*. New York, NY: Herder and Herder.

Frum, D. (2009), "Reading by Ear," *Commentary* 127(5): 94–6.

Furedi, F. (2016), "Moral Panic and Reading: Early Elite Anxieties about the Media Effect," *Cultural Sociology* 10(4): 523–37.

Furnham, A. (2001), "Remembering Stories as a Function of the Medium of Presentation," *Psychological Reports* 89: 483–6.

Furnham, A., and Gunter, B. (1989), "The Primacy of Print: Immediate Cued Recall of News as a Function of the Channel of Communication," *Journal of General Psychology* 116(3): 305–10.

Gardner, H. (July 18, 2002), "Test for Aptitude, Not for Speed," *New York Times*. Available at https://www.nytimes.com/2002/07/18/opinion/test-for-aptitude-not-for-speed.html

Garfinkle, A. (2020), "The Erosion of Deep Literacy," *National Affairs* 45(Fall). Available at https://www.nationalaffairs.com/publications/detail/the-erosion-of-deep-literacy

Garrett, H. J. (2019), "Why Does Fake News Work? On the Psychosocial Dynamics of Learning, Belief, and Citizenship," in W. Journell, ed., *Unpacking Fake News: An Educator's Guide to Navigating the Media with Students*. New York, NY: Teachers College Press, pp. 15–29.

Gibson, J. J. (1979). *The Ecological Approach to Visual Perception*. Boston, MA: Houghton Mifflin Harcourt.

Gilovich, T., Kumar, A., and Jampol, L. (2015), "A Wonderful Life: Experiential Consumption and the Pursuit of Happiness," *Journal of Consumer Psychology* 25(1): 152–65.

Gitelman, L. (1999). *Scripts, Grooves, and Writing Machines: Representing Technology in the Edison Age*. Stanford, CA: Stanford University Press.

Glaser, E. M. (1941). *An Experiment in the Development of Critical Thinking*. New York, NY: Teachers College, Columbia University.

Gojkov, G., Stojanović, A., and Rajić, A. G. (2015), "Critical Thinking of Students—Indicators of Quality in Higher Education," *Procedia: Science and Behavioral Sciences* 191: 591–6.

Golan, D. D., Barzillai, M., and Katzir, T. (2018), "The Effect of Presentation Mode on Children's Reading Preferences, Performance, and Self-Evaluations," *Computers & Education* 126: 346–58.

Goldberg, D. R. (June 2, 2009), "Aspirin: Turn-of-the-Century Miracle Drug," *Distillations*. Science History Institute. Available at https://www.sciencehistory.org/distillations/aspirin-turn-of-the-century-miracle-drug

Goldman, C. (September 7, 2012), "This is Your Brain on Jane Austen, and Stanford Researchers are Taking Notes," *Stanford University News*. Available at http://news.stanford.edu/news/2012/september/austen-reading-fmri-090712.html

Goldstein, D. (February 15, 2020), "An Old and Contested Solution to Boost Reading Scores: Phonics," *New York Times*. Available at https://www.nytimes.com/2020/02/15/us/reading-phonics.html

Gormley, W. T. (2017). *The Critical Advantage: Developing Critical Thinking Skills in School.* Cambridge, MA: Harvard Education Press.

Greenfield, S. (2015). *Mind Change: How Digital Technologies are Leaving Their Mark on Our Brains.* New York, NY: Random House.

Grimshaw, S., Dungworth, N., McKnight, C., and Morris, A. (2007), "Electronic Books: Children's Reading and Comprehension," *British Journal of Educational Technology* 38(4): 583–99.

Guernsey, L., and Levine, M. (2015). *Tap, Click, Read: Growing Readers in a World of Screens.* San Francisco, CA: Jossey-Bass.

Guernsey, L., Levine, M., Chiong, C., and Severns, M. (2014), "Pioneering Literacy in the Digital Wild West: Empowering Parents and Educators," New America and the Joan Ganz Cooney Center. Available at https://joanganzcooneycenter.org/publication/pioneering-literacy/

Guillory, J. (2010), "Close Reading: Prologue and Epilogue," *ADE Bulletin* 149: 8–14.

Guimarães, N. M., and Carriço, L. M. (2010). *Hypermedia Genes: An Evolutionary Perspective on Concepts, Models, and Architectures.* San Rafael, CA: Morgan & Claypool.

Hakvoort, B., van den Boer, M., Leenaars, T., Bos, P., and Tijms, J. (2017), "Improvements in Reading Accuracy as a Result of Increased Interletter Spacing are Not Specific to Children with Dyslexia," *Journal of Experimental Child Psychology* 164: 101–16.

Halamish, V., and Elbaz, E. (2020), "Children's Reading Comprehension and Metacomprehension on Screen Versus on Paper," *Computers & Education* 145, Article 103737. Early View Online.

Halverson, K., Siegel, M., and Freyermuth, S. (2010), "Non-Science Majors' Critical Evaluation of Websites in a Biotechnology Course," *Journal of Science Education and Technology* 19: 612–20.

Hammersley, B. (February 11, 2004), "Audible Revolution," *Guardian*. Available at https://www.theguardian.com/media/2004/feb/12/broadcasting.digitalmedia

Hanewald, R., and Ifenthaler, D. (2014), "Digital Knowledge Mapping in Educational Contexts," in D. Ifenthaler and R. Hanewald, eds., *Digital Knowledge Maps in Education*. New York, NY: Springer, pp. 3–15.

Hanson, F. A. (1993). *Testing Testing: Social Consequences of the Examined Life.* Berkeley, CA: University of California Press.

Hargittai, E., Fullerton, L., Menchen-Trevino, E., and Thomas, K. Y. (2010), "Trust Online: Young Adults' Evaluation of Web Content," *International Journal of Communication* 4: 468–94.

Harris-Warrick, R., and Marsh, C. G. (1994). *Musical Theatre at the Court of Louis XIV.* Cambridge, UK: Cambridge University Press.

Hart Research Associates (2015), "Falling Short? College Learning and Career Success. Selected Findings from Online Surveys of Employers and College Students." Conducted on Behalf of the Association of American Colleges and Universities. Washington, DC. Available at https://www.aacu.org/leap/public-opinion-research/2015-survey-falling-short

Have, I., and Stougaard Pedersen, B. (2016). *Digital Audiobooks: New Media, Users, and Experiences.* New York, NY: Routledge.

Hayles, N. K. (2012). *How We Think: Digital Media and Contemporary Technogenesis.* Chicago, IL: University of Chicago Press.

Hazelrigg, N. (July 25, 2019), "Textbook Spending Continues Slow Decline," *Inside HigherEd.* Available at https://www.insidehighered.com/news/2019/07/25/spending-and-costs-textbooks-continue-decrease-according-surveys?utm_source=Inside+Higher+Ed&utm_campaign=c9014fd456-DNU_2019_COPY_01&utm_medium=email&utm_term=0_1fcbc04421-c9014fd456-197800657&mc_cid=c9014fd456&mc_eid=2508470a88

Heilweil, R. (January 21, 2019), "Infoporn: College Esports Players Cashing in Big," *Wired.* Available at https://www.wired.com/story/infoporn-college-esports-players-cashing-in-big/

Higgins, J., Russell, M., and Hoffmann, T. (2005), "Examining the Effect of Computer-Based Passage Presentation of Reading Test Performance," *Journal of Technology, Learning and Assessment* 3(4).

Hildyard, A., and Olson, D. R. (1982), "On the Comprehension and Memory of Oral vs. Written Discourse," in D. Tannen, ed., *Spoken and Written Language: Exploring Orality and Literacy.* Norwood, NJ: Ablex Publishing Corporation, pp. 19–33.

Hilton, W. (1997). *Dance and Music of Court and Theater: Selected Writings of Wendy Hilton.* Stuyvesant, NY: Pendragon Press.

Hollis, R. B., and Was, C. A. (2016), "Mind Wandering, Control Failures, and Social Media Distractions in Online Learning," *Learning and Instruction* 42: 104–12.

Horowitz, R., and Samuels, S. J. (1985), "Reading and Listening to Expository Text," *Journal of Reading Behavior* 17(3): 185–98.

Horowitz, R., and Samuels, S. J. (1987), "Comprehending Oral and Written Language: Critical Contrasts for Literacy and Schooling," in R. Horowitz and S. J. Samuels, eds., *Comprehending Oral and Written Language.* San Diego, CA: Academic Press, pp. 1–52.

Huang, S. H., Capps, M., Blacklock, J., and Garza, M. (2014), "Reading Habits of College Students in the United States," *Reading Psychology* 35(5): 437–67.

Hubert, P. G. (1889), "The New Talking-Machines," *The Atlantic Monthly* 63 (376): 256–61.

Ifenthaler, D., and Hanewald, R., eds. (2014). *Digital Knowledge Maps in Education.* New York, NY: Springer.

Ingraham, C. (September 7, 2016), "The Long, Steady Decline of Leisure Reading," *Washington Post.* Available at https://www.washingtonpost.com/news/wonk/wp/2016/09/07/the-long-steady-decline-of-literary-reading/

Ingraham, C. (June 29, 2018), "Leisure Reading in the US is at an All-Time Low," *Washington Post.* Available at https://www.washingtonpost.com/news/wonk/wp/2018/06/29/leisure-reading-in-the-u-s-is-at-an-all-time-low/

Ingraham, C. (June 21, 2019), "Screen Time is Rising, Reading is Falling, and It's Not Young People's Fault," *Washington Post.* Available at https://www.washingtonpost.com/business/2019/06/21/screen-time-is-rising-reading-is-falling-its-not-young-peoples-fault/

Jabr, F. (April 11, 2013), "The Reading Brain in the Digital Age: The Science of Paper Versus Screens," *Scientific American*. Available at https://www.scientificamerican.com/article/reading-paper-screens/

Jackson, H. (1932). *The Fear of Books*. London, UK: The Soncino Press.

Jackson, H. J. (2001). *Marginalia: Readers Writing in Books*. New Haven, CT: Yale University Press.

Japan Times (February 28, 2018), "Majority of Japanese University Students Don't Read Books for Pleasure, Poll Shows." Available at https://www.japantimes.co.jp/news/2018/02/28/national/majority-japanese-university-students-dont-read-books-pleasure-poll-shows/#.XNFy1C2B3_S

Jaschik, S., and Lederman, D. (2019), *2019 Survey of Faculty Attitudes on Technology*. A Study by Inside HigherEd and Gallup. *Inside HigherEd.*

Jerrim, J., and Moss, G. (2019), "The Link Between Fiction and Teenagers' Reading Skills: International Evidence from the OECD PISA Study," *British Educational Research Journal* 45(1): 181–200.

Johnson, D. (n.d.), "Benefits of Audiobooks for All Readers." Reading Rockets. Available at https://www.readingrockets.org/article/benefits-audiobooks-all-readers

Johnson, S. (April 21, 2019), "The Fall, and Rise, of Reading," *Chronicle of Higher Education.*

Jones, P. (August 24, 2011), "Music to Read Words by (or the Enhancement Nobody Wanted)?," *The Bookseller*. Available at https://www.thebookseller.com/futurebook/music-read-words-or-enhancement-nobody-wanted

Joo, S. J., White, A. L., Strodtman, D. J., and Yeatman, J. D. (2018), "Optimizing Text for an Individual's Visual System: The Contributions of Visual Crowding to Reading Difficulties," *Cortex* 103: 291–301.

Journell, W., ed. (2019). *Unpacking Fake News: An Educator's Guide to Navigating the Media with Students*. New York, NY: Teachers College Press.

Just, M. A., and Carpenter, P. A. (1987). *The Psychology of Reading and Language Comprehension*. Boston, MA: Allyn & Bacon.

Kalyuga, S., and Sweller, J. (2014), "The Redundancy Principle in Multimedia Learning," in R. E. Mayer, ed., *The Cambridge Handbook of Multimedia Learning*, 2nd edition. Cambridge, UK: Cambridge University Press, pp. 247–62.

Kaspersky Lab (June 19, 2015a), "The Rise and Impact of Digital Amnesia. Why We Need to Protect What We Can No Longer Remember [European data]." [No longer available online]

Kaspersky Lab (July 1, 2015b), "The Rise and Impact of Digital Amnesia. Why We Need to Protect What We Can No Longer Remember [US data]." Available at https://media.kasperskycontenthub.com/wp-content/uploads/sites/100/2017/03/10084613/Digital-Amnesia-Report.pdf

Kaspersky Lab (August 17, 2016), "From Digital Amnesia to the Augmented Mind." Available at https://media.kaspersky.com/pdf/Kaspersky-Digital-Amnesia-Evolution-report-17-08-16.pdf

Kaufman, G., and Flanagan, M. (2016), "High-Low Split: Divergent Cognitive Construal Levels Triggered by Digital and Non-Digital Platforms," *CHI '16 Proceedings of the 2016 CHI Conference on Human Factors in Computing Systems*. New York, NY: ACM, pp. 2773–7.

Khazan, O. (April 11, 2018), "The Myth of 'Learning Styles'," *The Atlantic*. Available at https://www.theatlantic.com/science/archive/2018/04/the-myth-of-learning-styles/557687/

Kintsch, W., and Kozminsky, E. (1977), "Summarizing Stories After Reading and Listening," *Journal of Educational Psychology* 69(5): 491–9.

Korat, O., and Falk, Y. (2019), "Ten Years After: Revisiting the Question of e-Book Quality as Early Language and Literacy Support," *Journal of Early Childhood Literacy* 19(2): 206–23.

Kornmann, J., Kammerer, Y., Anjewierden, A., Zettler, I., Trautwein, U., and Gerjets, P. (2016), "How Children Navigate a Multiperspective Hypermedia Environment: The Role of Spatial Working Memory Capacity," *Computers in Human Behavior* 55: 145–8.

Krashen, S. (2004). *The Power of Reading: Insights from the Research*, 2nd edition. Portsmouth, NH: Heinemann.

Kretzschmar, F., Pleimling, D., Hosemann, J., Fuessel, S., Bornkessel-Schlesewsky, I., et al. (2013), "Subjective Impressions Do Not Mirror Online Reading Effort: Concurrent EEG-Eyetracking Evidence from the Reading of Books and Digital Media," *PLoS ONE* 8(2). Available at https://journals.plos.org/plosone/article?id=10.1371/journal.pone.0056178

Kucirkova, N. (2018). *How and Why to Read and Create Children's Digital Books: A Guide for Primary Practitioners*. London, UK: UCL Press.

Kucirkova, N. (2019), "Children's Reading with Digital Books: Past Moving Quickly to the Future," *Child Development Perspectives* 13(4): 208–14.

Kucirkova, N., and Cremin, T. (2020). *Children Reading for Pleasure in the Digital Age: Mapping Reader Engagement*. London, UK: Sage.

Kucirkova, N., and Littleton, K. (2016). *The Digital Reading Habits of Children. A National Survey of Parents' Perceptions of and Practices in Relation to Children's Reading for Pleasure with Print and Digital Books*. Book Trust. London, UK: Art Council England.

Kucirkova, N., Messer, D., and Sheehy, K. (2014a), "The Effects of Personalisation on Young Children's Spontaneous Speech during Shared Book Reading," *Journal of Pragmatics* 71: 45–55.

Kucirkova, N., Messer, D., and Sheehy, K. (2014b), "Reading Personalized Books with Preschool Children Enhances Their Word Acquisition," *First Language* 34(3): 227–43.

Kucirkova, N., and Zuckerman, B. (2017), "A Guiding Framework for Considering Touchscreens in Children Under Two," *International Journal of Child-Computer Interaction* 12: 46–9.

Kuzmičová, A. (2016), "Audiobooks and Print Narratives: Similarities in Text Experience," in J. Mildorf and T. Kinzel, eds., *Audionarratology: Interfaces of Sound and Narrative* (Vol. 52). Boston, MA: Walter de Gruyter.

Kuzmičová, A., Dias, P., Vogrinčič Čepič, A., Albrechtslund, A.-M., Casado, A., Kotrla Topić, M., Mínguez-López, X., Nilsson, S. K., and Teixeira-Botelho, I. (2018), "Reading and Company: Embodiment and Social Space in Silent Reading Practices," *Literacy* 52(2): 70–7.

Langin, K. (March 8, 2018), "Fake News Spreads Faster Than True News," *Science*. Available at http://www.sciencemag.org/news/2018/03/fake-news-spreads-faster-true-news-twitter-thanks-people-not-bots

Lankshear, C., and Knobel, M. (2011). *New Literacies*, 3rd edition. New York, NY: Open University Press.

Lapowsky, I. (April 8, 2015), "What Schools Must Learn from LA's iPad Debacle," *Wired*. Available at https://www.wired.com/2015/05/los-angeles-edtech/

Latini, N., Bråten, I., Anmarkrud, Ø., and Salmerón, L. (2019), "Investigating Effects of Reading Medium and Reading Purpose on Behavioral Engagement and Textual Integration in a Multiple Text Context," *Contemporary Educational Psychology* 59, Article 101797. Early View Online.

Lauterman, T., and Ackerman, R. (2014), "Overcoming Screen Inferiority in Learning and Calibration," *Computers in Human Behavior* 35: 455–63.

Lazarsfeld, P. (1948). *Radio Listening in America*. New York, NY: Prentice-Hall. Reprinted by Aron Press, 1979.

Lee, H. Y., and List, A. (2019), "Processing of Texts and Videos: A Strategy-Focused Analysis," *Journal of Computer Assisted Learning* 35: 268–82.

Leith, S. (August 14, 2011), "Is This the End for Books?," *Guardian*. Available at https://www.theguardian.com/books/2011/aug/14/kindle-books

Lenhard, W., Schroeders, U., and Lenhard, A. (2017), "Equivalence of Screen and Print Reading Comprehension Depends on Task Complexity and Proficiency," *Discourse Processes* 54(5–6): 427–45.

Leu, D. J., Kinzer, C. K., Coiro, J. L., and Cammack, D. W. (2004), "Toward a Theory of New Literacies Emerging from the Internet and Other Information and Communication Technologies," in R. B. Ruddell and N. J. Unrau, eds., *Theoretical Models and Processes of Reading*, 5th edition. Newark, DE: International Reading Association, pp. 1570–613.

Li, L.-Y., Chen, G.-D., and Yang, S.-J. (2013), "Construction of Cognitive Maps to Improve e-Book Reading and Navigation," *Computers & Education* 60: 32–9.

List, A. (2018), "Strategies for Comprehending and Integrating Texts and Videos," *Learning and Instruction* 57: 34–46.

Luchini, P. L. (2015), "Simultaneous Reading and Listening is Less Effective Than Reading Alone: A Study Based on Cognitive Load Theory," in E. Piechurska-Kuciel and M. Szyszka, eds., *The Ecosystem of the Foreign Language Learner*. Cham, Switzerland: Springer International, pp. 71–80.

Macedo-Rouet, M., Rouet, J.-F., Epstein, I., and Fayard, P. (2003), "Effects of Online Reading on Popular Science Comprehension," *Science Communications* 25(2): 99–128.

Macedo-Rouet, M., Salmerón, L., Ros, C., Pérez, A., Stadtler, M., and Rouet, J.-F. (2020), "Are Frequent Users of Social Network Sites Good Information Evaluators? An Investigation of Adolescents' Sourcing Abilities," *Journal for the Study of Education and Development/ Infancia y Aprendizaje* 43(1): 101–38.

Mangen, A. (2008), "Hypertext Fiction Reading: Haptics and Immersion," *Journal of Research in Reading* 31(4): 404–19.

Mangen, A. (2016), "What Hands May Tell Us About Reading and Writing," *Educational Theory* 66(4): 457–77.

Mangen, A., Olivier, G., and Velay, J.-L. (2019), "Comparing Comprehension of a Long Text Read in Print Book and on Kindle: Where in the Text and When in the Story?," *Frontiers in Psychology* 10, Article 38. Available at https://www.frontiersin.org/articles/10.3389/fpsyg.2019.00038/full

Mangen, A., Walgermo, B. R., and Brønnick, K. (2013), "Reading Linear Texts on Paper Versus Computer Screen: Effects on Reading Comprehension," *International Journal of Educational Research* 58: 61–8.

Margolin, S., Driscoll, C., Toland, M., and Kegler, J. (2013), "E-Readers, Computer Screens, or Paper: Does Reading Comprehension Change Across Media Platforms?," *Applied Cognitive Psychology* 27(4): 512–9.

Marken, S. (December 12, 2019), "Half in the U.S. Now Consider College Education Very Important," Gallup. Available at https://news.gallup.com/poll/270008/half-consider-college-education-important.aspx

Maryniak, A. (2014), "Effectiveness of Reading, Listening and Reading-while-Listening—Quasi-Experimental Study," Paper presented at International Conference: ICT for Language Learning. Available at https://pdfs.semanticscholar.org/8f72/d757f1ff24a8fae3958cfbbba8 25211fc4e6.pdf?_ga=2.200608682.52292669.1577564546-194054829.1547465777

Mayer, R. E., ed. (2014). *Cambridge Handbook of Multimedia Learning*, 2nd edition. New York, NY: Cambridge University Press.

Maynard, S. (2010), "The Impact of e-Books on Young Children's Reading Habits," *Publishing Research Quarterly* 26: 236–48.

McAllister, T., Whittingham, J., Huffman, S., and Christensen, R. (2014), "Developing Independent Readers with Audiobooks," *AMLE Magazine* (October): 19–21.

McConnell, K. D., and Rhodes, T. L. (December 1, 2017), "On Solid Ground: VALUE Report 2017." Association of American Colleges and Universities. Available at https://www.aacu. org/publications-research/publications/solid-ground-value-report-2017

McGrew, S., Breakstone, J., Ortega, T., Smith, M., and Wineburg, S. (2018), "Can Students Evaluate Online Sources? Learning from Assessments of Civic Online Reasoning," *Theory & Research in Social Education* 46(2): 165–93.

McGrew, S., Breakstone, J., Ortega, T., Smith, M., and Wineburg, S. (2019), "How Students Evaluate Digital News Sources," in W. Journell, ed. (2019), *Unpacking Fake News: An Educator's Guide to Navigating the Media with Students*. New York, NY: Teachers College Press, pp. 60–73.

McKenzie, L. (November 14, 2017), "Do Professors Need Automated Help Grading Online Comments?," *Inside HigherEd*. Available at https://www.insidehighered.com/news/2017/ 11/14/professors-have-mixed-reactions-blackboard-plan-offer-tool-grading-online

McKenzie, L. (December 12, 2018), "Shifting Focus of Publishers Signals Tough Times for Textbook Authors," *Inside HigherEd*. Available at https://www.insidehighered.com/news/ 2018/12/12/switch-digital-first-products-publishers-are-signing-fewer-textbook-authors

McKenzie, L. (November 4, 2019), "A Window of Opportunity for Alternative Textbook Providers," *Inside HigherEd*. Available at https://www.insidehighered.com/digital-learning/ article/2019/11/04/window-opportunity-alternative-textbook-providers

McReynolds, E. (June 27, 2016), "For Kids with Reading Challenges, Just Add Listening," Audio Range. The Official Blog of Audible Inc. Available at https://www.audible.com/blog/ the-listening-life/for-kids-with-reading-challenges-just-add-listening/

Merchant, G. (2015), "Keep Taking the Tablets: iPads, Story Apps, and Early Literacy," *Australian Journal of Language and Literacy* 38(1): 3–11.

Merga, M., and Roni, S. M. (2017), "The Influence of Access to eReaders, Computers and Mobile Phones on Children's Book Reading Frequency," *Computers & Education* 109: 187–96.

Merkt, M., Weigand, S., Heier, A., and Schwan, S. (2011), "Learning from Videos vs. Learning with Print: The Role of Interactive Features," *Learning and Instruction* 21: 687–704.

Middaugh, E. (2019), "Teens, Social Media, and Fake News," in W. Journell, ed., *Unpacking Fake News: An Educator's Guide to Navigating the Media with Students*. New York, NY: Teachers College Press, pp. 42–59.

Miedema, J. (2009). *Slow Reading*. Duluth, MN: Litwin Books.

Milani, A., Lorusso, M. L., and Molteni, M. (2010), "The Effects of Audiobooks on the Psychosocial Adjustment of Pre-Adolescents and Adolescents with Dyslexia," *Dyslexia* 16: 87–97.

Miller, K., Lukoff, B., King, G., and Mazur, E. (March 2018), "Use of a Social Annotation Platform for Pre-Class Reading Assignments in a Flipped Introductory Physics Class," *Frontiers in Education* 3, Article 8. Available at https://www.frontiersin.org/articles/10.3389/feduc.2018.00008/full

Miranda, T., Williams-Rossi, D., Johnson, K. A. and McKenzie, N. (2011), "Reluctant Readers in Middle School: Successful Engagement with Text Using the E-reader," *International Journal of Applied Science and Technology* 1(6): 81–91.

Misra, S., Cheng, L., Genevie, J., and Yuan, M. (2016), "The iPhone Effect: The Quality of In-Person Social Interactions in the Presence of Mobile Devices," *Environment and Behavior* 48(2): 275–98.

Mizrachi, D., and Salaz, A. M. (2020), "Beyond the Surveys: Qualitative Analysis from the Academic Reading Format International Study (ARFIS)," *College & Research Libraries* 81(5): 808–21.

Mizrachi, D., Salaz, A. M., Kurbanoglu, S., and Boustany, J. (May 30, 2018), "Academic Reading Format Preferences and Behaviors Among University Students Worldwide: A Comparative Survey Analysis," *PLoS ONE* 13(5). Available at https://journals.plos.org/plosone/article?id=10.1371/journal.pone.0197444

Mohn, T. (December 31, 2012), "Silencing the Smartphone," *New York Times*. Available at https://www.nytimes.com/2013/01/01/business/some-companies-seek-to-wean-employees-from-their-smartphones.html

Mokhtari, K., Reichard, C. A., and Gardner, A. (2009), "The Impact of Internet and Television Use on the Reading Habits and Practices of College Students," *Journal of Adolescent and Adult Literacy* 52(7): 609–19.

Mol, S. E., and Bus, A. G. (2011), "To Read or Not to Read: A Meta-Analysis of Print Exposure from Infancy to Early Adulthood," *Psychological Bulletin* 137(2): 267–96.

Moore, B. N., and Parker, R. (2016). *Critical Thinking*, 12th edition. New York, NY: McGraw-Hill.

Moore, J., and Cahill, M. (2016), "Audiobooks: Legitimate 'Reading' Material for Adolescents?," *School Library Research* 19: 1–17.

Mueller, P. A., and Oppenheimer, D. M. (2014), "The Pen is Mightier Than the Keyboard," *Psychological Science* 25: 1159–68.

Munzer, T. G., Miller, A. L., Weeks, H. M., et al. (2019), "Differences in Parent-Toddler Interactions with Electronic Versus Print Books," *Pediatrics* 143(4):e20182012.

NACE (November 2017), "Job Outlook 2018." Bethlehem, PA: National Association of Colleges and Employers.

National Center for Education Statistics (2019), Digitally Based Assessments. Available at https://nces.ed.gov/nationsreportcard/dba/

National Center for Education Statistics (n.d.), PIRLS and ePIRLS Results, 2016. Available at https://nces.ed.gov/surveys/pirls/pirls2016/tables/pirls2016_table10.asp

National Endowment for the Arts (2007), *To Read or Not to Read: A Question of National Consequence*. Washington, DC. Available at https://www.arts.gov/publications/read-or-not-read-question-national-consequence-0

National Endowment for the Arts (2012), *How a Nation Engages with Art: Highlights from the 2012 Survey of Public Participation in the Arts*. Washington, DC. Available at https://www.arts.gov/sites/default/files/highlights-from-2012-sppa-revised-oct-2015.pdf

National Survey of Student Engagement (2019), Summary Tables: Summary Means and Standard Deviations. Available at https://nsse.indiana.edu/html/summary_tables.cfm

Nation's Report Card (2017), *NAEP Reading Report Card 2017*. National Assessment of Educational Progress. Washington, DC: National Center for Education Statistics. Available at https://www.nationsreportcard.gov/reading_2017?grade=4

Naumann, J. (2015), "A Model of Online Reading Engagement: Linking Engagement, Navigation, and Performance in Digital Reading," *Computers in Human Behavior* 53: 263–77.

Naumann, J., and Salmerón, L. (2016), "Does Navigation Always Predict Performance? Effects of Navigation on Digital Reading are Moderated by Comprehension Skills," *International Review of Research in Open and Distributed Learning* 17(1): 42–59.

Nicholas, M., and Paatsch, L. (2018), "Mothers' Views on Shared Reading with Their Two-Year-Olds Using Printed and Electronic Texts: Purpose, Confidence and Practice," *Journal of Early Childhood Literacy* Early View Online.

Nielsen Company (2018), "A Marketer's Guide to Podcasting: Third-Quarter 2018." Available at https://www.nielsen.com/wp-content/uploads/sites/3/2019/04/marketers-guide-to-podcasting-q3-2018.pdf

Nielsen Company (2019), "Audio Today 2019: How America Listens." Available at https://www.nielsen.com/wp-content/uploads/sites/3/2019/06/audio-today-2019.pdf

Nix, E. (August 30, 2018), "When was the First U.S. Driver's License Issued?" History.com. Available at https://www.history.com/news/when-was-the-first-u-s-drivers-license-issued

Norman, D. (1988). *The Psychology of Everyday Things*. New York, NY: Basic Books.

Novak, J. D. (1991), "Clarify with Concept Maps: A Tool for Students and Teachers Alike," *The Science Teacher* 58(7): 45–9.

Nuwer, R. (January 24, 2016), "Are Paper Books Really Disappearing?", *BBC Future*. Available at https://www.bbc.com/future/article/20160124-are-paper-books-really-disappearing

Odom, W., Sellen, A., Harper, R., and Thereska, E. (2012), "Lost in Translation: Understanding the Possession of Digital Things in the Cloud," *Proceedings of the SIGCHI Conference on Human Factors in Computing Systems*. New York, NY: ACM, pp. 781–90.

Odom, W., Zimmerman, J., and Forlizzi, J. (2011), "Teenagers and Their Virtual Possessions: Design Opportunities and Issues," *Proceedings of the SIGCHI Conference on Human Factors in Computing Systems*. New York, NY: ACM, pp. 1491–500.

OECD (2011), *PISA in Focus 8: Do Students Today Read for Pleasure?* Available at https://www.oecd.org/pisa/pisaproducts/pisainfocus/48624701.pdf

OECD (2015). *Students, Computers, and Learning: Making the Connection*, PISA. Paris, France: OECD Publishing.

OECD (2019a), *PISA 2018 Assessment and Analytical Framework*. Available at https://www.oecd-ilibrary.org/education/pisa-2018-assessment-and-analytical-framework_b25efab8-en

OECD (2019b), *PISA 2018 Results: Combined Executive Summaries*, Volumes I, II & III. Available at https://www.oecd.org/pisa/Combined_Executive_Summaries_PISA_2018.pdf

Ong, W. J. (1982). *Orality and Literacy: The Technologizing of the Word*. London, UK: Methuen.

"Online Learning Graduation Requirements" (September 25, 2018), *Digital Learning Collaborative*. Available at https://www.digitallearningcollab.com/online-learning-graduation-requirements

Parish-Morris, J., Mahajan, N., Hirsh-Pasek, K., Golinkoff, R. M., and Collins, M. F. (2013), "Once upon a Time: Parent-Child Dialogue and Storybook Reading in the Electronic Era," *Mind, Brain, and Education* 7(3): 200–11.

Paul, R., and Elder, L. (2008). *The Miniature Guide to Critical Thinking*. Dillon Beach, CA: Foundation for Critical Thinking.

Payne, S. J., and Reader, W. R. (2006), "Constructing Structure Maps of Multiple On-Line Texts," *International Journal of Human-Computer Studies* 64: 461–74.

Pearson (July 16, 2019), "Pearson Turns the Page on College Textbooks as Digital Courseware Demand Grows," Pearson.com. Available at https://www.pearson.com/corporate/news/media/news-announcements/2019/07/pearson-turns-the-page-on-college-textbooks-as-digital-coursewar.html

Perrin, A. (October 19, 2015), "Slightly Fewer Americans are Reading Print Books, New Survey Finds," Pew Research Center. Available at https://www.pewresearch.org/fact-tank/2015/10/19/slightly-fewer-americans-are-reading-print-books-new-survey-finds/

Perrin, A. (March 8, 2018), "Nearly One-in-Five Americans Now Listen to Audiobooks," Pew Research Center. Available at https://www.pewresearch.org/fact-tank/2018/03/08/nearly-one-in-five-americans-now-listen-to-audiobooks/

Perrin, A. (September 25, 2019a), "One-in-Five Americans Now Listen to Audiobooks," Pew Research Center. Available at https://www.pewresearch.org/fact-tank/2019/09/25/one-in-five-americans-now-listen-to-audiobooks/

Perrin, A. (September 26, 2019b), "Who Doesn't Read Books in America?," Pew Research Center. Available at https://www.pewresearch.org/fact-tank/2019/09/26/who-doesnt-read-books-in-america/

Peterson, E. M., and Alexander, P. A. (2020), "Navigating Print and Digital Sources: Students' Selection, Use, and Integration of Multiple Sources Across Mediums," *Journal of Experimental Education* 88(1): 27–46.

Pfost, M., Dörfler, T., and Artelt, C. (2013), "Students' Extracurricular Reading Behavior and the Development of Vocabulary and Reading Comprehension," *Learning and Individual Differences* 26: 89–102.

Philipp, M. (2019). *Multiple Dokumente verstehen: Theoretische und empirische Perspektiven auf Prozesse und Produkte des Lesens mehrerer Dokumente*. Weinheim, Germany: Beltz Juventa.

Picton, I., and Clark, C. (2015), "The Impact of Ebooks on the Reading Motivation and Reading Skills of Children and Young People: A Study of Schools using RM Books." National Literacy Trust. Available at https://literacytrust.org.uk/research-services/research-reports/impact-ebooks-reading-motivation-and-reading-skills-children-and-young-people/

Podcast Insights (December 11, 2019), "2019 Podcast Stats & Facts (New Research from Dec 2019)." Available at https://www.podcastinsights.com/podcast-statistics/

Pollan, M. (January 28, 2007), "Unhappy Meals," *New York Times Magazine*. Available at https://www.nytimes.com/2007/01/28/magazine/28nutritionism.t.html

Pommerich, M. (2004), "Developing Computerized Versions of Paper-and-Pencil Tests: Mode Effects for Passage-Based Tests," *Journal of Technology, Learning and Assessment* 2(6).

Popken, B. (August 6, 2015), "College Textbook Prices Have Risen 1,041 Percent Since 1977," *NBC News*. Available at https://www.nbcnews.com/feature/freshman-year/college-textbook-prices-have-risen-812-percent-1978-n399926

Pressley, M., and Afflerbach, P. (1995). *Verbal Protocols of Reading: The Nature of Constructively Responsive Reading*. Hillsdale, NJ: Lawrence Erlbaum Associates.

Price, L. (2009), "Reading as If for Life," *Michigan Quarterly Review* 48(4): 483–98.

Price, L. (2019). *What We Talk About When We Talk About Books*. New York, NY: Basic Books.

Protopapas, A., Simos, P. G., Sideridis, G. D., and Mouzaki, A. (2012), "The Components of the Simple View of Reading: A Confirmatory Factor Analysis," *Reading Psychology* 33(3): 217–40.

Prouty, C. (1954), "Introduction," *Mr. William Shakespeares Comedies, Histories, & Tragedies*, facsimile edition prepared by H. Kokeritz. New Haven, CT: Yale University Press.

RAND Reading Study Group (2002), *Reading for Understanding: Toward an R&D Program in Reading Comprehension*. RAND Corporation. Available at https://www.rand.org/pubs/monograph_reports/MR1465.html

Rayner, K., Pollatsek, A., Ashby, J., and Clifton, C. (2012). *Psychology of Reading*, 2nd edition. New York, NY: Psychology Press.

Rea, A. (January 6, 2020), "Reading Through the Ages: Generational Reading Survey," *Library Journal*. Available at https://www.libraryjournal.com/?global_search=generational%20reading%20survey%202019%20library%20journal

Rée, J. (1999). *I See a Voice*. New York, NY: Metropolitan Books.

Ribera, A., and Wang, R. L. (2015), "To Read or Not to Read? Investigating Students' Reading Motivation," Presentation at the 40th Annual POD Conference, San Francisco, CA. Available at https://scholarworks.iu.edu/dspace/handle/2022/24302

Rice, P., Beeson, P., and Blackmore-Wright, J. (2019), "Evaluating the Impact of a Quiz Question Within an Educational Video," *TechTrends* 63(5): 522–32.

Rideout, V. J., and Robb, M. B. (2019), *The Common Sense Census: Media Use by Tweens and Teens*. San Francisco, CA: Common Sense Media. Available at https://www.commonsensemedia.org/sites/default/files/uploads/research/2019-census-8-to-18-full-report-updated.pdf

Rieh, S. Y., Kim, Y.-M., and Markey, K. (2012), "Amount of Invested Mental Effort (AIME) in Online Searching," *Information Processing and Management* 48: 1136–50.

Robins, D., and Holmes, J. (2008), "Aesthetics and Credibility in a Website Design," *Information Processing & Management* 44: 386–99.

Rogowsky, B. A., Calhoun, B. M., and Tallal, P. (2016), "Does Modality Matter? The Effects of Reading, Listening, and Dual Modality," *SAGE Open* (July–September): 1–9. Available at https://journals.sagepub.com/doi/full/10.1177/2158244016669550

Roskos, K., Burstein, K., and You, B.-K. (2012), "A Typology for Observing Children's Engagement with eBooks at Preschool," *Journal of Interactive Online Learning* 11(2): 47–66.

Rouet, J.-F., Ros, C., Goumi, A., Macedo-Rouet, M., and Dinet, J. (2011), "The Influence of Surface and Deep Cues in Primary and Secondary School Students' Assessment of Relevance in Web Menus," *Learning and Instruction* 21: 205–19.

Rowold, K. (2010). *The Educated Woman: Minds, Bodies, and Women's Higher Education in Britain, Germany, and Spain, 1865–1914*. New York, NY: Routledge.

Rubery, M. (2016). *The Untold Story of the Talking Book*. Cambridge, MA: Harvard University Press.

Rubery, M., and Price, L., eds. (2020). *Further Reading*. Oxford: Oxford University Press.

Rubin, D. L., Hafer, T., and Arata, K. (2000), "Reading and Listening to Oral-Based Versus Literate-Based Discourse," *Communication Education* 49(2): 121–33.

Salmerón, L., García, A., and Vidal-Abarca, E. (2018a), "The Development of Adolescents' Comprehension-Based Internet Reading Activities," *Learning and Individual Differences* 61: 31–9.

Salmerón, L., Gil, L., and Bråten, I. (2018b), "Effects of Reading Real Versus Print-Out Versions of Multiple Documents on Students' Sourcing and Integrated Understanding," *Contemporary Educational Psychology* 52: 25–35.

Salmerón, L., and Llorens, A. (2019), "Instruction of Digital Reading Strategies Based on Eye-Movement Modeling Examples," *Journal of Educational Computing Research* 57(2): 343–59.

Salmerón, L., Naumann, J., García, V., and Fajardo, I. (2017), "Scanning and Deep Processing of Information in Hypertext: An Eye Tracking and Cued Retrospective Think-Aloud Study," *Journal of Computer Assisted Learning* 33: 222–33.

Salmerón, L., Sampietro, A., and Delgado, P. (2020), "Using Internet Videos to Learn About Controversies: Evaluation and Integration of Multiple and Multimodal Documents by Primary School Students," *Computers & Education* 148, Article 103796. Early View Online.

Salmerón, L., Strømsø, H., Kammerer, Y., Stadtler, M., and van den Broek, P. (2018c), "Comprehension Processes in Digital Reading," in M. Barzillai, J. Thomson, S. Schroeder, and P. van den Broek, eds., *Learning to Read in a Digital World*. Amsterdam, The Netherlands: John Benjamins, pp. 91–120.

Salomon, G. (1984), "Television is 'Easy' and Print is 'Tough': The Differential Investment of Mental Effort in Learning as a Function of Perceptions and Attributions," *Journal of Educational Psychology* 76(4): 647–58.

Sanchez, C. A., and Wiley, J. (2009), "To Scroll or Not to Scroll: Scrolling, Working Memory Capacity, and Comprehending Complex Texts," *Human Factors* 51(5): 730–8.

Sarı, B., Başal, H. A., Takacs, Z., and Bus, A. G. (2019), "A Randomized Controlled Trial to Test Efficacy of Digital Enhancements of Storybooks in Support of Narrative Comprehension and Word Learning," *Journal of Experimental Child Psychology* 179: 212–26.

Schlueter, J. (June 7, 2016), "Higher Ed's Biggest Gamble," *Inside HigherEd*. Available at https://www.insidehighered.com/views/2016/06/07/can-colleges-truly-teach-critical-thinking-skills-essay

Schneps, M. H., Thomson, J. M., Chen, C., Sonnert, G., and Pomplun, M. (2013a), "E-Readers Are More Effective Than Paper for Some with Dyslexia," *PLoS ONE* 8(9). Available at https://journals.plos.org/plosone/article?id=10.1371/journal.pone.0075634

Schneps, M. H., Thomson, J. M., Sonnert, G., Pomplun, M., Chen, C., et al. (2013b), "Shorter Lines Facilitate Reading in Those Who Struggle," *PloS ONE* 8(8). Available at https://journals.plos.org/plosone/article?id=10.1371/journal.pone.0071161

Scholastic (2013), *Kids & Family Reading Report*, 4th edition. Available at http://mediaroom.scholastic.com/files/kfrr2013-noappendix.pdf

Scholastic (2017), *Kids & Family Reading Report*, 6th edition. Available at https://www.scholastic.com/readingreport/past-reports.html

Scholastic (2019a), *Kids & Family Reading Report*, 7th edition. Available at https://www.scholastic.com/readingreport/home.html

Scholastic (2019b), *Kids & Family Reading Report*, 7th edition, Third Installment: "The Summer Reading Imperative." Available at https://www.scholastic.com/content/dam/KFRR/SummerReading/KFRR_SummerReadingImperative.pdf

Schüler, A., Scheiter, K., and Gerjets, P. (2013), "Is Spoken Text Always Better? Investigating the Modality and Redundancy Effect with Longer Text Presentation," *Computers in Human Behavior* 29: 1590–601.

Schulz-Heidorf, K., and Støle, H. (2018), "Gender Differences in Norwegian PIRLS 2016 and ePIRLS 2016 Results at Test Mode, Text and Item Format Level," *Nordic Journal of Literacy Research* 4(1): 167–83.

Schwarzenegger, A. (June 7, 2009), "Digital Textbooks Can Save Money, Improve Learning," *San Jose Mercury News.* Available at https://www.mercurynews.com/2009/06/06/schwarzenegger-digital-textbooks-can-save-money-improve-learning/

Science Daily (August 19, 2019), "A Map of the Brain Can Tell What You're Reading About." Available at https://www.sciencedaily.com/releases/2019/08/190819175719.htm

Scutter, S., Stupans, I., Sawyer, T., and King, S. (2010), "How Do Students Use Podcasts to Support Learning?," *Australasian Journal of Educational Technology* 26(2): 180–91.

Seaman, J. E., and Seaman, J. (2020), "Inflection Point: Educational Resources in U.S. Higher Education, 2019." Bay View Analytics. Available at http://www.onlinelearningsurvey.com/reports/2019inflectionpoint.pdf

Segall, A., Crocco, M. S., Halvorsen, A.-L., and Jacobsen, R. (2019), "Teaching in the Twilight Zone of Misinformation, Disinformation, Alternative Facts, and Fake News," in W. Journell, ed., *Unpacking Fake News: An Educator's Guide to Navigating the Media with Students.* New York, NY: Teachers College Press, pp. 74–91.

Seidenberg, M. (2017). *Language at the Speed of Sight: How We Read, Why So Many Can't, and What Can Be Done About It.* New York, NY: Basic Books.

Serafini, F., and Gee, E., eds. (2017). *Remixing Multiliteracies: Theory and Practice from New London to New Times.* New York, NY: Teachers College Press.

Sidi, Y., Shpigelman, M., Zalmanov, H., and Ackerman, R. (2017), "Understanding Metacognitive Inferiority on Screen by Exposing Cues for Depth of Processing," *Learning and Instruction* 51: 61–73.

Siegenthaler, E., Wurtz, P., Bergamin, P., and Groner, R. (2011), "Comparing Reading Processes on e-Ink Displays and Print," *Displays* 32(5): 268–73.

Singer, L. M., and Alexander, P. A. (2017a), "Reading Across Mediums: Effects of Reading Digital and Print Texts on Comprehension and Calibration," *Journal of Experimental Education* 85(1): 155–72.

Singer, L. M., and Alexander, P. A. (2017b), "Reading on Paper and Digitally: What the Past Decades of Empirical Research Reveal," *Review of Educational Research* 87(6): 1007–41.

Singer Trakhman, L. M., Alexander, P. A., and Berkowitz, L. E. (2019), "Effects of Processing Time on Comprehension and Calibration in Print and Digital Mediums," *Journal of Experimental Education* 87(1): 101–5.

Smeets, D. J., and Bus, A. G. (2012), "Interactive Electronic Storybooks for Kindergartners to Promote Vocabulary Growth," *Journal of Experimental Child Psychology* 112(1): 36–55.

Smith, D. G. (December 2017), "Parents in a Remote Amazon Village Barely Talk to Their Babies—and the Kids are Fine," *Scientific American.* Available at https://www.scientificamerican.com/article/parents-in-a-remote-amazon-village-barely-talk-to-their-babies-mdash-and-the-kids-are-fine/

Smith, M. D. (2017), "Cognitive Validity: Can Multiple-Choice Items Tap Historical Thinking Processes?," *American Educational Research Journal* 54(6): 1256–87.

Sorrel, C. (August 24, 2011), "Bad Ideas: Booktrack Adds Sound Effects, Music to Books," *Wired.* Available at https://www.wired.com/2011/08/bad-ideas-booktrack-adds-sound-effects-and-music-to-books/

Sosnoski, J. (1999), "Hyper-Readings and Their Reading Engines," in G. E. Hawisher and C. L. Selfe, eds., *Passions, Pedagogies, and Twenty-First Century Technologies*. Logan, UT: Utah State University Press/National Council of Teachers of English, pp. 161–77.

Sparrow, B., Liu, J., and Wegner, D. M. (2011), "Google Effects on Memory: Cognitive Consequences of Having Information at Our Fingertips," *Science* 333(6043): 776–8. Available at https://science.sciencemag.org/content/333/6043/776.full

Spence, C. (2020), "The Multisensory Experience of Handling and Reading Books," *Multisensory Research* 33(8): 902–28.

Stadtler, M., Scharrer, L., Brummernhenrich, B., and Bromme, R. (2013), "Dealing with Uncertainty: Readers' Memory for and Use of Conflicting Information from Science Texts as Function of Presentation Format and Source Expertise," *Cognition and Instruction* 31(2): 130–50.

Stallybrass, Peter (2002), "Books and Scrolls: Navigating the Bible," in J. Andersen and E. Sauer, eds., *Books and Readers in Early Modern England: Material Studies*. Philadelphia, PA: University of Pennsylvania Press, pp. 42–79.

Stavanger Declaration Concerning the Future of Reading (2019). COST E-READ. Available at https://ereadcost.eu/wp-content/uploads/2019/01/StavangerDeclaration.pdf

St Clair-Thompson, H., Graham, A., and Marsham, S. (2018), "Exploring the Reading Practices of Undergraduate Students," *Education Inquiry* 9(3): 284–98.

Stokoe, W. (1960). *Sign Language Structure: An Outline of the Visual Communication Systems of the American Deaf.* Studies in Linguistics, Occasional Paper 8. Buffalo, NY: University of Buffalo.

Støle, H., Mangen, A., Frønes, T. S., and Thomson, J. (2018), "Digitisation of Reading Assessment," in M. Barzillai, J. Thomson, S. Schroeder, and P. van den Broek, eds., *Learning to Read in a Digital World*. Amsterdam, The Netherlands: John Benjamins, pp. 205–23.

Støle, H., Mangen, A., and Schwippert, K. (2020), "Assessing Children's Comprehension on Paper and Screen: A Mode-Effect Study," *Computers & Education* 151, Article 103861. Early View Online.

Strouse, G. A., and Ganea, P. A. (2017a), "A Print Book Preference: Caregivers Report Higher Child Enjoyment and More Adult-Child Interactions When Reading Print Than Electronic Books," *International Journal of Child-Computer Interaction* 12: 8–15.

Strouse, G. A., and Ganea, P. A. (2017b), "Parent-Toddler Behavior and Language Differ When Reading Electronic and Print Picture Books," *Frontiers in Psychology* 8, Article 677. Available at https://www.frontiersin.org/articles/10.3389/fpsyg.2017.00677/full

Szpunar, K. K., Jing, H. G., and Schacter, D. L. (2014), "Overcoming Overconfidence in Learning from Video-Recorded Lectures: Implications of Interpolated Testing for Online Education," *Journal of Applied Research in Memory and Cognition* 3: 161–4.

Takacs, Z. K., Swart, E. K., and Bus, A. G. (2014), "Can the Computer Replace the Adult for Storybook Reading? A Meta-Analysis on the Effects of Multimedia Stories as Compared to Sharing Print Stories with an Adult," *Frontiers in Psychology* 5, Article 1366. Available at https://www.frontiersin.org/articles/10.3389/fpsyg.2014.01366/full

Takacs, Z. K., Swart, E. K., and Bus, A. G. (2015), "Benefits and Pitfalls of Multimedia and Interactive Features in Technology-Enhanced Storybooks: A Meta-Analysis," *Review of Educational Research* 85: 698–739.

Tenner, E. (1996). *Why Things Bite Back: Technology and the Revenge of Unintended Consequences.* New York, NY: Alfred A. Knopf.

Thurlow, C. (2006), "From Statistical Panic to Moral Panic: The Metadiscursive Construction and Popular Exaggeration of New Media Language in the Print Media," *Journal of Computer-Mediated Communication* 11(3). Available at https://onlinelibrary.wiley.com/doi/full/10.1111/j.1083-6101.2006.00031.x

TIMMS & PIRLS International Study Center (n.d. -1), PIRLS 2016 International Results in Reading. Available at http://timssandpirls.bc.edu/pirls2016/international-results/pirls/summary/

TIMMS & PIRLS International Study Center (n.d. -2), PIRLS 2021. Available at https://timssandpirls.bc.edu/pirls2021/downloads/P2021_PIRLS_Brochure.pdf

Tønnessen, E. S., and Hoel, T. (2019), "Designing Dialogs Around Picture Book Apps," in J. E. Kim and B. Hassinger-Das, eds., *Reading in the Digital Age: Young Children's Experiences with E-books*. Cham, Switzerland: Springer Nature, pp. 197–215.

Torppa, M., Niemi, P., Vasalampi, K., Lerkkanen, M.-K., Tolvanen, A., and Poikkeus, A.-M. (2019), "Leisure Reading (But Not Any Kind) and Reading Comprehension Support Each Other—A Longitudinal Study Across Grades 1 and 9," *Child Development* 91(3): 876–900.

Townsend, D. J., Carrithers, C., and Bever, T. (1987), "Listening and Reading Processes in College and Middle School Age Readers," in R. Horowitz and S. J. Samuels, eds., *Comprehending Oral and Written Language*. San Diego, CA: Academic Press, pp. 217–42.

Troseth, G. L., Strouse, G. A., Flores, I., Stuckelman, Z. D., and Johnson, C. R. (2020), "An Enhanced eBook Facilitates Parent-Child Talk During Shared Reading by Families of Low Socioeconomic Status," *Early Childhood Research Quarterly* 50: 45–58.

Turner, K. H., and Hicks, T. (2015). *Connected Reading: Teaching Adolescent Readers in a Digital World*. Urbana, IL: National Council of Teachers of English.

Turner, K. H., Hicks, T., and Zucker, L. (2020), "Connected Reading: A Framework for Understanding How Adolescents Encounter, Evaluate, and Engage with Texts in the Digital Age," *Reading Research Quarterly* 55(2): 291–309.

Turner, K. H., and Zucker, L. (2020), "Taking Annotation Digital: A Strategy for Online Teaching & Learning," *K-12 Talk*. W.W. Norton and Company. Available at https://k-12talk.com/2020/04/09/taking-annotation-digital-a-strategy-for-online-teaching-learning/

Tveit, Å. K., and Mangen, A. (2014), "A Joker in the Class: Teenage Readers' Attitudes and Preferences to Reading on Different Devices," *Library & Information Science Research* 36(3): 179–84.

Tyo-Dickerson, K., Mangen, A., Baron, N. S., and Hakemulder, F. (2019), "Print and Digital Reading Habits Survey." International School of Stavanger, Stavanger, Norway. Unpublished study.

U.S. Department of Education (2008), "Structure of the U.S. Education System: Credit Systems." International Affairs Office. Available at http://www.ed.gov/international/usnei/edlite-index.html

Uston, K. (1983), "9,250 Apples for the Teacher," *Creative Computing* 9(10): 178.

Uzanne, O., and Robida, A. (1894), "The End of Books," *Scribner's Magazine Illustrated* 16 (July–December): 221–31.

Vaikutytė-Paškauskė, J., Vaičiukynaitė, J., and Pocius, D. (2018), "Research for CULT Committee—Digital Skills in the 21st Century," European Parliament, Policy Department for Structural and Cohesion Policies, Brussels. Available at http://www.europarl.europa.eu/RegData/etudes/STUD/2018/617495/IPOL_STU(2018)617495_EN.pdf

Vajoczki, S., Watt, S., Marquis, N., and Holshausen, K. (2010), "Podcasts: Are They an Effective Tool to Enhance Student Learning? A Case Study from McMaster University, Hamilton, Canada," *Journal of Educational Multimedia and Hypermedia* 19(3): 349–62.

Varao Sousa, T. L., Carriere, J. S. A., and Smilek, D. (2013), "The Way We Encounter Reading Material Influences How Frequently We Mind Wander," *Frontiers in Psychology* 4, Article 892. Available at https://www.frontiersin.org/articles/10.3389/fpsyg.2013.00892/full

Verhallen, M. J., and Bus, A. G. (2010), "Low-Income Immigrant Pupils Learning Vocabulary Through Digital Picture Storybooks," *Journal of Educational Psychology* 102(1): 54–61.

Waite, S. (2018), "Embracing Audiobooks as an Effective Educational Tool." Master's thesis. The College at Brockport: State University of New York.

Wakefield, J. F. (1998), "A Brief History of Textbooks," Paper presented at the meeting of Text and Academic Authors, St. Petersburg, FL, June 12–13. Available at https://files.eric.ed.gov/fulltext/ED419246.pdf

Walgermo, B. R., Mangen, A., and Brønnick, K. (2013), "Lesing av sammenhengende tekster på skjerm og papir: Apropos digitalisering av leseprøver," Conference Paper, Skriv! Les! Trondheim, Norway, May 6–8.

Wang, S., Jiao, H., Young, M. J., Brooks, T., and Olson, J. (2008), "Comparability of Computer-Based and Paper-and-Pencil Testing in K-12 Reading Assessments," *Educational and Psychological Measurement* 68(1): 5–24.

Ward, A. F., Duke, K., Gneezy, A., and Bos, M. W. (2017), "Brain Drain: The Mere Presence of One's Own Smartphone Reduces Available Cognitive Capacity," *Journal for the Association of Consumer Research* 2(2): 140–54.

Warner, J. (February 27, 2017), "The Holy Grail of Critical Thinking," *Inside HigherEd*. Available at https://www.insidehighered.com/blogs/just-visiting/holy-grail-critical-thinking

Wästlund, E. (2007), "Experimental Studies of Human-Computer Interaction: Working Memory and Mental Workload in Complex Cognition." Gothenberg, Sweden: Gothenburg University, Department of Psychology.

Wästlund, E., Reinikka, H., Norlander, T., and Archer, T. (2005), "Effects of VDT and Paper Presentation on Consumption and Production of Information: Psychological and Physiological Factors," *Computers in Human Behavior* 21: 377–94.

WeAreTeachers Staff (September 18, 2013), "10 Ways to Boost Literacy Using Audiobooks in the Classroom," We Are Teachers. Available at https://www.weareteachers.com/want-to-support-student-readers-have-them-listen-in/

Weissmann, J. (January 21, 2014), "The Decline of the American Book Lover," *The Atlantic*. Available at https://www.theatlantic.com/business/archive/2014/01/the-decline-of-the-american-book-lover/283222/

Whalen, A. (July 17, 2019), "Biggest Textbook Publisher Pushing Students to Ebooks Undermining Resale Market," *Newsweek*. Available at https://www.newsweek.com/textbook-colleges-cheap-publisher-pearson-ebook-resell-1449860

Whitehead, A. N. (1929). *The Aims of Education and Other Essays*. New York, NY: Macmillan Company.

Whittingham, J., Huffman, S., Christensen, R., and McAllister, T. (2013), "Use of Audiobooks in a School Library and Positive Effects of Struggling Readers' Participation in a Library-Sponsored Audiobook Club," *School Library Research* 16. Available at http://www.ala.org/aasl/sites/ala.org.aasl/files/content/aaslpubsandjournals/slr/vol16/SLR_Use_of_AudiobooksV16.pdf

Wickelgren, W. A. (1977), "Speed-Accuracy Tradeoff and Information Processing Dynamics," *Acta Psychologica* 41(1): 67–85.

Wiley, J., and Voss, J. F. (1996), "The Effects of 'Playing Historian' on Learning in History," *Applied Cognitive Psychology* 10: S63–S72.

Willingham, D. T. (November 25, 2017), "How to Get Your Mind to Read," *New York Times*, Sunday Review. Available at https://www.nytimes.com/2017/11/25/opinion/sunday/how-to-get-your-mind-to-read.html

Willingham, D. T. (December 8, 2018), "Is Listening to a Book the Same as Reading It?," *Washington Post*. Available at https://www.nytimes.com/2018/12/08/opinion/sunday/audiobooks-reading-cheating-listening.html

Willingham, D. T., Hughes, E. M., and Dobolyi, D. G. (2015), "The Scientific Status of Learning Styles Theories," *Teaching of Psychology* 42(3): 266–71.

Wilson, K. E., Martinez, M., Mills, C., D'Mello, S., Smilek, D., and Risko, E. F. (2018), "Instructor Presence Effect: Liking Does Not Always Lead to Learning," *Computers & Education* 122: 205–20.

Wineburg, S. (1991), "Historical Problem Solving: A Study of Cognitive Processes Used in Evaluation of Documentary and Pictorial Evidence," *Journal of Educational Psychology* 83(1): 73–87.

Wineburg, S., and McGrew, S. (2017), "Lateral Reading: Reading Less and Learning More When Evaluating Digital Information," Stanford History Education Group Working Paper No. 2017-A1. Available at https://papers.ssrn.com/sol3/papers.cfm?abstract_id=3048994

Wolf, M. (2007). *Proust and the Squid: The Story and Science of the Reading Brain*. New York, NY: HarperCollins.

Wolf, M. (2018). *Reader, Come Home: The Reading Brain in a Digital World*. New York, NY: HarperCollins.

Wolf, M., and Barzillai, M. (2009), "The Importance of Deep Reading," *Educational Leadership* 66(6): 32–7.

Wolf, M. C., Muijselaar, M. M. L., Boonstra, A. M., and de Bree, E. H. (2019), "The Relationship Between Reading and Listening Comprehension: Shared and Modality-Specific Components," *Reading and Writing* 32(7): 1747–67.

Wood, S. G., Moxley, J. H., Tighe, E. L., and Wagner, R. K. (2018), "Does Use of Text-to-Speech and Related Read-Aloud Tools Improve Reading Comprehension for Students with Reading Disabilities? A Meta-Analysis," *Journal of Learning Disabilities* 51(1): 73–84.

Woodall, B. (2010), "Simultaneous Listening and Reading in ESL: Helping Second Language Learners Read (and Enjoy Reading) More Efficiently," *TESOL Journal* 1(2): 186–205.

Wu, Y.-C., and Samuels, S. J. (2004), "How the Amount of Time Spent on Independent Reading Affects Reading Achievement: A Response to the National Reading Panel," Paper presented at the 49th Annual Convention of the International Reading Association. Available at http://citeseerx.ist.psu.edu/viewdoc/download?doi=10.1.1.539.9906&rep=rep1&type=pdf

Zabrucky, K., and Ratner, H. H. (1992), "Effects of Passage Type on Comprehension Monitoring and Recall in Good and Poor Readers," *Journal of Reading Behavior* 24: 373–91.

Zambarbieri, D., and Carniglia, E. (2012), "Eye Movement Analysis of Reading from Computer Displays, eReaders, and Printed books," *Ophthalmic and Physiological Optics* 32: 390–6.

Zickuhr, K. (May 28, 2013), "In a Digital Age, Parents Value Printed Books for Their Kids," Pew Research Center. Available at https://www.pewresearch.org/fact-tank/2013/05/28/in-a-digital-age-parents-value-printed-books-for-their-kids/

Zucker, L. (2019), "Embracing Visual Notetaking. Review of T. McGregor, *Ink and Ideas: Sketchnotes for Engagement, Comprehension, and Thinking*. Heineman, 2018," *English Journal* 108(6): 97–9.

Zucker, L., and Turner, K. H. (2019), "Adolescents' Preferences for Print and Digital Annotation," Presentation at Roundtable on "Medium Matters: Connecting Research and Practice in Print and Digital Reading." National Council of Teacher of English Convention, Baltimore, MD, November 23.

Index